Equilibrium Exchange Rates of Central and Eastern European Countries on the Road to the European Monetary Union

European University Studies

Europäische Hochschulschriften

Publications Universitaires Européennes

Series V

Economics and Management

Reihe V Série V

Volks- und Betriebswirtschaft

Sciences économiques, gestion d'entreprise

Vol./Bd. 3161

PETER LANG

Frankfurt am Main · Berlin · Bern · Bruxelles · New York · Oxford · Wien

Jörg Rahn

Equilibrium Exchange Rates of Central and Eastern European Countries on the Road to the European Monetary Union

PETER LANG
Europäischer Verlag der Wissenschaften

Bibliographic Information published by Die Deutsche Bibliothek
Die Deutsche Bibliothek lists this publication in the Deutsche Nationalbibliografie; detailed bibliographic data is available in the internet at <http://dnb.ddb.de>.

Zugl.: Hamburg, Univ., Diss., 2005

D 18
ISSN 0531-7339
ISBN 3-631-54243-7
US-ISBN 0-8204-7753-2

www.peterlang.de

Acknowledgements

I wish to take this opportunity to thank all the people who have contributed to my studies and the successful completion of this book.

First and foremost, I would like to express my gratitude to Prof. Dr. Michael Funke for supervising my work. His guidance and fruitful ideas have contributed greatly to the success of this project. I am also grateful for all the helpful comments I have received from the participants of the seminars where I have presented my work. Special thanks go to my university colleagues and all my friends for their suggestions and the good times we have spent together.

This thesis would not have been undertaken without the support of my parents. Their love and continuous encouragement to ascend all steps of education have provided the way for this book. At this point I would also like to mention my sister Sonja who has given me the strength to cope with any difficulties and who will always live in my heart.

I would like to express my deepest thanks to my girl friend Larissa who without complaining accepted many sacrifices while I was working on this project. Her love and support and her help especially on language issues have been invaluable throughout.

Index

Figures

Tables

Abbreviations

ADF	Augmented Dickey-Fuller
AKAIKE	Akaike Information Criterion
ARDL	Autoregressive Distributed Lag
ARIMA	Autoregressive Integrated Moving Average
AS	Austrian Schilling
BEER	Behavioural Equilibrium Exchange Rate
CA	Current Account
CEEC	Central and Eastern European Countries
CHEER	Capital-Enhanced Equilibrium Exchange Rate
CHF	Swiss Franc
CPI	Consumer Price Index
DEER	Desired Equilibrium Exchange Rate
DM	German Mark
DOLS	Dynamic Ordinary Least Squares
ECB	European Central Bank
ECU	European Currency Unit
EMU	European Monetary Union
ERM2	Exchange Rate Mechanism II
EU	European Union
FEER	Fundamental Equilibrium Exchange Rate
FFR	French Franc
FMOLS	Fully Modified Ordinary Least Squares
GBP	Great Britain Pound
GDP	Gross Domestic Product
GMM	Generalized Method of Moments
GNI	Gross National Income
HP	Hodrick-Prescott
ICP	International Comparison Program
IFS	International Financial Statistics
IMF	International Monetary Fund
ITMEER	Intermediate-Term Model-based Equilibrium Exchange Rate
MG	Mean Group
NAIRU	Non-Accelerating Inflation Rate of Unemployment
NATREX	Natural Real Exchange Rate
NFA	Net Foreign Asset Position
OLS	Ordinary Least Squares
PEER	Permanent Equilibrium Exchange Rate

PMG	Pooled Mean Group
PPI	Producer Price Index
PPP	Purchasing Power Parity
PROD	Productivity Differential
RER	Real Exchange Rate
ROW	Rest of the World
SDR	Special Drawing Rights
SUR	Seemingly Unrelated Regression
TOT	Terms Of Trade
ULC	Unit Labour Costs
UNECE	United Nations Economic Commission for Europe
USD	US Dollar
VAR	Vector Autoregression
VECM	Vector Error Correction Model

1 Introduction

On May 1, 2004 ten new countries joined the 15 existing members of the European Union (EU). Among the entrants are the central and eastern European countries (CEEC) Poland, Hungary, the Czech Republic, Slovenia, Estonia, Lithuania, Latvia, and Slovakia. Two other states, Bulgaria and Romania, are expected to follow in January 2007. For these economies accession implies a tighter linking of the local currencies to the euro. The first step of this integration is participation in the European Exchange Rate Mechanism II (ERM2) system, under which these local currencies will be allowed to fluctuate by ± 15 percent around a fixed reference rate against the euro. Slovenia, Estonia, and Lithuania were the first to enter the system on June 28, 2004, and the others will follow as soon as the economic outlook is sufficiently positive to suggest that membership would be a success. New members must participate in ERM2 for at least two years before they are eligible to join the European Monetary Union (EMU), which is also conditioned upon meeting the Maastricht criteria.[1]

Entering the ERM2 implies a fixing of the reference rate, which has profound economic implications for the new members. On one hand, if the selected exchange rate is too high the new member harms its export sector and faces a lack of competitiveness by making its domestic goods comparatively more expensive. Moreover, a substantial overvaluation leaves the country vulnerable to speculative attacks and exchange rate crises. A subsequent lowering of the reference rate during participation in the ERM2 system would considerably delay the country's entry into European Monetary Union (EMU). On the other hand, a reference rate below the equilibrium value unnecessarily reduces national wealth and prolongs the country's convergence towards western European economic standards. Furthermore, undervalued currencies tend to increase inflation through higher prices for imported goods and could thereby impede fulfilment of the Maastricht criterion regarding the appropriate level of inflation. The importance of a proper reference rate is accentuated when the accession to the EMU is also considered. If past experience is any guide, the selected ERM2 reference rates are likely to become the official fixed conversion rates against the euro at the time of entry. Given these implications, it is not premature to consider what the appropriate

[1] In contrast to Denmark and the United Kingdom, who had the possibility to opt out of EMU participation, the new member countries are essentially obliged to join the EMU as soon as they fulfil the Maastricht criteria. Although the example of Sweden demonstrates that this compulsory step can simply be avoided by not meeting the Maastricht criteria, the CEEC presently show a keen interest in joining the EMU as soon as possible.

reference rates for the CEEC should be if these new EU entrants are to avoid economic distortions.

Determination of an exchange rate that is neither undervalued nor overvalued raises the issue of equilibrium exchange rates. This area of research has undergone major strides in recent years; fairly sophisticated methods that go well beyond traditional Purchasing Power Parity (PPP) models are now readily available for calculating equilibrium exchange rates. These newer approaches have typically been applied to the euro, the dollar or the exchange rates of other western industrialized countries. The forthcoming accession to the EMU has only recently drawn the attention to the currencies of the central and eastern European transition economies.

In this paper, equilibrium real exchange rates for the ten CEEC are determined by three different approaches, namely the Behavioural Equilibrium Exchange Rate (BEER), the Permanent Equilibrium Exchange Rate (PEER), and an adjusted version of the PPP. The estimation comprises time series studies for each country as well as panel estimations for groups of CEEC. This work also contributes to the existing literature by applying an algebraic transformation to extract bilateral nominal equilibrium exchange rates against the euro that allows to directly assess possible reference rates for ERM2 participation.

This work is organised as follows. Chapter 2 provides an overview of the exchange rates of central and eastern European transition economies and gives attention to the choice of exchange rate regimes. Chapter 3 surveys the literature on equilibrium exchange rates. In the first subsection, different concepts to determine equilibrium levels of real exchange rates are summarised. In the second subsection, empirical applications of the various approaches to CEEC are considered. Chapter 4 presents the time series and panel estimations of the BEER concept. In chapter 5 the estimation procedure and the results of the PEER concept are discussed. Absolute and relative PPP figures are calculated and evaluated in chapter 6. Chapter 7 summarises the results and discusses some important implications arising from this study. Finally, chapter 8 provides concluding remarks.

2 Exchange rate developments, "de jure" and "de facto" exchange rate regimes of central and eastern European countries

This chapter deals with the development of exchange rates in the central and eastern European transition economies. The evolution of nominal exchange rates will be presented for each of the ten countries under consideration. Although nominal exchange rates do not directly affect equilibrium levels of exchange rates, a thorough analysis can be very informative. On the one hand, certain developments in the nominal rate can explain why significant deviations from equilibrium emerged. Maintenance of a fixed peg against the currency of a country with a notably deviating economic development or a revaluation of the exchange rate are just two examples. On the other hand, determined equilibrium levels can help to understand why swift or large nominal adjustments, e.g. currency crisis or strong nominal appreciation, occurred.

Since the evolution of exchange rates depends to a certain extend on the adopted exchange rate system, the officially proclaimed exchange regimes ("de jure") are discussed in this chapter as well. In this context, however, it has to be considered that officially stated positions sometimes differ from their actual practise. Such a discrepancy can occur for several reasons. Some countries officially adopt a more flexible exchange rate regime for political reasons, but retain a longing for more stability and thus use frequent interventions to prevent large fluctuations. Calvo and Reinhart (2002) introduce the terminology "fear of floating" for this common phenomenon. Other countries officially peg their currencies, but frequently adjust the exchange rates to account for changes in terms of trade ("fear of pegging"). In all of these cases it is advisable to cross-check the officially announced regimes for their practical validity, so that "de facto" exchange regimes are presented here as well.

Before each country is investigated in detail, some general economic developments of the eastern and central European countries that moved from a planned to a market-based economic system shall be addressed. These economies have shared many similar economic experiences during the transition process, which have to a certain extent influenced the evolution of exchange rates. The inspection of the general economic development in the transition economies will thus help to understand some of the underlying forces behind the exchange rate evolution later.

2.1 General economic development affecting the exchange rates of central and eastern European transition economies

The shift to a market-based economy required a comprehensive reform of the trading and exchange rate system. Until 1989 trade between the communist eastern and central European countries was organised by the *comecon*, the "council for mutual economic cooperation". Prices for exports and imports were not related to world market prices but controlled and determined by the governments. Payments for imported goods were settled in transferable roubles, an artificial currency.[2] Transferable roubles were exclusively used for bilateral trade settlements, which means that the trade surplus against one country could not be used to balance deficits against other trading partners. In addition to the exchange rate of the domestic currency against the transferable rouble a whole bundle of other exchange rates existed, e.g. for transactions with non-members of the *comecon* or for non commercial payments as used for travel expenses. With the breakdown of the *comecon* this artificial exchange rate system became obsolete and had to be replaced by an internationally convertible currency, a prerequisite for the integration into the world market (Williamson, 1991).[3] The path to a convertible currency, however, proved to be difficult and often painful. The authorities had to cope with a number of different objectives. First, laws and regulations had to be designed to accommodate the needs of a market-based system. Second, institutions had to be established that could steer the economy and that have the power to achieve internal and external stability. Third, existing exchange rates had to be unified and the unified exchange rate ought to be accepted by all market participants. Fourth, the foreign exchange regime rate had to be selected in a way so that it could possibly help to build up confidence in the new currency. Fifth, the appropriate level at which the exchange rate should initially be set had to be found since the authorities lacked any reliable information about equilibrium value. Sixth, the authorities had to decide which degree of convertibility they should agree on or how rapidly they should move to free convertibility.

---

2 The name transferable rouble is actually misleading as it was not really transferable and certainly not convertible.

3 Only the introduction of convertibility combined with liberalization of trade and capital transactions brings about an efficient allocation of resources and a competitive production structure through increased competition from abroad and the import of an undistorted price system. Moreover, convertibility is considered a precondition to attract foreign investments and with it the import of modern technologies and know-how.

Given the complexity of these objectives and the lack of experience in the transition economies it was not surprising that the economies were soon faced with serious economic problems. Price liberalisation in the presence of a monetary overhang led to strong inflationary pressures.[4] As a consequence, high inflation rates arose in most transition countries. Figure A1 in appendix 1 shows that all countries experienced at least double-digit if not even triple-digit inflation at the beginning of the transition. Inflation peaks were usually seen in the first years, or more accurately one year before a stabilisation program was introduced (Fischer et al., 1996). As a consequence of high inflation rates, nominal exchange rates either declined or real exchange rates appreciated if the nominal rates were fixed. In many cases exchange rates were used as nominal anchors since pegging a currency towards a highly reputed foreign currency or a basket of foreign currencies can import a certain degree of stability if the peg is credible.

Another characteristic experience of transition economies is a tremendous contraction of output as a result of non-competitiveness of products on the world market and the massive collapse of state-owned enterprises.[5] Figure A2 in appendix 1 shows that most CEEC were faced with high negative real GDP growth rates in the first years of transition.[6] The length of decline and the speed of recovery varies among the countries and depends on a broad range of factors, such as the initial economic condition, the dependency on trade with Russia, and the speed of reforms. Fischer et al. (1996) show that positive growth rates can be expected to emerge about two years after the stabilisation of the economy. After recovery, the transition economies have enjoyed comparatively high and sustainable growth rates. Economic downturn and recovery have had impacts on nominal and real exchange rates through a number of channels, which will be discussed in detail later in this work.

Transition economies also share many experiences as far as exchange rate movements are concerned. However, there are substantial differences among the countries as well. Each of the CEEC has opted for its individual way in terms of exchange rate policy. The policies deviate with respect to various aspects, such as the official choice of exchange rate regimes, the practical implementation of the regimes, the government preferences either towards stabilisation or towards inter-

---

4 The monetary overhang resulted from long-time repressed demand for foreign assets, which could not instantly be met by adequate supply of goods.

5 See Mundell (1997) for a thorough analysis of the causes of the economic collapse.

6 Countries like the Czech Republic and Slovakia that do not exhibit the economic downturn were founded after the break-down.

national trade competitiveness, and the exposure and reaction to currency crises. All these issues affect the equilibrium levels of nominal and real exchange rates, so that a more detailed discussion of exchange rate developments is required. The following sections will therefore investigate these issues for each country separately.

2.2 Poland

Figure 2.1 presents the nominal exchange rate of the Polish zloty against the euro and its predecessor, the ECU.[7] The picture shows that the zloty - starting with a rate close to parity in 1990 - depreciated continuously to a level of about 4.4 zloty for one euro in 1999. In 2000 and the first half of 2001 the zloty regained some of its value against the euro to attain a level of about 3.4 before it began depreciating again.[8]

Figure 2.1. The nominal exchange rate of Poland against the ECU/Euro

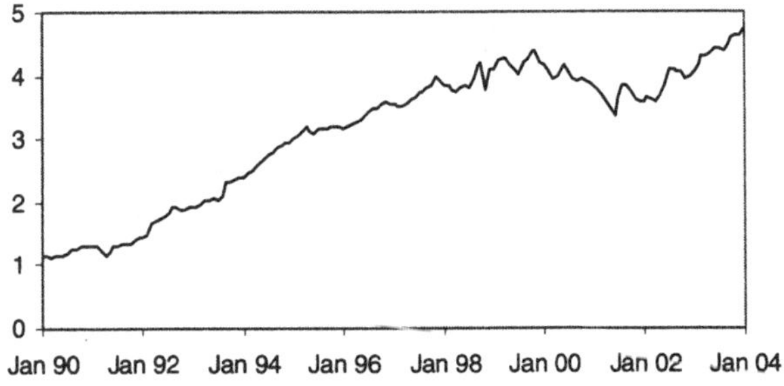

Data sources: International Financial Statistics and http://oanda.com.

The evolution of the nominal zloty exchange rate is closely linked to the various exchange rate regimes during the transition process. In the beginning Poland opted for a fixed exchange rate regime. The Polish zloty was pegged against the US dollar. Such a peg against a "hard" currency, i.e. a currency with good reputation and relatively low inflation in the home country, was considered to be a

---

[7] ECU = European Currency Unit.

[8] The fluctuations of the zloty against the euro in recent years are more a reflection of the fluctuating international value of the euro than of shifts in the value of the zloty.

reasonable way to import stability from abroad. During this period from 1990 to mid 1991 the depreciation against the euro was only marginal. However, high inflation rates in Poland made this system unsustainable in the long run, so that the Polish government decided to switch to a pre-announced crawling peg regime in October 1991. In a crawling peg the exchange rate is pegged against an anchor currency, or alternatively against a currency basket, and devalued with a fixed rate, the rate of crawl, on a regular basis. Typically, the rate of crawl is used to compensate for inflation differentials between the home country and the anchor countries. However, if the system is selected in order to reduce inflation in the long run, the rate of crawl ought to be set below the projected inflation differential and it should decrease gradually. Accordingly, the rate of crawl was initially set to 1.8 percent per month and lowered in several steps to 0.3 percent. Figure 2.1 illustrates the declining speed of depreciation against the euro. Starting in mid 1995 the band width around the parity in which the exchange rate was allowed to fluctuate was progressively widened until in April 2000 the system was abandoned. Since then, the exchange rate is officially allowed to fluctuate freely and the nominal exchange rate appreciated moderately against the euro until 2002. Table 2.1 summarises the development of the exchange rate regimes in Poland.

Several papers investigate whether the "de facto" exchange rate regime deviated from the officially announced "de jure" position in the CEEC. Von Hagen and Zhou (2002) seek to determine the "de facto" exchange rate regimes for a broad set of 25 transition economies. The procedure is based on work from Levy-Yeyati and Sturzenegger (2000) and makes use of cluster analysis. Three different volatility measures (exchange rate, exchange rate change, and reserve volatility) are considered to define features of exchange rate regime groups. Afterwards, the exchange rate systems are classified into clusters of fixed, intermediate and flexible regimes. In the case of Poland, von Hagen and Zhou (2002) determine four different periods. The year 1990 is classified as a fixed regime, 1991 to 1993 as flexible, 1994 to 1997 again as fixed and the period from 1998 to 1999 as an intermediate regime. That means, the period between 1991 and 1993 does not match with the "de jure" exchange rate regime, but the other periods do.

Frömmel and Schobert (2004) analyse the exchange rate regimes of six CEEC (Poland, Hungary, the Czech Republic, Slovenia, Slovakia, and Romania) based on two different approaches. The first approach examines volatilities and frequency distributions of three indicators (exchange rates, interest rates, and reserves). In the second approach co-movements with possible anchor currencies are explored. For Poland the authors find inconclusive results for the period before April 2000 and a flexible exchange rate regime for the period afterwards.

In another study Schnabl (2004) examines low- and high-frequency exchange rate stability against the euro and the US dollar for all CEEC over the period from 1999 to 2004. While the low frequency stability criterion exploits the above mentioned three indicators (exchange rates, interest rates, and reserves), the high frequency stability criterion investigates daily exchange rate movements. According to both criteria, Poland can be classified as a free floater.

Table 2.1. De jure exchange rate regimes of Poland

Date	Exchange Rate Regime	Specification
01/1990-05/1991	Fixed exchange rate	Peg against USD
05/1991-10/1991	Fixed exchange rate	Initial devaluation of 17 %; peg against a currency basket (45 % USD, 35 % DM, 10 % GBP, 5 % FFR, 5 % CHF)
10/1991-05/1995	Crawling peg	Monthly devaluations of initially 1.8 % decreasing gradually to 1.2 %; devaluations of 10.7 % and 7.4 % in 02/1992 and 08/1993 respectively
05/1995-12/1998	Crawling band	Band of ± 7 % widening gradually to ± 12.5 %; monthly devaluations of 1.2 % decreasing gradually to 0.5 %; 6 % revaluation in 12/1995
01/1999-04/2000	Crawling band	Peg against a new currency basket (55 % Euro, 45 % USD); band of ± 12.5 % widening gradually to ± 15 %; monthly devaluations of 0.5 % decreasing gradually to 0.3 %
Since 04/2000	Free float	

Sources: Nuti (2000); National Bank of Poland "Annual Report" (various issues); International Monetary Fund (IMF) "Exchange rate arrangements and exchange restrictions: annual report" (various issues).

2.3 Hungary

Hungary was the first country of the CEEC to move from a centrally planned to a market economy. Already at the end of the 1980s the first steps towards price liberalisation and exchange rate convertibility were accomplished, so that Hungary was in a comparatively advanced situation in 1990. Nevertheless, Hungary also opted for a nominal anchor to gain stability and credibility. However, in contrast to Poland, Hungary chose an adjustable peg right from the start. Until 1995 nominal exchange rate adjustments were frequent, but irregular and not pre-announced. These adjustments were made to compensate for the positive inflation differential against the basket of anchor currencies. Beginning in March 1995 Hungary adjusted the exchange rate on a more regular basis in the framework of a crawling peg system. Figure 2.2 shows that the nominal exchange rate against the euro declined gradually. In 2001, Hungary turned to a more flexible exchange rate regime by introducing a crawling band (see table 2.2 for details). Later on in 2001 the rate of crawl was abolished and Hungary moved to a horizontal band exchange rate regime with a band width of ± 15 percent. Remaining restrictions on capital mobility were also abolished and the Hungarian central bank switched to an inflation targeting system. In the following months the nominal exchange rate did not depreciate further, but appreciated towards the stronger bound of the band. Speculators induced such strong appreciative pressure that the Hungarian central bank had to massively buy euros to defend the band. However, at the beginning of 2003 the direction of the exchange rate turned towards the weaker bound of the band. In June 2003 the government initiated a downward shift of the central parity from 276.11 forint against the euro to 282.36 in order to improve the competitiveness of Hungarian enterprises. This measure, however, harmed the confidence in the forint and triggered a far greater nominal depreciation than expected.

Figure 2.2. The nominal exchange rate of Hungary against the ECU/Euro

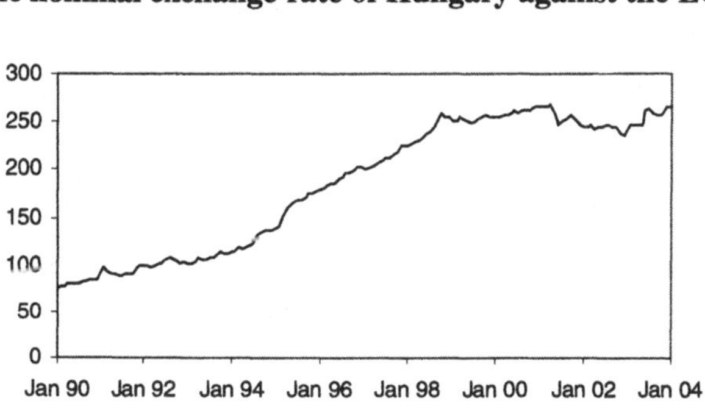

Data sources: International Financial Statistics and http://oanda.com

In terms of "de facto" exchange rates, Hungary's official announcements seem to be consistent with the practical implementation. The cluster analysis to determine "de facto" exchange rate regimes from von Hagen and Zhou (2002) reveals that

Hungary's regime can be classified as fixed from 1991 to 1999, which matches the "de jure" position. The study from Frömmel and Schobert (2004) confirms that the "de facto" regimes have always been in line with the officially declared, even with respect to the proclaimed anchor currencies. According to Schnabl (2004), low- and high-frequency exchange rate stability criteria reveal that Hungary effectively pegs its exchange rate against the euro since 1999.

Table 2.2. De jure exchange rate regimes of Hungary

Date	Exchange Rate Regime	Specification
01/1990-12/1991	Adjustable fixed exchange rate	Peg against a currency basket depending on the composition of previous year's foreign trade
12/1991-03/1995	Adjustable fixed exchange rate	Peg against a currency basket; slightly changing compositions including USD and either ECU or DM; frequent devaluations of varying magnitude
03/1995-05/2001	Crawling peg	Peg against a currency basket (70 % ECU, 30 % USD); later on the ECU was replaced by the DM and thereafter by the euro; since 01/2000 peg against the euro; daily devaluations of initially 0.06 % decreasing gradually to 0.00654 %; tight band of ± 2.25 %
05/2001-09/2001	Crawling band	Band of ± 15 % against the euro; daily devaluations of 0.00654 %
Since 10/2001	Horizontal band	Band of ± 15 %; in 06/2003 devaluation of central parity by 2.26 %

Sources: Magyar Nemzeti Bank "Annual Report" (various issues); IMF "Exchange rate arrangements and exchange restrictions: annual report" (various issues).

2.4 Czech Republic

When Czechoslovakia split up at the end of 1993, the Czech Republic inherited its fixed peg against a basket of five countries. The Czech Republic maintained the fixed exchange rate system for several years, but adjusted the basket in May 1993. This new basket consisted of German mark and US dollar exclusively. As a result, the nominal exchange rate against the euro did not fluctuate very much and stayed at a level of about 34 koruna for one euro (see figure 2.3).

The fixed peg served its goal in stabilising the economy in the first years and brought down inflation rapidly. In February 1996, the Czech National Bank decided to widen the band around the parity in response to large capital inflows. The more flexible version, however, proved to be unsustainable. Against the backdrop of growing internal and external imbalances - in particular a huge current account deficit - speculators triggered an attack on the koruna in May 1997. After a few days of defending the band, the government let the koruna float (see table 2.3). As a consequence, the koruna depreciated rapidly by 15 percent to about 38 koruna per euro. The Czech National Bank intervened promptly and increased interest rates sharply. Moreover, administrative measures were introduced that restricted access to the exchange market. At the same time, the government launched a stabilisation reform program aimed at reducing inflation and government spending. These measures proved to be successful and the koruna regained most of its value by the end of 1998.[9] The Czech currency slipped again at the beginning of 1999, but mostly as a result of overshooting. Since then the nominal exchange rate of the Czech koruna has appreciated against the euro.

Figure 2.3. The nominal exchange rate of the Czech Republic against the ECU/Euro

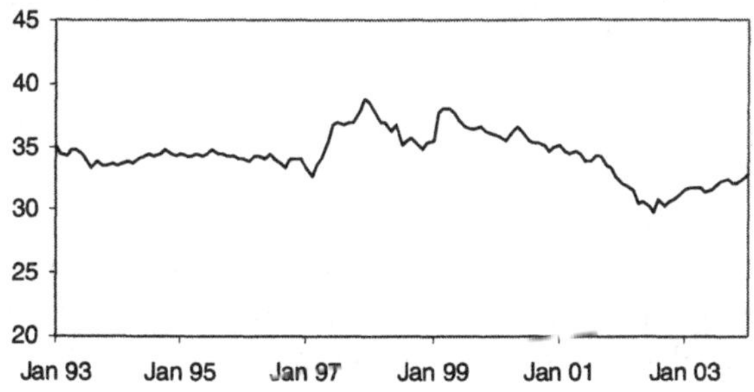

Data sources: International Financial Statistics and http://oanda.com.

According to von Hagen and Zhou (2002) the "de facto" exchange rate regimes are to a large extent consistent with the "de jure" regimes. The period until 1996 is classified as a fixed regime, the years 1997 and 1998 as intermediate regimes, and 1999 as a flexible exchange rate regime. Schnabl (2004) finds low exchange rate

9 Despite the successful reforms, the Czech Republic experienced two years with negative growth rates (see figure A2 in appendix 1).

volatility against the euro throughout the period, but also relatively low reserve and interest rate volatility. The Czech National Bank officially admits various exchange market interventions, so that a the managed float seems to be consistent with real practise after mid 1997.[10] Frömmel and Schobert (2004) additionally reveal that there is still co-movement of the Czech koruna and the euro, even after 1997.

Table 2.3. De jure exchange rate regimes of the Czech Republic

Date	Exchange Rate Regime	Specification
01/1993-05/1993	Fixed peg	Peg against a basket of five currencies (49.07 % USD, 36.15 % DM, 8.07 % AS, 3.79 % CHF, 2.92 % FFR); until 01/1993 currency union with Slovakia
05/1993-07/1996	Fixed peg	Peg against a currency basket (65 % DM; 35 % USD)
07/1996-05/1997	Horizontal band	Band of ± 7.5 % against a currency basket (65 % DM; 35 % USD)
Since 05/1997	Managed float	No pre-announced path

Sources: Czech National Bank "Annual Report" (various issues); IMF "Exchange rate arrangements and exchange restrictions: annual report" (various issues).

2.5 Slovenia

In contrast to most of the other transition economies, Slovenia opted for a flexible exchange rate regime. This step was controversially discussed in Slovenia, but the government argued that lack of foreign exchange reserves and low credibility of the newly established institutions in the young country did not leave any other option (Oesterreichische Nationalbank, 1994). However, the following months proved that not only fixed exchange rate regimes could stabilize the economy. Inflation rates fell quickly and Slovenia's economic development outperformed that of many other transition economies.[11] Foreign exchange reserves summed up fast and could have given the option to switch to a fixed peg, but the success of

[10] See Czech National Bank (2003) for a summary of monetary policies over the first decade of independence.

[11] Figure A2 in appendix 1 reveals constantly high growth rates over the entire period after 1992.

the managed float did not give reasons to do so. Accordingly, the Bank of Slovenia maintained the flexible exchange rate system.

The evolution of the nominal exchange rates is depicted in figure 2.4. The graph displays a continuous depreciation against the euro. The stability of the nominal exchange rate path is highly remarkable for an officially flexible currency regime and Schnabl (2004) reveals that its volatility against the euro is one of the lowest of all CEEC. It is thus not surprising that von Hagen and Zhou (2002) determine that the Slovenian exchange rate regime should rather be classified as fixed than as flexible. In February 2002, the International Monetary Fund (IMF) more precisely reclassified Slovenia's exchange rate system as an implicit crawling band (IMF, 2002). This step, however, does not reflect a change in the exchange rate policy, but rather a correction of the initial classification as Slovenia did not modify its policy officially.

Figure 2.4. The nominal exchange rate of Slovenia against the ECU/Euro

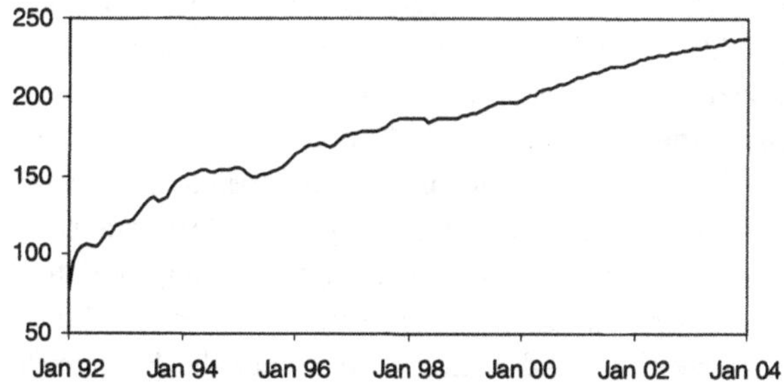

Data sources: International Financial Statistics and http://oanda.com.

Frömmel and Schobert (2004) find support for the IMF classification and determine that at least since 1997 a "de facto" crawling peg has been managed against the German mark and later against the euro. Very high reserve volatility also indicates that the Bank of Slovenia regularly intervenes in the foreign exchange rate market. In June 2004 Slovenia entered the ERM2 system. This step implies the end of the crawl since the Slovenian tolar is now fixed against the euro within a band of ± 15 percent (see table 2.4).

Table 2.4. De jure exchange rate regimes of Slovenia

Date	Exchange Rate Regime	Specification
01/1992-06/2004	Managed float	No pre-announced path
Since 06/2004	Fixed peg	Participation in the ERM2; peg against the euro with band width of ± 15 %.

Source: Bank of Slovenia "Monthly Bulletin" (various issues).

2.6 Estonia

Estonia, separating in August 1991 from the former Soviet Union, introduced its own currency, the Estonian kroon, in June 1992. Prior to the launch the selection of the exchange rate regime had been discussed extensively. The experience of the hyperinflation of the Russian rouble in 1991 and 1992 had led to a high propensity in the public towards very rapid stabilisation. Monetary stability and credibility were considered the most important preconditions for economic reforms (Sepp and Randveer, 2002). In such a context, it is easy to understand that the Estonian government decided to implement a currency board system at the same time with the introduction of the new currency.[12] The currency board system was chosen because of the difficulties in establishing an independent monetary policy in an environment of high uncertainty regarding monetary transmission channels (Knöbl et al., 1996). It was also believed to be the appropriate way to rapidly reduce inflation through the credible implementation of a solid nominal anchor. The backing of money is broader than usual under the Estonian currency board since not only currency in circulation, but also currency in current accounts and in accounts of a fixed date are secured by reserves (Bank of Estonia, 1992).

[12] A simple definition of a currency board is given by Williamson (1995): "A currency board is an arrangement under which a country fixes its exchange rate and maintains 100 percent backing of its money supply with foreign exchange." Three main characteristics determine a currency board, i.e. a fixed exchange rate against an anchor currency, full convertibility of current account as well as capital account transactions, and a full coverage of at least coins and notes by foreign reserves or gold (Schuler, 2002). Currency boards deviate with respect to two features. First, orthodox currency boards are distinguished from unorthodox currency boards. Under orthodox currency boards no central bank exists, i.e. the sole function of a currency board is to exchange its notes and coins for the anchor currency at a fixed rate. Under unorthodox currency boards the central bank retains some functions such as a lender of last resort or supervision of the banking system. Second, currency boards differ with respect to a broader or narrower interpretation of reserve coverage. Some currency board arrangements do not only cover M0, but M1 or even M2.

Berensmann (2002) calculates that the backing of monetary base with gross foreign reserves amounted to about 130 percent between 1992 and 2001. The Estonian system, however, is not an orthodox currency board since the central bank retains some rights to conduct monetary policy. Concerning the anchor currency, a number of options was considered, such as the ECU or a currency basket. Finally, however, the Estonian kroon was pegged against a single currency, at eight Estonian kroon for one German mark. The government argued that pegging against a single well established currency would increase transparency and credibility (Sepp et al., 2002).

In the following years, inflation rates fell quickly and the Estonian economy was the first of the Baltic States to recover from the turmoil. The currency board strengthened the stabilisation process and Estonia has managed to maintain the peg against the German mark and since 1999 against the euro at the same level until today (see figure 2.5).

Figure 2.5. The nominal exchange rate of Estonia against the ECU/Euro

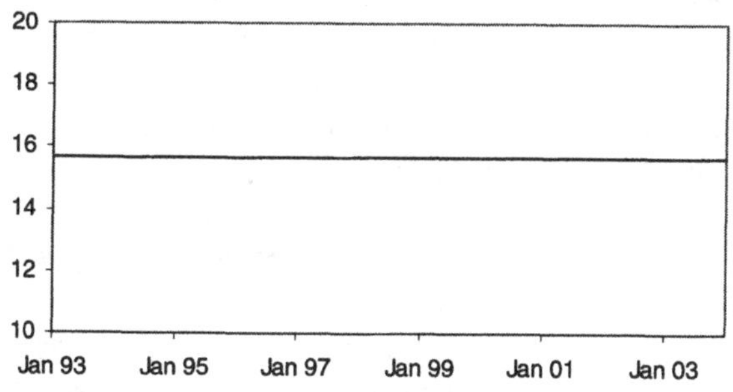

Data sources: International Financial Statistics and http://oanda.com.

However, two critical situations had to be managed. In 1997 the Asian crisis led to a drain of foreign capital inflows in several emerging market economies, which affected Estonia as well. First concerns about the sustainability of the currency board arose. The situation became even more dangerous when in mid 1998 the Russian crisis hit Estonia. The terms of trade with Russia, one of Estonia's most important trading partners, deteriorated substantially and devaluation expectations led to speculative pressure against the currency board system. However, given the high commitment to the currency board, Estonia also managed to overcome this critical situation.[13] Bauer and Herz (2004) even show that the system is also highly credible. Since June 2004 Estonia participates in the ERM2 system, but retains the currency board system (see table 2.5).

Table 2.5. De jure exchange rate regimes of Estonia

Date	Exchange Rate Regime	Specification
Since 06/1992	Currency board	Until 12/1998 against the DM and against the euro thereafter; since 06/2004 participation in the ERM2

Source: Bank of Estonia "Annual Report" (various issues).

2.7 Latvia

The development of the Latvian nominal exchange rate differs from that of other CEEC as it did not depreciate but appreciate initially in 1993 (see figure 2.6). The reason for this can be ascribed to the circumstances after the breakdown of the Soviet Union. In mid 1992 Latvia faced a severe shortage of Russian roubles in circulation. This shortage forced the Latvian government to introduce a local currency. The situation in Latvia, however, did not allow to immediately establish an independent currency since a trustworthy currency reform required a substantial backing of foreign reserves, which Latvia could not provide. Therefore, the Latvian government decided to introduce a temporary currency and in May 1992 the Latvian rouble became legal tender. In the first two months the Latvian rouble was fixed to the Russian rouble with a conversion rate of 1:1 (see table 2.6), but very high inflation rates in Russia in 1992 quickly led to the decision to terminate the fixed parity (Garry and Vanags, 1995). From now on the Latvian rouble became the sole legal tender. Initially, the exchange rate was set at 130 Latvian roubles per US dollar and the Bank of Latvia decided to let the exchange rate float, but already in September 1992 the central bank intervened in the foreign exchange rate market to reduce the nominal appreciation against the US dollar (Saavalainen, 1995). In the following, the Bank of Latvia officially pursued the policy of a managed float. Frequent interventions were intended to stabilise the external value of the Latvian currency. In October 1993, the Latvian rouble was replaced by the Latvian lat at a conversion rate of 1 lat against 200 Latvian

[13] A detailed analysis of the Estonian currency board and its sustainability is given in Sepp and Randveer (2002).

roubles. At first, the exchange rate regime remained unchanged. However, high real interest rates (intended to combat inflation) led to strong foreign capital inflows, so that alternative exchange rate regimes became optional. In this period the nominal exchange rate appreciated strongly and Latvia decided to halt this process.[14] In February 1994 the Bank of Latvia pegged the exchange rate of the lat to the Special Drawing Rights (SDR).[15] The decision of the Bank of Latvia to peg the lat to the SDR basket was based on the fact that Latvian entrepreneurs used more than one single foreign currency in international trade (Bank of Latvia, 1994). Although the formal legislation of the Latvian exchange rate system is not congruent to a currency board, there is practically little difference to the formal adoption of the currency board system as foreign reserves have usually exceeded the reserve money.

Figure 2.6. The nominal exchange rate of Latvia against the ECU/Euro

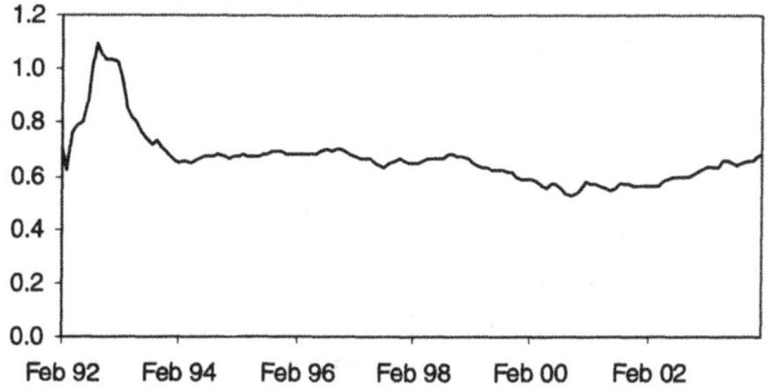

Data sources: International Financial Statistics and http://oanda.com

According to von Hagen and Zhou (2002) Latvia's "de facto" exchange rate system can also be classified as a fixed regime since the end of 1993, although some observations are noted as inconclusive. Bauer and Herz (2004) find evidence for a high credibility of the quasi currency board. Schnabl (2004) reveals that the low- and high-frequency exchange rate stability against the euro is substantially lower than for Estonia.

---

[14] Garry and Vanags (1995) argue that the Latvian central bank implicitly pursued a "crawling appreciation" against the SDR.

[15] The SDR is an international reserve asset, created by the IMF in 1969 to supplement the existing official reserves of member countries. SDRs are allocated to member countries in proportion to their IMF quotas. Its value is based on a basket which consists of the US dollar (43 %), the euro (26 %), the British pound (19 %) and the Japanese yen (12 %).

Table 2.6. De jure exchange rate regimes of Latvia

Date	Exchange Rate Regime	Specification
05/1992-07/1992	Fixed peg	Temporary currency "Latvian rouble"; 1:1 peg against Russian rouble
07/1992-10/1993	Managed float	No pre-announced path
10/1993-02/1994	Managed float	New currency "lat" single official means of payment
Since 02/1994	Fixed peg	Peg against SDR

Source: Bank of Latvia "Monetary Bulletin" (various issues).

2.8 Lithuania

Lithuania was the first Baltic State to declare independence from the Soviet Union. As such it was the first to be affected by a supply shortage of Russian roubles, so that already in August 1991 the coupon-like currency named talonas was issued to overcome this problem (Bank of Lithuania, 1992). Its value was equivalent to the Russian rouble and for more than one year both currencies circulated together in Lithuania. In October 1992, Lithuania left the rouble zone and the talonas was declared as sole legal tender. The talonas floated freely on currency auctions organised by the Bank of Lithuania (IMF, 1994). The talonas was always regarded as a temporary currency only and in June 1993 the litas was introduced at a conversion rate of 100 talonas for 1 litas. Soon the litas started to appreciate even in nominal terms (see figure 2.7), which posed competitiveness problems to Lithuanian producers. Even though the Central Bank interfered with the foreign exchange market to stabilise the litas, the industry was pushing for fixing the litas. In April 1994 Lithuania followed Estonia's example and introduced a currency board and the currency was fixed at 4 litas per US dollar (see table 2.7). The choice of the anchor currency was a rational step since 90 percent of trade and most foreign assets and liabilities were denominated in US dollars in 1994 (Alonso-Gamo et al., 2002). In Lithuania, besides coins and notes also accounts kept with the Bank of Lithuania as well as all other liquid liabilities of the Bank upon demand are covered by reserves (Bank of Lithuania, 1994).[16] As the Bank of Estonia, the Bank of Latvia also preserves the right to provide credits to the banking sector. The definition of the Lithuanian currency board is less

[16] In the beginning the Bank of Lithuania could not cover the monetary base fully by its own assets, but required loans from the IMF to guarantee full coverage.

stringent than the Estonian as not only net foreign reserves can be put to discretionary use to conduct monetary policy. However, the backing of the monetary base with gross foreign reserves amounted to an average of 132 percent over the period ranging from 1994 to 2001, which means it was on a comparable level to Estonia (Berensmann, 2002). Since the beginning of 2002 the litas has been pegged against the euro. In June 2004 Lithuania, together with Estonia and Slovenia, recorded a level of nominal convergence that allowed it to participate in the ERM2.

Figure 2.7. The nominal exchange rate of Lithuania against the ECU/Euro

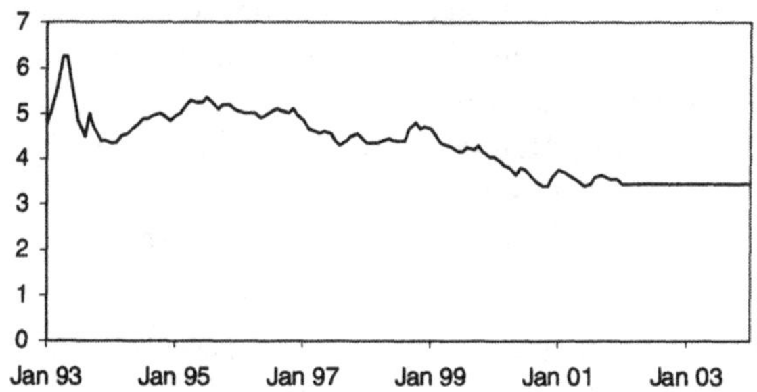

Data sources: International Financial Statistics and http://oanda.com.

Von Hagen and Zhou (2002) verify that Lithuania's "de jure" currency board can be also be categorized "de facto" as a fixed regime. Bauer and Herz (2004) further note that the Lithuanian exchange rate policy is highly credible.

Table 2.7. De jure exchange rate regimes of Lithuania

Date	Exchange Rate Regime	Specification
08/1991-10/1992	Fixed peg	Temporary currency "talonas"; 1:1 peg against Russian rouble
10/1992-06/1993	Free float	Temporary currency "talonas"
06/1993-04/1994	Managed float	New currency "litas"
Since 04/1994	Currency board	Until 12/2001 peg against the USD and against the euro thereafter; since 06/2004 participation in the ERM2

Sources: Rudgalvis (1996); Bank of Lithuania "Quarterly Bulletin" (various issues).

2.9 Bulgaria

Bulgaria's political and economic reform process towards a market economy lagged behind many of the other CEEC's at the beginning of the transition process. The break-down of the *comecon* had hit the Bulgarian economy particularly hard as most of Bulgaria's trade had been conducted with other *comecon* members and as its products were far from being competitive on world markets. However, the main reason for the slow recovery was that though economic reforms were inevitable a fundamental political change did not take place until 1997. Concerning the exchange rate policy, the first reform step was implemented in May 1990, when the existing system of multiple exchange rates was replaced by three exchange rates for dollar transactions. In the second step the three different exchange rates were abolished and a free interbank exchange rate market established in February 1991 (Hughes, 1991). However, convertibility was limited and the volume of transactions was relatively low. The daily exchange rate was quoted by the Bulgarian National Bank depending on the developments in the interbank exchange market.

Until 1997 Bulgaria experienced several critical periods with extremely high inflation rates and large devaluation. At the end of 1994 an overoptimistic interest rate cut of the Bulgarian National Bank led to speculative pressure on the exchange market. Since efforts to defend the currency were unsuccessful the Bulgarian lev declined quickly. The situation remained unstable until mid 1995, before a certain degree of stabilisation set in. At the beginning of 1996 Bulgaria got hit by a new crisis, which was far more severe than the crisis in 1994 since it was accompanied by a collapse of the country's banking sector. Hence, the crisis had strong negative impacts on the real sector and Bulgaria went into a deep recession.[17] The causes of the crisis included delays in vital structural reforms, weak banking supervision, soft budget constraints, and a continued central bank financing of the budget deficit (Vasileva, 2002). In February 1997 the crisis mounted when the monthly inflation rate hit 243 percent and the Bulgarian lev devalued correspondingly (see figure 2.8). In this situation of turmoil, the government of Bulgaria took the risk and introduced a currency board system in July 1997 (see table 2.8). The Bulgarian lev was pegged against the German mark - with a symbolic exchange rate of one lev for one mark - and since 1999 against the euro. In view of earlier stabilisation attempts, the rule-based currency board

[17] Figure A2 in appendix 1 shows that the Bulgarian economy experienced two subsequent years of real economic decline.

system was thought to be the only way to gain the trust and support of the population. Surprisingly, despite the unfavourable overall economic situation the crisis helped to introduce the currency board, since the hyperinflation reduced the real value of domestic debt and the banking crisis forced the execution of necessary reforms (Gulde, 1999). The design of the Bulgarian currency board deviates from the orthodox currency board system as the central bank also works - under restricted circumstances - as a lender of last resort. The central bank may also grant credits to the government, but only on the basis of funds from the IMF in excess of its reserve requirements (Pavlov, 1999). Furthermore, the coverage of reserves is extended to comprise not only notes and coins but also all deposits made with the central bank. In terms of stabilisation the currency board system has been very successful and has even served to strengthen financial and fiscal discipline (Vasileva, 2002). It has remained in operation until today.

Figure 2.8. The nominal exchange rate of Bulgaria against the ECU/Euro

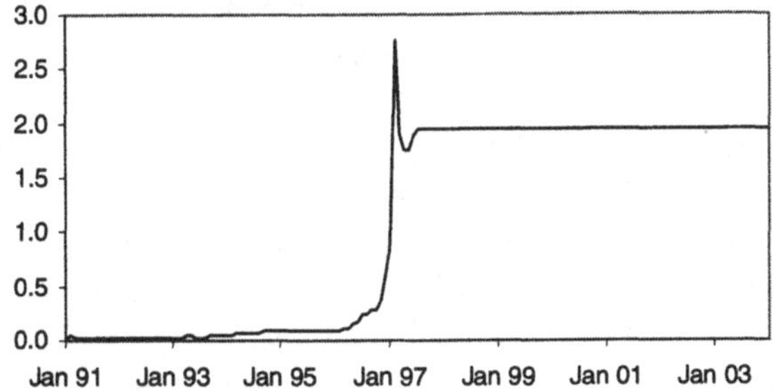

Data sources: International Financial Statistics and http://oanda.com.

The officially announced free float until June 1997 may be questioned. Von Hagen and Zhou (2002) determine a "de facto" fixed exchange rate regime until 1995 and a floating regime only in 1996. Moreover, frequent central bank interventions to stabilise the currency and a thin auction trade volume hint at an implicit managed float rather than a free float. The currency board system since 1997, however, is highly credible according to the study from Bauer and Herz (2004).

Table 2.8. De jure exchange rate regimes of Bulgaria

Date	Exchange Rate Regime	Specification
01/1991-06/1997	Free float	
Since 07/1997	Currency board	Until 12/1998 peg against the DM; peg against the euro thereafter

Source: Bulgarian National Bank "Monthly Bulletin" (various issues).

2.10 Romania

Romania's economic performance during the transition process can be considered as disappointing, at least for the first ten years. Often enough necessary reforms were delayed for years or implemented only slowly. The exchange rate market is no exception from the general development. In January 1991, Romania - faced with the breakdown of the *comecon* - was forced to abandon the system of transferable roubles, and all commercial and non-commercial transactions began to be effected in convertible currencies. However, the exchange market exhibited many imperfections and the convertibility of the Romanian leu remained very limited until the end of 1996 (Scutaru and Ghita, 1999). Moreover, governmental control of exchange transactions led to the coexistence of three different exchange rates: an official rate fixed by the central bank on a daily interbank foreign exchange market, an implicitly free rate used by firms to link import and export transactions, and a free rate for individuals (Daianu and Vranceanu, 2001). The official exchange rate depreciated consistently throughout this period. At the beginning of 1997 the leu was allowed to float and became convertible on current account, which led to a swift drop of its nominal value.[18] Since then, the leu has declined steadily, but on a relatively constant path (see figure 2.9).

According to the IMF, Romania pursued a free float exchange regime until the end of 1997.[19] However, given the frequency of adjustments by the authorities and the exchange market imperfection this official view is not consistent with reality (Budina et al., 2002). Von Hagen and Zhou (2002) determine a "de facto" fixed peg for the years 1992, 1993 and 1997, and an intermediate regime for 1994 to 1996.[20] At the beginning of 1998 the central bank of Romania officially switched

[18] At the same time, most of the price controls were abolished.

[19] See IMF "Exchange rate arrangements and exchange restrictions: annual report" (various issues) for details.

[20] Only 1991 is classified as a free float.

to a managed float (see table 2.9). Daianu and Vranceanu (2001), however, notice that the volume and the frequency of central bank interventions in the foreign exchange market exceed the normal definition of a managed float. Consequently, the IMF later reclassified Romania's regime as a crawling band and noted that the exchange rate is used as a soft nominal anchor.[21]

Figure 2.9. The nominal exchange rate of Romania against the ECU/Euro

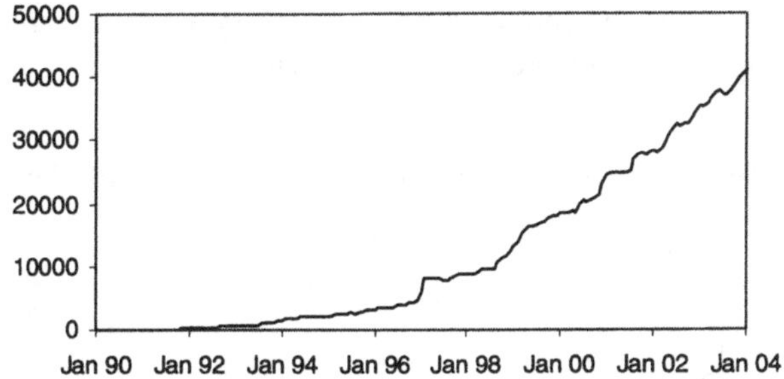

Data sources: International Financial Statistics and http://oanda.com.

According to official statements a basket of euro and US dollar serves as reference for managing the leu.[22] Frömmel and Schobert (2004) investigate whether the observed exchange rate movement is consistent with a crawling band. The authors find a significant rate of crawl, which however follows German mark and euro only until the end of 1998. For the period since 1999, the German mark and the US dollar both enter regression for the exchange rate determination of the Romanian leu insignificantly.

Table 2.9. De jure exchange rate regimes of Romania

Date	Exchange Rate Regime	Specification
01/1991-12/1997	Free float	
Since 1/1998	Managed Float	No pre-announced path

Source: National Bank of Romania "Annual Report" (various issues).

[21] See IMF "Exchange rate arrangements and exchange restrictions: annual report" (various issues) for details.

[22] Since March 2003 the euro has taken the role as the only reference currency according to official statements (National Bank of Romania, 2003).

2.11 Slovakia

The nominal exchange rate of Slovakia against the euro remained relatively stable in a range of 34 to 46 koruna per euro over the entire period (see figure 2.10). However, certain periods can be distinguished. From 1993 to 1998 the Slovak koruna was pegged against a currency basket (see table 2.10 for the exact composition of the basket), so that large fluctuations of the nominal exchange rate did not occur. The only exception was a nominal devaluation by 10 percent in July 1993. This step became inevitable due to low reserves when market participants anticipated a devaluation in view of fiscal and external deficits.[23]

Figure 2.10. The nominal exchange rate of Slovakia against the ECU/Euro

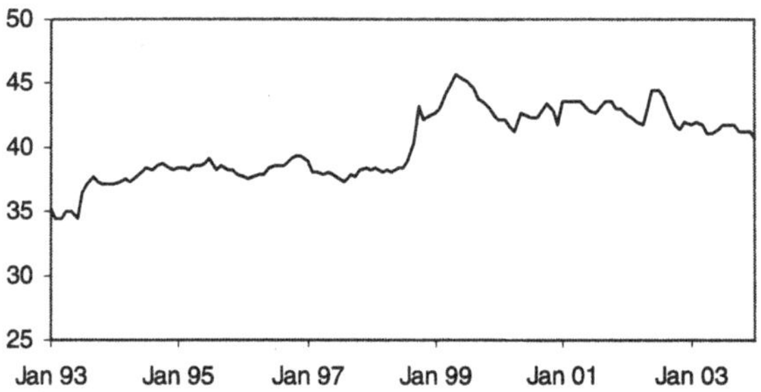

Data sources: International Financial Statistics and http://oanda.com

The fixed exchange rate system was quite successful as inflation rates declined and the Slovak economy stabilized quickly. In mid 1998, however, pressure on Slovakia's exchange rate peg surged due to political uncertainties, the exchange rate crises in Russia and in the Czech Republic, and the build-up of post-election devaluation expectations. Against the backdrop of macroeconomic imbalances, Slovakia abandoned its exchange rate peg and switched to a managed float in October 1998. As a result, the Slovak koruna depreciated sharply until about mid 1999. In response to some degree of overshooting the depreciation was partly

[23] Detailed background information about the exchange rate policies of Slovakia is given in Beblavý (2002).

reversed in the second half of 1999. Since then the exchange rate against the euro has remained relatively stable at around a level of 42 koruna per euro.

Studies on "de facto" exchange regimes find support for the currency peg until 1998. Von Hagen and Zhou (2002), for example, determine a fixed regime from 1994 to 1998, and an intermediate regime in 1993 and 1999. However, the managed float seems to have been administered rather tightly. Beblavý (2002) shows that after abandoning the fixed exchange rate regime officially, the exchange rate volatility against the euro remained very low. Interventions on the exchange rate market occurred occasionally.

Table 2.10. De jure exchange rate regimes of Slovakia

Date	Exchange Rate Regime	Specification
01/1993-07/1994	Fixed peg	Peg against a basket of five currencies (49.07 % USD, 36.16 % DM, 8.07 % AS, 3.79 % CHF, 2.92 % FFR); until 01/1993 currency union with the Czech Republic; in 07/1993 devaluation by 10 %
07/1994-10/1998	Fixed peg	Peg against a currency basket (60 % DM; 40 % USD)
Since 10/1998	Managed float	No pre-announced path

Sources: National Bank of Slovakia "Annual Report" (various issues); Beblavý (2002).

In this chapter the evolution of nominal exchange rates and exchange rate regimes of ten transition countries from central and eastern Europe has been presented. This overview has provided a rational understanding of nominal and real exchange rate developments. It will also serve to interpret deviations of exchange rates from equilibrium values later. The next chapter will now turn to the question how equilibrium exchange rate levels are determined. The chapter will give a detailed survey of the existing concepts to calculate equilibrium exchange rates and will present its applications to the central and eastern European transition economies.

3 Concepts to determine equilibrium exchange rates

3.1 General classification of concepts to determine equilibrium exchange rates

The growing economic globalisation has led to a rapid increase of trade flows and capital movements. Along with this development the importance of exchange rate movements and their economic implications in macroeconomics has continuously risen. Exchange rates are deemed to affect not only the international competitiveness but also the nation's trade deficit, the government budget deficit, and even employment. As a consequence, exchange rate movements are closely monitored by economists. Whenever large shifts of the exchange rate occur or when shifts are expected to take place, economists tend to have simple explanations for these fluctuations. They typically claim that the exchange rate has been "overvalued" or "undervalued". These terms have become so frequently used that almost nobody questions the meaning. Obviously, the terms over- and undervaluation imply that there has to be a certain level at which the exchange rate is correctly valued, or more precisely, at which the exchange rate is in equilibrium. However, although this implication is straight-forward concrete quantitative assessments of equilibrium values are rarely given.

A reason for this shortcoming may be that equilibrium values of exchange rates are rather difficult to determine. Predictions of exchange rate movements with structural macroeconomic models have not proven very successful. In particular medium-run forecasts have lacked accuracy. The short run is apparently easier to determine and in the long run the well known PPP has been given credit. Recently, however, a number of innovative concepts to calculate measures of equilibrium have been suggested in order to determine equilibrium levels for the medium or long run. In the following the most important approaches for the assessment of equilibrium exchange rates in the CEEC are presented in detail. The remaining concepts are briefly summarized as well.

3.1.1 The Behavioural Equilibrium Exchange Rate (BEER)

The Behavioural Equilibrium Exchange Rate (BEER) approach is founded on the notion that the real exchange rate cannot be isolated from real factors. More precisely, a set of economic fundamentals is assumed to drive the real exchange rate. Obviously, not all fluctuations of the real exchange rates are caused by innovations of economic fundamentals. It is the medium-run or long-run component of the real exchange rate, which is assumed to be determined.

Consider the equation

$$(3.1) \qquad q_t = \delta_1 FD_t + \delta_2 TF_t + \varepsilon_t .$$

In this equation, the real exchange rate q_t is explained by a vector of economic fundamentals $\boldsymbol{FD_t}$ that affect the real exchange rate in the medium or long run, a vector of transitory factors $\boldsymbol{TF_t}$ that affect the real exchange rate in the short run only, and a random error term ε_t; δ_1 and δ_2 are vectors of coefficients. The variable q_t displays the actual value of the real exchange rate. The equilibrium exchange rate $\bar{q}_t$ of the BEER concept is defined as

$$(3.2) \qquad \bar{q}_t = \delta_1 FD_t .$$

The BEER is thus the medium- and long-run component of the real exchange rate that can be explained by economic fundamentals. Any deviations from equilibrium are reflected in the terms $\boldsymbol{TF_t}$ and ε_t, so that total misalignment Mis_t is given as

$$(3.3) \qquad Mis_t = \delta_2 TF_t + \varepsilon_t .$$

Fundamental variables driving the real exchange rate have been formally introduced in a number of exchange rate models.[24] However, the BEER is more a statistical approach than a theoretical model. As a result, there is no unambiguous definition, which economic variables are deemed to be fundamental variables, and in empirical work a number of variables have been considered. However, two fundamental variables have been figured out both theoretically and empirically as main determinants of the real exchange rate, which are the productivity differential between the home country and abroad and the net foreign asset position.[25] The influence of these variables on the real exchange rate will therefore be discussed in more detail.

---

[24] A commonly referred exchange rate model has been advanced by Faruqee (1995). Alternative exchange rate models have been suggested Elbadawi (1994) and Edwards (1994).

[25] The theoretical derivation of the productivity differential and net foreign assets as main determinants of the real exchange rate goes back to Faruqee (1995). Alberola et al. (1999), Hansen and Roeger (2000), Clark and MacDonald (2000), as well as Maeso-Fernandez et al. (2001), among others have given empirical support for this theory.

The impact of the ***productivity differential*** on the real exchange rate is commonly known as the Balassa-Samuelson effect (Balassa, 1964; Samuelson, 1964). This effect can be described with a two-country model (home and foreign) which comprises two sectors, producing either traded goods or non-traded goods. It is assumed that prices for traded goods are exogenously given for both countries and that wages in the traded goods sector are determined by productivity. The Balassa-Samuelson effect arises when a productivity increase in the traded goods sector of one country, e.g. the home country, occurs. This rise in productivity raises wages in this sector. Assuming intersectoral labour mobility, wages in the non-traded goods sector are also driven upward in the home country. Since higher wages in the non-traded sector are not matched by productivity improvements, prices for non-traded goods have to shift upwards. These price increases constitute a positive inflation differential against the foreign country, which in turn will be reflected in a real appreciation.

The Balassa-Samuelson effect is most evident in catch-up countries, which are characterised by relatively high productivity gains compared to industrialised countries. The CEEC are most likely candidates for such a process of catching-up. Highly inefficient production inherited from the centrally planned era and low wages described the situation at the beginning of the 1990s. High growth rates, huge foreign direct investment, and increasing trade with western industrialised countries are indicators for productivity improvements. Rising wages and appreciated currencies support the evidence of the Balassa-Samuelson effect.

Hence, several empirical studies investigate the Balassa-Samuelson effect in the CEEC. In a study commissioned by the United Nations Economic Commission for Europe (UNECE), Halpern and Wyplosz (2001) confirm the presence of the Balassa-Samuelson effect in a panel analysis of various central and eastern transition economies. The authors determine a persistent annual real appreciation of around 3 percent. Sinn and Reutter (2001) calculate the productivity-driven inflation potential of five CEEC. The results suggest annual inflation rates in a range of 2.8 percent to 6.9 percent for a period in the second half of the 1990s. In a cointegration framework, Golinelli and Orsi (2002) seek to determine the contribution of the relative productivity of traded to non-traded goods sectors to overall inflation. The estimates range from 0.6 to 5.8 percent for Hungary, Poland, and the Czech Republic. Using cointegration as well as panel estimation techniques, Égert (2002a, 2002b) investigates the impact of productivity improvements on overall inflation of five CEEC and computes the average inflation differential against Germany. His finding is that the Balassa-Samuelson effect can only explain part of the observed appreciation with figures varying between –0.4 and

2.4 percent. Fischer (2002) determines that about half of the real exchange rate appreciation in CEEC may be attributed to the Balassa-Samuelson effect. He notes further that this effect seems to work not only through a supply channel but also through an investment demand channel.

Overall, there is strong empirical support for the presence and importance of the Balassa-Samuelson effect in the CEEC. Nevertheless, the effect cannot explain the entire level of appreciation. Other factors, such as the net foreign asset position, have implications on the real exchange rate development as well.[26]

The ***net foreign asset position*** affects the real exchange rate through different channels. An important channel arises from interest payments. For instance, a worsening of the net foreign asset position means higher interest payments for net debtor countries on their debt or smaller incomes from interest payments for creditor countries. This has to be financed by an improvement in the trade balance, which in turn requires a depreciation of the currency. Another channel links net foreign assets and the real exchange rate through the risk of default. Increasing debt leads to a rise in the risk premium, which demands higher yield expectations. At some point, however, a higher yield can only be guaranteed if the domestic currency depreciates.[27]

Gagnon (1996) examines the link between exchange rates and various variables in a panel data set with 20 industrial countries. His main finding is a significant and robust relationship between the real exchange rates and the net foreign asset position of the economy. In a cross-country study, Lane and Milesi-Ferretti (2000) investigate the same relationship and show that countries with net external liabilities tend to have more depreciated real exchange rates. In another paper, Lane and Milesi-Ferretti (2002) provide evidence for a negative long-run relationship between the real exchange rate and the trade balance, which again directly affects the net foreign asset position. Overall, there is strong empirical support for a positive link between net external wealth and the real exchange rate.

---

[26] In transition economies some of the inflation can be attributed to price liberalization. At the beginning of transition, many prices of goods, particularly services like public transport, energy supply, or communication, remained under government control. Later on, prices were either adjusted to real costs or liberalized. As a result, thereby fuelling inflation.

[27] Obstfeld and Rogoff (1995) have argued that a strong long-run relationship exists between persistent deficits (surpluses) in the current account balance and the depreciation (appreciation) of the real exchange rate. Faruqee (1995) has motivated the NFA variable from a stock-flow model of the exchange rate.

Aside from the productivity differential and the net foreign asset position ***other fundamental variables*** may have impact on the real exchange rate and may thus be also considered in the BEER approach. For example, the real exchange rate may be affected by the terms of trade. A deterioration of terms of trade in a country weakens its international competitiveness and ought to result in a depreciation of its currency.[28] However, the terms of trade across countries varies so that comparing the impact of terms of trade in a broad panel of countries is difficult. Another possible source of influence on the real exchange rate arises from the fiscal position. Frankel and Mussa (1988) argue that a fiscal consolidation in a country results in an improvement of its net foreign asset position and subsequently in an appreciation of its currency if this consolidation is permanent. However, a fiscal contraction could also lead to a negative demand shock, at least in the short term, which could have the opposite effect on the real exchange rate via relative prices. Another negative impact could arise if the marginal propensity of the public sector on non-traded goods is high, so that prices for non-traded goods fall with the reduction in government spending and consequently exchange rates depreciate (Dibooglu, 1996). Alternatively, in some BEER approaches the real interest rate differential is included.[29] It reflects the empirical evidence that interest rates deviate between countries over time although according to economic theory they should tend to equalise across countries. However, interest rate differentials are rather short term, so that they will not be considered in this study.

Considering the productivity differential (*prod*) and the level of net foreign assets (*nfa*) as main determinants of the real exchange rate, the BEER can be expressed as

$$\bar{q}_t = f(\, prod_t , nfa_t \,). \tag{3.4}$$

Estimation of the BEER approach involves the determination of a long-run relationship of equation (3.4). Cointegration analysis is the standard tool of BEER estimation.

---

[28] Dibooglu (1996) has studied the effects of real oil price increases on the real exchange rates of various currencies against the dollar. He found that the dollar appreciates when the oil price goes up.

[29] See Clark and MacDonald (2000) and Maeso-Fernandez et al. (2001) for examples.

3.1.2 The Permanent Equilibrium Exchange Rate (PEER)

The BEER approach is providing a long-run relationship between the real exchange rate and a set of fundamental variables. The fundamentals entering the calculations, however, are not necessarily at equilibrium values. This weakness is typically less serious if highly persistent time series are used as fundamentals. Nevertheless, there are certain ways to deal with this issue. A straight-forward method is to enter long-run or sustainable values in the cointegration relationship. This procedure obviously involves knowledge of these long-run or sustainable levels of fundamental variables.

An alternative is to decompose the real exchange rate times series into permanent (q_t^P) and transitory components (q_t^T)

(3.5) $$q_t = q_t^P + q_t^T \ .$$

The transitory component is characterised as having limited memory, i.e. the effects of the shock die away over time. The permanent component on the contrary is expected to have a persistent impact. The permanent component of the real exchange rate is then taken as a measure of equilibrium and forms the so-called Permanent Equilibrium Exchange Rate (PEER).

A rather simple way to deal with the issue of extracting permanent and transitory factors is to use mechanical filters such as the Hodrick-Prescott (HP) filter suggested by Hodrick and Prescott (1997) or the band-pass filter proposed by Baxter and King (1999). These filters essentially remove the business cycle from the data. The smoothed series are then interpreted as permanent or equilibrium values. However, mechanical filters have been criticised. Harvey and Jaeger (1993) show that the HP filter induces spurious dynamics in the cyclical component when it is used with integrated data. Moreover, mechanical filters become ill-defined at the beginning and the end of samples (Baxter and King, 1999).

The alternative is based on the idea of separating stationary from non-stationary components. The permanent component is associated with a non-stationary, i.e. I(1), process, while the transitory component is stationary or I(0). The main technical question is how to identify both components, since the sum of I(1) and I(0) is also I(1). In a seminal paper, Beveridge and Nelson (1981) use an ARIMA model to prove that the real exchange rate consists of a random walk and a stationary term. Subsequently, several authors have employed the Beveridge-Nelson decomposition to investigate the relative importance of permanent and transitory components. Huizinga (1987) uses the univariate Beveridge-Nelson decompositiona and finds that innovations in the permanent component account for around 90 percent of the volatility. This result is confirmed qualitatively by Baxter (1994) for univariate decompositions. However, Baxter (1994) also finds that with multivariate Beveridge-Nelson decompositions the temporary component is more important. Cumby and Huizinga (1990) use a bivariate vector autoregression of monthly changes in the real exchange rate and the inflation differential, and notice that the temporary components of real exchange rates are substantial.

Clarida and Gali (1994) use a methodology proposed by Blanchard and Quah (1989) to identify shocks that explain the volatility of the real exchange rate. In a trivariate vector autoregression including exchange rates, output and inflation, three types of shocks - supply, demand and money - are distinguished. Supply and demand side shocks are expected to have long-run effects, while money shocks are expected to have a temporary influence only. Results suggest that supply shocks only explain a small fraction of the exchange rate.

Another decomposition method to identify permanent and transitory components is proposed by Gonzalo and Granger (1995). This approach is based on the Johansen (1995) cointegration method and explicitly takes account of potential cointegrating relationships amongst the variables. A desirable feature of this decomposition is that the transitory component does not Granger-cause the permanent component in the long-run. That means movements in the transitory component will not have an impact on the long-run values of the permanent values of the variables. Clark and MacDonald (2000) have used this method to identify the permanent component for the exchange rates of the United States, Canada and the United Kingdom. Other applications on industrialised countries include Alberola et al. (1999) and Maeso-Fernandez et al. (2001).

3.1.3 The Purchasing Power Parity (PPP)

The purchasing power parity concept has a long tradition in economics and has been widely applied as a method to estimate equilibrium exchange rates. Cassel (1922) developed the idea that the nominal exchange rate should reflect the purchasing power of one currency against another. Cassel (1922) defined the purchasing power exchange rate as the reciprocal of the home country's price level against the foreign country's. Expressed in logarithms, the relationship is formally given as

(3.6) $$s_t = p_t - p_t^* ,$$

where s is the log of the nominal exchange rate as the ratio of foreign to local currency, p is the log of the domestic price, and p^* is the log of the foreign price of the good. Cassel (1922) noted that the purchasing power rate is the rate towards which the nominal exchange rate tends as long as free trade takes place.

Equation (3.6) may be interpreted as the law of one price, which states that once converted to a common currency an identical good should sell for the same price in different countries. This law of one price has been criticised for several reasons. Price differences may exist because of transaction costs like transportation expenses and tariffs. Moreover, data is typically only available for bundles of goods with different weights, compositions and with non-traded goods included. Therefore, *absolute PPP* as described above may not hold. Alternatively, *relative PPP* is postulated. Relative PPP posits that changes in the exchange rate are equal to changes in relative domestic to foreign prices. Algebraically this means

$$(3.7) \qquad \Delta s_t = \Delta p_t - \Delta p_t^*,$$

where Δ constitutes the first difference in time. Instead of using equation (3.7) tests for relative PPP are based on the equation

$$(3.8) \qquad q_t = \beta_0 + \beta_1 q_{t-1} + \varepsilon_t ,$$

where q is the log of the real exchange rate, given as

$$(3.9) \qquad q_t = s_t + p_t^* - p_t .$$

Considering equation (3.8) relative PPP simply relies on real exchange rates being stationary or mean-reverting (Taylor, 2001). In order to confirm the relative PPP hypothesis the parameter β_1 in equation (3.8) ought to be smaller than one. Therefore, empirical studies focus on testing for $\beta_1 < 1$.

The literature on PPP is extensive.[30] Many empirical applications on industrialised countries with relatively short time series fail to reject the hypothesis that the real exchange rate is non-stationary (Rogoff, 1996). As a consequence, long historical data sets have been used and Frankel (1986) and Edison (1987) among others find evidence in favour of PPP. However, the use of long historical time series has been criticised for the so-called "survivorship bias", since the sample is limited to countries for which long span time series exist. Another more promising approach

[30] For an overview on PPP refer to Breuer (1994) or Froot and Rogoff (1995).

involves the use of panel data. Studies from Frankel and Rose (1996), Oh (1996), and MacDonald (1996) get results that support PPP. However, O'Connell (1998) shows that these tests may suffer from cross-sectional correlation. In such a case empirical tests are biased towards over-acceptance of the PPP hypothesis. Recently, further innovations in panel time series analysis have again drawn the attention towards PPP. Papers from Pedroni (2001, 2004), Wu and Wu (2001) and Papell (1997, 2002), among others, employ new econometric testing procedures and take account of the above mentioned shortcomings. The results indicate that more powerful tests may tend to support the PPP hypothesis. In general, however, the evidence of PPP still remains an open question with mixed results.

3.1.4 The Fundamental Equilibrium Exchange Rate (FEER)

The idea of the fundamental equilibrium exchange rate (FEER) approach originates from Williamson (1983, 1994). He defines the FEER as the exchange rate that simultaneously satisfies internal and external balance. Internal balance is identified when an economy has full employment along with low inflation. External balance is characterised as the current account balance that is sustainable in the medium or long run when all countries under consideration are in internal equilibrium.

This basic definition may require some further explanations. Two equations are central to the FEER approach. First, output Y ought to be at the potential level $\overline{Y}$, which is consistent with the nonaccelerating inflation rate of unemployment (NAIRU). This assumption should hold for all countries, or simplified for domestic output Y and foreign output Y^*

(3.10) $$Y = \overline{Y} \text{ and } Y^* = \overline{Y}^*.$$

Second, the current account balance CA, which depends on the real exchange rate q as well as on foreign and domestic output, ought to be at a sustainable level $\overline{CA}$

(3.11) $$CA(q, Y^*, Y) = \overline{CA}.$$

The FEER is defined as the real exchange rate that satisfies both equations (3.10) and (3.11) simultaneously, which means the equilibrium exchange rate equilibrium $\overline{q}$ is a function of $\overline{Y}^*$, $\overline{Y}$ and $\overline{CA}$

(3.12) $$\overline{q} = f(\overline{CA}, \overline{Y}^*, \overline{Y}).$$

Equation (3.12) shows that the FEER is as "a *method of calculation* of a real exchange rate which is consistent with *medium-term macroeconomic equilibrium*" (Wren-Lewis, 1992, p. 75). Furthermore, unless the economies are permanently away from equilibrium, equation (3.12) includes the implicit assumption that the real exchange rate will converge to the FEER over time. Barisone et al. (2004) provide empirical evidence that FEERs act as attractors of the real exchange rate in the medium-run.

A major criticism of the FEER approach is that the estimated equilibrium exchange rate essentially depends on assumptions about a level of sustainable current account balance. In this respect, the FEER contains a strong normative element as these assumptions involve an arbitrary judgement. There are, of course, ways to retrieve estimates or judgements of potential and sustainable levels. The potential output may be either empirically generated, e.g. using the Hodrick-Prescott filter, or derived from economic theory. The sustainable current account balance can be determined as the level of capital inflow (or outflow) that stabilises the external debt-to-GDP ratio at a given level. Alternatively, instead of judging the sustainable current account directly, Isard and Faruqee (1998) use the accounting identity, which states that the current account equals the difference between aggregate saving S and aggregate investment I. The equilibrium current account may then be viewed as the difference between desired savings $\bar{S}$ and desired investment $\bar{I}$, and equation (3.11) becomes to

$$(3.13) \qquad CA(q,\bar{Y}^*,\bar{Y}) = \overline{CA} = \bar{S} - \bar{I}.$$

This so-called macroeconomic balance approach provides a more satisfactory method to estimate the equilibrium current account when economic variables such as the fiscal position, consumption smoothing or population demographics are used to determine the sustainable levels of savings and investment.

Another reason for criticism is due to the fact that the FEER approach does not guarantee stock-flow consistency. Artis and Taylor (1995) point out that the FEER is subject to hysteresis since temporary shocks may alter the underlying stocks and thus affect the sustainable current account balance. For this reason, the FEER is considered as a medium-run and not a long-run concept. Bayoumi et al. (1994) consider a time horizon of four to six years.

Estimation of FEERs can essentially be carried out in two ways. One way, as originally proposed and applied by Williamson (1994), is to use a fully specified macroeconomic model. Assuming internal and external balance, the model is solved for the real exchange rate, which then defines the FEER. This approach, however, has the disadvantage that a large and often intransparent macroeconomic model is required to determine the FEER for a set of countries simultaneously. Wren-Lewis (1992) suggests an alternative way, where equation (3.13), i.e. the relationship for the external balance, is estimated in a partial equilibrium model for each country separately. Isard et al. (2001) refine and extend this method in the line of the macroeconomic balance approach.[31] Their estimation method essentially involves three steps. In the first step the value of the current account position that is likely to emerge at prevailing exchange rates when all economies are at potential output is estimated. The second step involves the determination of an equilibrium saving-investment position. In the last step the exchange rate is determined that would bring the underlying current account level back to the equilibrium current account. This exchange rate is defined as the medium-term equilibrium or FEER.

3.1.5 The Natural Real Exchange Rate (NATREX)

An alternative to the FEER, which does not have the above mentioned disadvantages of normative assumptions and stock flow inconsistency, is the Natural Real Exchange Rate (NATREX) concept as proposed by Stein (1994, 1999, 2002). Similar to the FEER, the NATREX is based on the accounting equation

(3.14) $$CA_t = S_t - I_t .$$

However, in the NATREX the levels of current account, savings and investment are determined by a broad set of fundamentals, which include productivity and thrift. Equations (3.15) to (3.17) summarize the key fundamentals of the NATREX approach [32]

(3.15) $$CA_t = f(\overset{-}{q_t}, \overset{-}{c_t}, \overset{+}{c_t^*}, \overset{+}{a_t}, \overset{+/-}{i_t}, \overset{+}{nfa_t}),$$

(3.16) $$S_t = f(\overset{-}{c_t}, \overset{+}{nfa_t}),$$

[31] Other applications that use the macroeconomic balance approach of the FEER include Isard and Faruqee (1998), Faruqee et al. (1999), and Borowski and Couharde (2003).

[32] See Stein (2002) for a thorough discussion of the fundamental variables and transmission mechanisms in the NATREX.

(3.17) $$I_t = f(\overset{-}{q_t}, \overset{+}{a_t}, \overset{-}{i_t}, \overset{+/-}{tot_t}).$$

The current account balance depends negatively on the real exchange rate[33] and domestic consumption[34] c, and positively on foreign consumption c^*, total factor productivity a, and the net foreign asset position. Real interest rates i have a positive impact if the net foreign asset position is positive (and negative otherwise), since the current account is the trade balance plus interest return (or less interest payment) on net foreign assets. Savings are negatively related to consumption and positively to the net foreign asset position. Investment reacts negatively to the real exchange rate since a rise in the real exchange rate negatively affects expected profits. An increase in total factor productivity encourages investment, whereas higher interest rates discourage investment. Foreign demand is reflected in the terms of trade *tot*.

Assuming internal balance to hold and real interest rates i to equal world real interest rates i^*, and solving for the real exchange rate yields

(3.18) $$R_t = f(\overset{-}{c_t}, \overset{+}{c_t^*}, \overset{+}{a_t}, \overset{+/-}{i_t^*}, \overset{+}{nfa_t}, \overset{+/-}{tot_t}).$$

Equation (3.18) constitutes the medium-run equilibrium of the NATREX. It shows that the real exchange rate is determined by consumption (at home and abroad), productivity, net foreign assets, the terms of trade, and the interest rate.

However, the NATREX is not only designed to deliver medium-run equilibrium. In the model, net foreign assets and productivity are considered as endogenous variables, so that changes in the net foreign asset position or in productivity feed back into the balance equation and thus alter the equilibrium exchange rate. The inclusion of stock variables in the system guarantees stock-flow consistency of the model. This feature distinguishes the NATREX from the FEER and enables the trajectory from medium to long run.

The linkage of the medium to the long run arises from the following two equations

(3.19) $$\frac{d\,nfa_t}{dt} = CA_t = S_t - I_t \;,$$

---

[33] An increase in the real exchange rate reflects an appreciation of the home country's currency.

[34] Consumption can also be considered as time preference. Consumption further depends on fiscal policy.

$$\frac{da_t}{dt} = f(\overset{+}{I_t}) . \tag{3.20}$$

The current account determines the change in the net foreign asset position and the productivity growth is positively related to the investment rate. In the long-run equilibrium net foreign asset position and productivity growth are assumed to be constant.

Although the NATREX is given in structural form, most empirical applications make use of a reduced-form equation that incorporates the fundamental variables of the model to estimate the equilibrium real exchange rate.[35] In this case, the NATREX becomes very similar to the BEER approach, albeit the choice of fundamental variables that drive the exchange rate is based on the model outlined above. A structural form of the NATREX model has been employed and calibrated by Detken et al. (2002) for the euro exchange rate.

3.1.6 Alternative concepts to determine equilibrium exchange rates

The above presented models are most commonly used. Still, there are other concepts to determine equilibrium exchange rates. However, the number of applications on CEEC is limited. The reasons may be manifold. Missing time series data may be one possible explanation. Some concepts may not (yet) be appropriate to determine equilibrium exchange rates of developing countries like the CEEC, since all concepts were originally applied and intended for industrialised countries. Moreover, some concepts may just not be as popular as others. Yet, these alternatives will be presented briefly.[36]

One alternative is the ***monetary-based exchange rate*** model, which has its starting point in the money demand function

$$m_t^D - p_t = \alpha_1 y_t - \alpha_2 i_t , \qquad \alpha_1, \alpha_2 > 0, \tag{3.21}$$

[35] See e.g. Stein (1999) for an application.

[36] Comprehensive overviews of all concepts are given in MacDonald (2000) or Driver and Westaway (2004).

where m_t^D is the log of demand for money and y_t is the log of domestic income. Assuming exogenously given money supply m_t^S (in logs) and equilibrium on the money market one obtains

$$(3.22) \qquad m_t^S - p_t = \alpha_1 y_t - \alpha_2 i_t\,, \quad \alpha_1, \alpha_2 > 0.$$

Taking equation (3.22) for the home country and the foreign country (denoted by *) and substituting both equations into the PPP relationship (equation (3.6)) gives – under the assumption of perfect capital mobility – the monetary model

$$(3.23) \qquad s_t = (m_t^S - m_t^{S^*}) - \alpha_1(y_t - y_t^*) + \alpha_2(i_t - i_t^*).$$

The term monetary model is defined since money plays the predominant role. Essentially it is excess money supply that drives the nominal real exchange rate and real variables influence the exchange rate through the money demand channel. A rise in domestic income, for example, increases the demand for money which for an exogenously given money supply can only be satisfied by a fall in prices and an exchange rate appreciation.

Empirically, MacDonald and Taylor (1994) find robust evidence of long-run relationships to give support to the link between exchange rates and monetary fundamentals. Chinn (2000) uses a variant of equation (3.23), which adds sticky prices to the model, to assess if the East Asian currencies were overvalued prior to the Asian crisis. Estimation is typically conducted with cointegration analysis.

Another approach is the ***Capital-Enhanced Equilibrium Exchange Rate (CHEER)*** model.[37] This concept combines the PPP hypothesis with the uncovered interest parity. The approach acknowledges that the real exchange rate may not be in equilibrium as a result of nonzero interest rate differentials. The deviations from PPP arising from the interest rate differential are assumed to have persistent effects, which stem from continuous current account imbalances that have to be financed through the capital account. Estimation involves cointegration analysis of a vector comprising the nominal exchange rate and both domestic and foreign price levels as well as interest rates. The CHEER is successful with respect to showing faster mean reversion to equilibrium levels than the PPP approach (see e.g. MacDonald and Marsh, 1997).

---

[37] The approach has been advanced by Juselius (1991) and Johansen and Juselius (1992). The terminology CHEER originates from MacDonald (2000).

The ***Intermediate-Term Model-based Equilibrium Exchange Rate (ITMEER)*** suggested by Wadhwani (1999) combines the uncovered interest parity with the FEER approach. The ITMEER assumes that the exchange rate moves to reflect interest differentials plus a risk premium. The risk premium is in turn influenced by asset-return differentials (such as differences in dividend yields) and the deviation of the exchange rate from equilibrium. The deviations of the exchange rate from equilibrium itself depends on a number of variables already known from other approaches like BEER or FEER, such as current account balances, unemployment, net foreign assets, and the relative price of non-traded and traded goods. The ITMEER focuses on the nominal rather than the real exchange rate. Unlike most other concepts the estimation is not based on cointegration analysis, but the use of macroeconomic models.

Closely related to the FEER concept is the ***Desired Equilibrium Exchange Rate (DEER)***. In this approach the equilibrium exchange rate is calculated to be "consistent with, and necessary for, achieving 'desired' positions of internal and external balance" (Bayoumi et al., 1994, p. 20). In this respect, the exchange rate is interpreted as a tool to achieve certain macroeconomic objectives. The estimation is based on the same macroeconomic models as used to determine the FEER.

3.1.7 Characteristic features of equilibrium exchange rate concepts

The discussion of the equilibrium exchange rates concepts has shown that the approaches differ with respect to certain issues, such as the time horizon, the estimation technique, or the statistical assumptions regarding the real exchange rate. As a consequence, calculated equilibrium values could be different only for these reasons. For the evaluation of empirical results, it is thus helpful to take a closer look at theses issues.

Figure 3.1 graphically illustrates the differences and similarities of the various approaches. As far as the time horizon is concerned, the CHEER, ITMEER and the monetary model have relatively seen the shortest time horizon. CHEERs may be interpreted as a medium-run or even short-run version of the PPP, where interest rate differentials are added. Interest rate differentials are rather volatile, thus inducing frequent alterations of equilibrium levels. The risk premium has a similar degree of volatility, so that ITMEERs are less appropriate to forecast long-run movements of the exchange rate. Monetary-based models are primarily intended to explain the behaviour of nominal exchange rates through the effects of money demand and supply. Since demand and supply for money alter over relatively short time frames, the monetary model is not appropriate to estimate long-run equilibrium. The time frame of the BEER varies with the selection of fundamental variables. If only slow moving variables like net foreign assets or productivity differentials are used in the model, the time horizon is more long term than if faster moving variables like interest rate differentials or terms of trade are included. FEER and DEER are typical concepts for the medium run with a time span of four to six years (Bayoumi et al., 1994). Both methods are not designed to determine long-run equilibrium values since they do not incorporate stock changes. Stock-flow consistency, however, is given in the NATREX, so that it is also able to capture long-run developments of the real exchange rate. The PEER uses statistical methods to filter out the transitory component from the BEER. The remaining permanent component is expected to describe the long-run behaviour of the real exchange rate. The slow adjustment speed of the PPP to equilibrium makes it the classical long-run concept.

Figure 3.1. Characteristic features of equilibrium exchange rate concepts

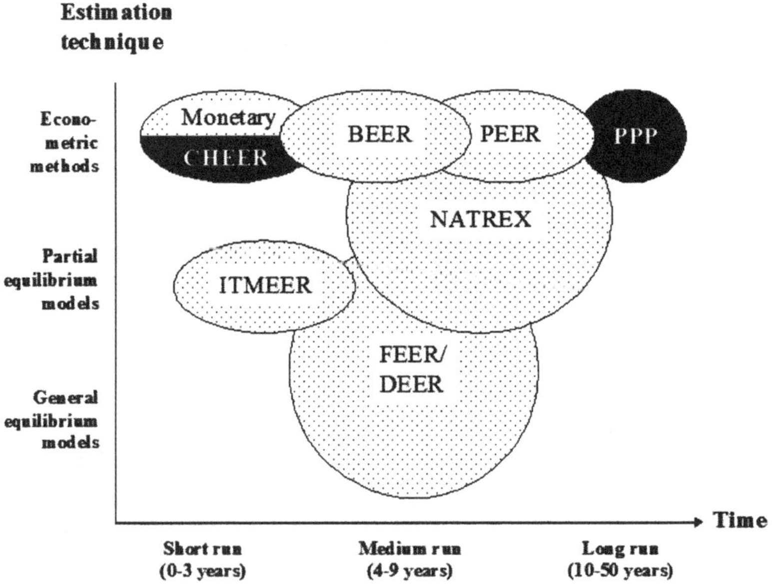

In terms of the estimation technique there are effectively three different approaches. One class of concepts is most commonly represented by reduced form equations, which are typically estimated in a cointegration framework. The monetary model, the CHEER, the BEER, and the PEER belong to this class. Most applications of the NATREX are based on such procedures as well, albeit the concept was originally designed as a partial equilibrium model. The ITMEER belongs to the class of concepts, which involve the calibration of partial equilibrium models. While many studies of the FEER or DEER approach are also based on the calibration of partial equilibrium models, general equilibrium models are also used for this concept. The absolute PPP does not require any specific methodology to determine the values. However, the examination of the validity of relative PPP is generally conducted in a reduced form equation, so that it is included in this type of methodology in the graph.

The colours of the ellipsoids add a third dimension to the classification. The black coloured ellipsoids indicate that these concepts assume stationarity of the real exchange rate, whereas the dotted approaches are based on the presumption of non-stationarity. The graph shows that while the CHEER and the PPP impose stationarity, all other approaches are based on non-stationarity of the exchange rate.

This section has provided a comprehensive summary of the various concepts to calculate equilibrium exchange rates. The next section will turn to the empirical applications of these concepts to CEEC in the literature and compare the qualitative and quantitative results of the studies.

3.2 Applications of equilibrium exchange rate concepts to central and eastern European countries

The empirical applications of equilibrium exchange rate concepts to CEEC can be distinguished with respect to a number of different criteria, such as the selected concept, the estimation techniques, the selected explanatory variables for the exchange rate determination, the reference currency or basket, the countries included in the analysis, or the time period. Given the multitude of possible estimation procedures, it is not surprising that quite different equilibrium exchange rate levels have been determined. The aim of this chapter is therefore to provide a brief, but rather comprehensive overview of the estimations and the associated results. The first three sections will present applications using the BEER, PPP and FEER approach respectively. Since panel estimations involve a very different approach than standard time series estimations, they will be grouped together in the last chapter.[38]

3.2.1 Behavioural equilibrium exchange rate studies

Kemme and Teng (2000) estimate a cointegration model for the monthly real exchange rate of ***Poland*** from December 1990 to May 1999. The real exchange rate is calculated by using four different deflators, such as the consumer price index (CPI), producer price index (PPI), wage rate and profits. A number of explanatory variables is considered, from which the ratio of government expenditures to industrial output as a measure of demand, the ratio of wages to producer prices as a proxy for productivity, the ratio of total trade to industrial output as an indicator for openness, and the current account balance turn out to be significant. An error correction model is estimated to obtain the long-run relationships, which define the equilibrium level of the real exchange rate. The calculated misalignment varies somewhat depending on the deflator. However, the general observation is that the real exchange rate of the Polish zloty was undervalued in the mid 1990s, but then appreciated strongly, so that it became overvalued in a range of 2 to 12 percent by 1999.

The work from *Sardà-Pons and Pérez-Lacasta (2003)* resembles the approach from Kemme and Teng (2000). In a cointegration framework, quarterly real exchange rate data of Poland are regressed on a wide range of explanatory variables, such as the ratio of government consumption to GDP, the ratio of total trade to GDP as a the measure for openness, the terms of trade, the interest rate differential against the United States level, domestic credit, and the trade balance relative to GDP. The estimated long-run relationship reveals an overvaluation of about 2 percent at the end of 1997. A key finding of the paper is that the real zloty exchange rate adjusts rather quickly to deviations from equilibrium. Misalignment is reduced by 40 to 50 percent within one quarter.

The exchange rate parity of the Polish zloty at entry to the EMU is in the focus of the paper from *Rawdanowicz (2002)*. Using quarterly data from the first quarter of 1995 to the second quarter of 2002, he employs cointegration techniques to obtain

---

[38] It has to be mentioned that this survey cannot claim to be fully comprehensive since the number of (unpublished) papers on real exchange rate determination in transition economies is too high. However, the aim of this chapter is to give an overview of the most influential and most valuable studies. In this respect, the emphasis is put on empirical studies that are closely related to this work. Another extensive summary, which also includes studies on the Balassa-Samuelson effect is provided by Égert (2004).

the long-run relationship between the real effective exchange rate and its fundamental determinants, which are the productivity differential against the euro zone, the terms of trade and the real interest rate differential against the Euribor. The results show that the appreciation of the zloty in 2001 was not matched by an equivalent appreciation of the equilibrium real exchange rate. As a result, the exchange rate appears to be overvalued in 2002.

Drummond et al. (2004) determine equilibrium exchange rates of ***Hungary*** for the period from the beginning of 1995 to the third quarter of 2003. The productivity differential and the net foreign asset position are selected as fundamentals to explain the CPI-based real effective exchange rate in a cointegration relationship. The productivity differential is proxied by the ratio of labour productivity in the industrial sector to labour productivity for the rest of the economy relative to the weighted average of trade partners. Net foreign assets are calculated by adding up current account balances and the resulting time series is normalised by the GDP. The results reveal a moderate undervaluation until 1999, followed by a period of overvaluation in a range of 2 to 10 percent. By the third quarter of 2003 the real exchange rate adjusted back to equilibrium.

In view of the Czech exchange rate crisis, *Frait and Komárek (1999)* study possible misalignments of the ***Czech Republic's*** koruna exchange rate till the end of 1998. A long-run cointegrating vector is obtained from an autoregressive distributed lag (ARDL) approach, which explains the CPI-based real exchange rate by GDP per capita, the terms of trade, the world interest rate, and a the ratio of savings to GDP. Substituting the long-run value of the fundamental determinants into the estimated equation, the outcome reveals a slight overvaluation prior to the crisis in 1997, followed by a short period of undervaluation, and again an overvaluation in 1998.

Two somewhat similar papers investigate real exchange rates and competitiveness of ***Estonia***. *Filipozzi (2000)* exploits quarterly data from the second quarter of 1993 to the second quarter of 1999. His estimation is based on the two-step Engle-Granger methodology. In the first step, ordinary least squares (OLS) estimation is used to regress the CPI-deflated real exchange rate on a list of possible explanatory variables. From this list, the productivity difference between the non-traded and traded goods sectors, the investment share of the economy, the ratio of the trade balance to GDP, and the effective nominal exchange rate turn out to be significant.[39] In the second step, an error correction model, which includes the

[39] It is noteworthy that Filipozzi (2000) does not calculate effective rates for the explanatory variables except for the nominal exchange rate.

four explanatory variables and a Russian crisis dummy, is employed to derive the long-run relationship. The author proceeds to assess equilibrium values of the explanatory variables. A number of alternative scenarios for deriving equilibrium values are considered, e.g. the HP filter or variable specific hypotheses. The outcome reveals initially declining real exchange rates with the peak undervaluation in 1994. Thereafter the real exchange rate appreciated strongly and arrived at 5 to 10 percent overvaluation in 1998 and 1999.

Randveeer and Rell (2002) investigate the impact of real exchange rate misalignment on the Estonian competitiveness. To calculate equilibrium exchange rate levels, the authors also employ the two-step Engle-Granger method, but the quarterly data now spans the time period from 1994 to 2000. From a long list of fundamental variables, they manage to find a single cointegration relationship between the CPI-deflated real effective exchange rate on the one hand side and the productivity differential as well as the terms of trade on the other hand side.[40] Two different procedures are applied to assess equilibrium values of the explanatory variables. The first approach makes use of the HP filter. In the second approach the authors attempt to determine a base period, at which the real exchange rate is believed to have been in equilibrium. Their ad hoc idea is to compare the Estonian price level with the implicit level, that is defined by the relationship between the level of per capita GDP and the price level. For this, they regress price levels of 52 countries on per capita GDP. It turns out that the Estonian real exchange rate seems to have been in equilibrium in 1996. The results of both approaches indicate that the Estonian kroon was highly undervalued at the beginning of 1994 with a deviation in the range of 15 to 30 percent. Most of the time, however, the exchange rate was close to equilibrium. Only during the Russian crisis the exchange rate was overvalued by about 5 percent.

Three papers deal with the case of ***Latvia***. *Kazaks (2000)* links the monthly real effective exchange rate to a broad set of fundamentals, which comprise labour productivity, unemployment, money velocity, and openness. He finds a cointegration relationship over the time period from January 1993 to June 1998. The fundamental equation is used to forecast the real exchange rate until the end of 1999. The calculations show no substantial misalignment.

Bitans (2002) follows the same approach for Latvia over the period from the fourth quarter of 1993 to the second quarter of 2001 as Randveer and Rell (2002) apply for Estonia. In the first step, the productivity differential, the openness of the economy, and the ratio of government consumption to GDP are determined as

---

[40] The productivity differential was calculated relative to the main trading partners.

fundamental variables influencing the real exchange rate. In the second step, the real exchange rate against a group of western European countries are found to form a stable long-run relationship. Fitting the HP filtered explanatory variables in the long-run equilibrium equation, Latvia's lat is found to have been undervalued until 1995 and overvalued from 1999 to 2000. By the third quarter of 2001 the real exchange rate seems to have readjusted to equilibrium.

Beguna (2002) employs the same idea over the same time period, but selects different explanatory variables. Besides openness and government consumption over GDP, the terms of trade and the net foreign direct investment are implemented in the error-correction model.[41] In order to determine the equilibrium exchange rate, the values of the explanatory variables are smoothened with a five-quarter moving average. The results indicate modest overvaluation of the lat since 1999. However, by the end of 2001, overvaluation has decreased to 2 percent.

The work of *Vetlov (2002)* on the ***Lithuanian*** real exchange rate is closely linked to the papers from Randveer and Rell (2002) and Bitans (2002). He also applies the two-step Engle-Granger framework, but focuses on the behaviour of PPI-deflated real effective exchange rates over the period beginning in the first quarter of 1995 and ending in the second quarter of 2001. The productivity differential, openness, the real price of oil as a proxy for terms of trade and the real interest rate differential are found to be robustly related to the real exchange rate. The HP-filtered explanatory variables reveal an undervalued currency from mid 1995 to 1998, before the Russian crisis led to a temporary overvaluation of up to 10 percent from 1999 to 2000. In the second quarter of 2001, however, the exchange rate was again undervalued by about 7 percent. As an alternative to the HP filter, various scenarios for equilibrium values of explanatory variables have been considered, which then again largely confirm the slight undervaluation in 2001.

Alonso-Gamo et al. (2002) are concerned with the competitiveness of the Lithuanian economy in view of the strong appreciation of the Lithuanian currency. The authors employ a cointegration model, where the real effective exchange rate is linked to relative sectoral prices as measured by the ratio of consumer prices to producer prices and the net foreign asset position relative to GDP.[42] In the resulting cointegrating relationship relative sectoral prices enter with a positive sign, but the net foreign asset position exhibits a negative sign, which contradicts the theory. One reason for this outcome could be that capital

---

[41] The coefficient of the net foreign direct investment, however, does not turn out to be significant.

[42] The term relative sectoral prices instead of productivity differential is used since the authors did not calculate effective rates against the rest of the world.

inflows have materialized in the form of productivity growth.[43] The computed equilibrium exchange rate reveals a 5 to 10 percent undervaluation of the litas from 1995 to 1998 and a period of overvaluation starting with the Russian crisis in the third quarter of 1998. At the beginning of 2001 the litas is found to have been slightly undervalued.

Burgess et al. (2003) closer inspect the exchange rates of all three ***Baltic States***. The productivity differential measured by the relative prices of non-traded to traded goods and the net foreign assets, which is derived by adding up current account data, are selected as explanatory variables for the real exchange rate. A cointegration relationship is estimated for each country separately. The coefficients of the productivity differential turn out to have the expected positive sign, but the net foreign assets are found to have negative impacts in all three cases. Despite this theoretically surprising outcome, the authors move on to determine equilibrium exchange rate values from the estimated cointegration vector. The results disclose a substantial overvaluation during the Russian crisis of about 10 to 15 percent. The effect of the Russian crisis, however, disappeared rather quickly, so that all three currencies appear to have been slightly undervalued in a range of 2 to 6 percent at the end of 2002.

Chobanov and Sorsa (2004) examine the real exchange rate behaviour of the ***Bulgarian*** lev for the period from the third quarter of 1997 to the first quarter of 2003. Since the authors do not consider the period before the introduction of the currency board, their analysis is largely restricted by the short time series. As a consequence, a mixture of BEER and NATREX approach is employed. The real effective exchange rate is regressed on the average labour productivity differential, the terms of trade, CPI deflated gross savings, world real interest rates measured by the LIBOR, and foreign direct investment. Autoregressive distributed lag (ARDL) estimation is used to obtain the long-run relationship. The authors proceed to determine actual and total misalignment, whereby the latter is determined by fitting HP-filtered fundamental variables in the long-run equation. The results indicate no serious actual misalignment of the Bulgarian lev. The total misalignment however peaked 7 percent at the beginning of 2002 and still amounted to 2 percent in the first quarter of 2003.

As part of a country report, the *IMF (1998)* evaluates the competitiveness of ***Slovakia*** by calculating equilibrium levels for the CPI-based, PPI-based, unit labour cost deflated real exchange rates as well as for an internal real exchange

[43] It is, however, most likely that this relation does only hold for the short time series used in their study and will thus eventually switch to the opposite.

rate. The study performs simple OLS regression based on monthly data with a number of long-run determinants of the real exchange rate, such as government consumption over GDP, investment over GDP, openness, and real wages as a proxy for productivity. Money (M2) over GDP is added to capture short-run fluctuations. The vector of coefficients for the long-run variables is used to compute the equilibrium rates. The resulting equilibrium rates were filtered with a moving average to remove remaining short-term noise. The paper reveals only modest departures from equilibrium and a slight overvaluation in mid 1997.

Égert and Lahrèche-Révil (2003) combine elements of the BEER and the FEER approach to determine equilibrium exchange rates of Poland, Hungary, the Czech Republic, Slovenia, and Slovakia. The authors apply a three-equation cointegration model. The first equation links the internal balance - defined as the price ratio of non-traded goods to traded goods - to the productivity differential as well as private consumption. The second equation constitutes the relationship between external balance - defined as the long-run sustainability of the current account - and terms of trade as well as openness. The third equation finally establishes the link of the real exchange rate to the internal and external balance. Data ranges from the first quarter of 1992 to the second quarter of 2001 and is expressed relative to the weighted average of US dollar and German mark.[44] Misalignment is calculated for the end of the observed period. The currencies of Poland, the Czech Republic, and Slovakia appear to be overvalued by 15 percent, 15 percent, and 8 percent respectively, whereas the Hungarian and the Slovenian currencies seem to be in equilibrium. The authors also provide some ad hoc determination of nominal exchange rate misalignment against the euro, which, however, due to the high weight of the euro in the two-currency basket does not deviate very much from the real misalignment.[45]

Table 3.1 summarizes key features of the presented BEER applications, such as the investigated country, the observed time period, the frequency of data, the estimation technique, and the explanatory variables used in the determination of the real exchange rate.

---

[44] In the case of Slovakia and Slovenia the data range starts in the first quarter of 1993.

[45] The authors basically compute the magnitude of nominal exchange rate adjustment against the euro required to eliminate the previously determined real misalignment.

Table 3.1. Key elements of studies using the BEER approach

Authors	Country	Period/ Frequency	Estimation technique	Explanatory variables
Kemme and Teng (2000)	Poland	1990:12-1999:5 Monthly	Error correction	Productivity (+) Current account (-) Govern. consumption (-) Openness (+)
Sardà-Pons and Pérez-Lacasta (2003)	Poland	1991:1-1997:4 Quarterly	Error correction	Govern. Consumption (+) Terms of trade (+) Interest rate differential (+) Openness (-) Credit expansion (+)
Rawdanowicz (2002)	Poland	1995:1-2002:2 Quarterly	Johansen cointegration	Productivity (+) Terms of trade (+) Interest rate differential (+)
Drummond et al. (2004)	Hungary	1995:1-2003:3 Quarterly	Johansen cointegration	Productivity (+) Net foreign assets (-)
Frait and Komárek (1999)	Czech Republic	1992:1-1998:4 Quarterly	ARDL cointegration	GDP per capita (+) Terms of trade (+) Interest rate (+) Savings (+)
Filipozzi (2000)	Estonia	1993:2-1999:2 Quarterly	Error correction	Productivity (+) Trade balance (+) Investment share (+) Nominal exchange rate (+)
Randveer and Rell (2002)	Estonia	1994:1-2000:4 Quarterly	Two-step Engle-Granger error correction	Productivity (+) Terms of trade (+)
Kazaks (2000)	Latvia	1993:1-1998:6 Monthly	Error correction	Productivity (+) Openness (-) Unemployment (+) Money velocity (-)
Bitans (2002)	Latvia	1993:4-2001:2 Quarterly	Two-step Engle-Granger error correction	Productivity (+) Govern. consumption (-) Openness (-)
Beguna (2002)	Latvia	1994:1-2001:4 Quarterly	Two-step Engle-Granger error correction	Govern. consumption (+) Terms of trade (+) Openness (+)
Vetlov (2002)	Lithuania	1995:1-2001:2 Quarterly	Two-step Engle-Granger error correction	Productivity (+) Terms of trade (+) Interest rate differential (-) Openness (-)
Alonso-Gamo et al. (2002)	Lithuania	1994:1-2001:3 Quarterly	Johansen cointegration	Productivity (+) Net foreign assets (-)
Burgess et al. (2003)	Estonia Latvia Lithuania	1994:1-2002:4 Quarterly	Johansen cointegration	Productivity (+) Net foreign assets (-)
Chobanov and Sorsa (2004)	Bulgaria	1997:3:2003:1 Quarterly	ARDL cointegration	Productivity (+) Terms of trade (+)

				Interest rate (+) Savings (-) Foreign direct investm. (-)
IMF (1998)	Slovakia	1990:1-1997:5 Monthly	OLS	Productivity (+) Govern. consumption (-) Investment share (-) Openness (+)
Égert and Lahrèche-Révil (2003)	Poland Hungary Czech Republic Slovenia Slovakia	1992:1-2001:2 Quarterly	Johansen cointegration	Productivity (+) Current account (+)

3.2.2 Purchasing power parity studies

Calculations of PPP values are not very popular for transition countries. However, some papers provide information on relative PPP rates in addition to BEER estimations. *Kemme and Teng (2000)*, for example, determine real exchange rate developments for ***Poland*** against the US dollar, whereby CPI, PPI, wage rates, or profits are used as deflators. Taking December 1990 as the base period, they find persistent overvaluation over the entire period based on CPI, PPI and wage rates, and undervaluation according to the profit-based real exchange rate. The magnitude of misalignment deviates substantially with respect to the price index. The CPI-based real exchange rate is overvalued by 50 percent, the PPI-based by 10 percent, the one based on wage rates by 110 percent in May 1999. Undervaluation based on profits sums up to 50 percent.

Sardà-Pons and Pérez-Lacasta (2003) also determine relative PPP with three different deflators (CPI, PPP, and wage rates) for Poland. Taking January 1991 as the base period, the authors detect rising overvaluation. The overvaluation is again the highest for the wage rate and the lowest for the PPI. Given the unrealistically high deviation from parity, the authors discard the relative PPP approach and proceed with a BEER-type model.

As part of their analysis on competitiveness of ***Estonia***, *Randveer and Rell (2002)* calculate a wide range of real exchange rate indicators. Besides CPI- and PPI-deflated real exchange rates, the ratios of export to import prices and of non-traded to traded goods were computed against the ten largest trading partners. Moreover, other indicators are used to determine real rates against specific country groups, like industrialised or transition countries. Most indices suggest substantial appreciation of more than 10 percent. Only the PPI against other transition countries and the unit labour costs against industrialized countries have depreciated.

Bitans (2002) also makes use of a number of deflators to determine real exchange rate movements of ***Latvia***. The appreciation, however, is lower than in case of Estonia. Competitiveness indicators like terms of trade and relative unit labour costs against western industrialized countries even reveal depreciation over time.

For ***Lithuania***, *Vetlov (2002)* computes real exchange rates based on CPI, PPI, terms of trade, internal prices, GDP-deflator, and unit labour costs. All calculations disclose a strong appreciation of the litas in a range of 25 to 85 percent. Indicators like terms of trade and unit labour costs suggest a significant loss of competitiveness.

The *IMF (1998)* investigates the evolution of PPP in ***Slovakia***. Taking January 1990 as the base period, they find overvaluation in a range of 2 to 10 percent in mid 1997, depending on the deflator. The authors further note that the real exchange rate appreciated against western industrialized countries, but depreciated against other transition countries. Table 3.2 provides a summary of the key elements of PPP studies described above.

Table 3.2. Key elements of studies using the PPP approach

Authors	**Country**	**Period**	**Frequency**	**Explanatory variables**	**Base Period**
Kemme and Teng (2000)	Poland	1990:12-1999:5	Monthly	CPI PPI Wage Profits	1990:12
Sardà-Pons and Pérez-Lacasta (2003)	Poland	1991:1-1997:4	Monthly	CPI PPI Wage	1991:1
Randveer and Rell (2002)	Estonia	1993:1-2000:4	Quarterly	CPI PPI Terms of Trade Internal	1993:1
Bitans (2002)	Latvia	1993:4-2001:2	Quarterly	CPI PPI Terms of Trade	1993:4
Vetlov (2002)	Lithuania	1993:6-2001:6	Monthly	CPI PPI Terms of Trade	1993:6
			Quarterly	Internal Unit labour costs GDP-deflator	1995:3
IMF (1998)	Slovakia	1990:1-1997:5	Monthly	CPI PPI Unit labour costs	1990:1

3.2.3 Fundamental equilibrium exchange rate studies

A comprehensive FEER study on CEEC is published by *Šmídková et al. (2002)*. Sustainable equilibrium values of real exchange rates are calculated for ***Poland***, ***Hungary***, the **Czech *Republic***, and ***Estonia***. The estimation employed in this paper is based on the general procedure presented in the chapter about FEER studies. The authors make use of the econometric model NiGEM of the National Institute of Economic and Social Research (NIESR) to retrieve trade elasticities. Instead of postulating sustainable current accounts, the study assumes a target value for the stock of external debt of 60 percent of GDP by 2022. The paper also takes the expected gains from economic integration such as the impact of foreign direct investment into account. The estimation reveals an appreciating tendency of the real exchange rates in all countries and significant overvaluation of at least four currencies, with the Slovenian tolar being the only exception in the first quarter of 2002.

Coudert and Couharde (2002) employ the FEER for the same five countries. Trade equations are also computed with the NiGEM model. The target current account is derived from a fixed effects model introduced by Doisy and Hervé (2001). The outcome exhibits an overvaluation of about 6 percent in 2000 and 2 percent in 2001 in the case of Poland, whereas the other currencies seem to be fairly valued. A sensitivity analysis suggests that the above values for Poland rather form the lower bound than the upper bound of misalignment.

Rawdonowicz (2002) performs some simple FEER calculations for the situation in ***Poland*** in 2002. Trade elasticities are taken from an earlier study. Three different scenarios for the potential output and the sustainable current account flows are assumed and some sensitivity analysis added. The calculations disclose a moderate nominal overvaluation against the euro in a range of 3 to 7 percent.

Hristov (2002) investigates real exchange rate misalignments of two countries that have established currency boards, i.e. ***Estonia*** and Argentina. In this study, the relationships are not based on a large model, but directly estimated from time series. Trade elasticities are evaluated with an error-correction model over the time period from 1993 to 1999. The level of potential output is determined from the time series trend, or alternatively with the HP filter. The sustainable level of the current account is calculated on the basis of a panel regression, which includes eleven transition economies. The results indicate that the Estonian kroon was overvalued until the end of 1996, then undervalued in 1997, and again overvalued in 1998. At the end of 1999 the exchange rate appears to be overvalued once more. Table 3.3 summarizes the FEER studies presented above. Table 3.3 summarizes the relevant characteristics of the FEER studies.

Table 3.3. Key elements of studies using the FEER approach

Authors	Countries	Macroeconomic Model	End period
Smidkova et al. (2002)	Poland Hungary Czech Republic Slovenia Estonia	NiGEM	2002
Coudert and Couharde (2002)	Poland Hungary Czech Republic Slovenia Estonia	NiGEM	2001
Rawdanowicz (2002)	Poland	No model	2002
Hristov (2002)	Estonia	Time series analysis	1999

Other concepts like the PEER, the monetary model, CHEER, or ITMEER have not yet been used in time series analysis to determine equilibrium exchange rates for CEEC. However, a panel study exists, which applies the monetary model and which will be discussed in the next chapter. Time series PEER estimates will be provided in chapter 5 of this study.

3.2.4 Panel studies

Most panel studies are very similar with respect to the selected concept since BEER type studies clearly dominate. However, there are essentially two different approaches. The first approach includes (only) the CEEC in the determination of long-run real exchange relationships and will therefore be referred as "in-sample" analysis. The alternative is the "out-of-sample" analysis where long-run relationships are estimated for a group of non-CEEC, before the resulting equation linking the real exchange rate to a set of fundamentals is used to determine equilibrium exchange rates for CEEC. Both approaches have their advantages and disadvantages.

The "out-of-sample" procedure was particularly useful at the beginning of the transition process, when time series were too short for direct estimation. Another rational argument for the "out-of-sample" approach is that estimations including the transition economies could lead to biased results. Economists advocating this method often argue that transition economies are characterised by group-specific factors like initially strongly undervalued currencies or sharp appreciation. Disregarding these aspects could bias the estimation results, so that it would be preferable to obtain the generally applicable relationship from non-CEEC first. However, the critical step of the "out-of-sample" approach is the application of the general estimation results on the CEEC. A one-to-one transformation typically produces implausible results since specific factors of transition economies are not considered. Any adjustment of the relationship, however, introduces a certain degree of arbitrariness. The "in-sample" analysis in turn does not have this disadvantage, but has to cope with data limitations in the CEEC.

Which of the two methodologies is selected, matters for the interpretation of the determined equilibrium levels and misalignments. Yet, there are other important criteria like the estimation technology or the selected time period that distinguish panel estimations as well. The following review will therefore be presented in chronological order to reflect the evolution of panel studies in terms of data, explanatory variables, and estimation techniques.

The first panel study on equilibrium exchange rates in transition economies was published by *Halpern and Wyplosz (1997)*. Confronted with the limitations of data at the time of publication, the authors do not estimate equilibrium exchange rates directly. They rather attempt to determine the equilibrium levels through a comparison with other countries of similar level of development. For this, Halpern and Wyplosz (1997) regress US dollar wages for about 80 countries from all over the world on a number of development indicators, such as GDP per worker, school enrolment, a ratio of agriculture to industry, the government share, and some dummies. Estimates are gained from a panel analysis with fixed effects, which includes data for five observations in the time series dimension, i.e. data from 1970, 1975, 1980, 1985, and 1990. The results of the panel regression are used to generate equilibrium levels for the real US dollar wage of six CEEC.[46] Comparing the outcome with the actual levels suggests that the currencies of Bulgaria, Czechoslovakia, Poland, and Romania were undervalued in 1990 while Hungary's currency appeared to be in equilibrium and Slovenia's seemed to have been even overvalued. By 1996 most of the undervaluation has diminished with

46 Besides the six CEEC, Croatia, Russia and China are included in the analysis.

only the Bulgarian and the Romanian exchange rates remaining undervalued and the other countries' rates close to equilibrium.

In a related paper, *Krajnyák and Zettelmeyer (1998)* regress US dollar wages on a number of development indicators. The main difference to the paper from Halpern and Wyplosz (1997) is that the authors focus on the time span from 1990 to 1995 and include the transition economies in the panel to perform an "in-sample" estimation. The results show that in the early 1990s the actual dollar wages in transition economies were very low in comparison to the equilibrium values. By 1995 the gap had narrowed but the magnitude of undervaluation was still between 45 and 55 percent.

Begg et al. (1999) extend and update the study from Halpern and Wyplosz (1997). A number of additional explanatory variables are added, such as an age dependence ratio, an openness indicator, the net foreign asset position of non-banks, and a ratio of credits to the private sector. The time series now includes the year 1995, so that six observations are available for the "out-of-sample" panel estimates. The outcome deviates in some cases from the previous study. The Slovenian exchange rate has now been overvalued throughout the period and also the Hungarian, Polish, and Romanian have more than offset any initial undervaluation by 1996. The currencies of the Czech Republic, Slovakia and Bulgaria as well as that of all three Baltic States now included in the sample remain below equilibrium.

The following three panel studies are concerned with the determination of explanatory variables for the real exchange rate development in the CEEC. Quantitative assessments of equilibrium exchange rates or real exchange rate misalignments, however, are not presented in these works. It is nevertheless instructive to present the selected estimation procedures and the resulting relationships between the real exchange rate and the set of fundamentals.

Maurin (2001) adjusts the traditional model on real exchange rate determination, so that it accounts for the typical characteristics of transition economies. According to the author the model should include factors like imperfect substitutability of traded goods, imperfect capital mobility, growing indebtedness, and high productivity gains. Maurin (2001) makes use of pooled least squares to estimate a regression, which includes relative productivity of non-traded to traded goods sectors, public consumption, the domestic real interest rate, and external debt as explanatory variables for the real exchange rate. The study comprises twelve countries over the time span from 1990 to 1998. The key finding of the paper is that public consumption and external debt have a significant impact on the real exchange rate in transition economies, whereas relative productivity and real interest rates turn out to be insignificant.

De Broeck and Sløk's (2001) main goal is to investigate whether the real exchange rate appreciation in transition economies is driven by productivity gains in the tradable goods sector. The authors use annual data from 1993 to 1998 for the same ten CEEC presented in this study. Two estimation techniques are employed, fixed effects and pooled mean group (PMG) estimates.[47] The CPI deflated real effective exchange rates are regressed on average labour productivities in the industrial, in the service, and in the agricultural sector, whereby all productivities are calculated relative to an average of productivities in OECD countries.[48] A number of control variables are also added to the regression, from which the government balance and openness turn out to be significant in the fixed effects regression, but not so in the pooled mean group estimation. The key finding of the paper is that an increase in productivity of 1 percent leads to a real exchange rate appreciation in a range of 0.2 to 0.6. percent.

The *Deutsche Bundesbank (2002)* is also concerned with the determination of fundamental variables influencing the real exchange rate evolution in the ten CEEC. In a first estimation, annual data ranging from 1994 to 1999 is used to regress real effective exchange rates on trade-weighted relative labour productivities of all three sectors, the trade-weighted relative ratio of government - or alternatively total consumption - to GDP, average real interest rates in the United States and Germany, and a price index for raw materials as a measure of the terms of trade. The results support the Balassa-Samuelson hypothesis of a positive link between productivity in the industrial production sector and real exchange rates. However, the relationship between productivity in the service sector and the real exchange rate also turns out to be positive, which contradicts the Balassa-Samuelson theory. The authors attempt to explain this by high demand for investment goods. Any increase in productivity leads to additional investment, which in an oligopolistic market for investment capital goods raises the prices for capital goods, thus inducing real appreciation. Therefore, in a second estimation, the authors select aggregated labour productivity, for which quarterly data is available. Using both seemingly unrelated (SUR) and PMG estimation the results reveal a relatively robust positive relationship between real effective exchange rates on the one hand side and labour productivity as well as

---

47 The PMG estimation will be presented in more detail in chapter 4.

48 The simplification of taking average OECD values is rather questionable, since effective rates are likely to deviate significantly in most CEEC.

consumption on the other hand side. Real interest rates have a negative impact on the appreciation of the local currencies and the measure for terms of trade turns out to be insignificant.

Kim and Korhonen (2002) perform an "out-of-sample" analysis. The authors employ the PMG and the fully modified ordinary least squares (FMOLS) estimator on a sample of 29 middle and high-income countries for the period from 1990 to 1999.[49] They regress real exchange rates on four fundamentals, such as GDP per capita, the ratio of government consumption to GDP as a proxy for fiscal policy, the external trade volume in relation to GDP as a measure of openness, and the ratio of gross fixed capital formation to GDP representing domestic supply capacity and technological progress. The resulting cointegration equation was applied to a sample of five central European transition economies to generate equilibrium real exchange rates of these countries. Kim and Korhonen (2002), however, encounter the problem that the results are not directly applicable to the CEEC since the deviation from real exchange rate equilibrium in the panel is positively related to per capita GDP. As a consequence, they introduce a common intercept for transition economies, which is based on the average per capita GDP in the transition economies.[50] The results show an overvaluation of the real effective exchange rate in a range of 8 to 20 percent for Poland and Slovakia, 12 to 19 percent for the Czech Republic and 40 to 49 percent for Hungary in 1999. For Slovenia real effective exchange rates were not calculated, but the authors determined that Slovenia's exchange rate was undervalued by 28 percent against the US dollar in 1999.

A somewhat different paper stems from *Crespo-Cuaresma et al. (2003),* who employ the monetary approach to six CEEC, i.e. Poland, Hungary, the Czech Republic, Slovenia, Romania, and Slovakia. Referring to the key equation (3.23) of the monetary-based model, they regress the nominal exchange rate against the euro on money supply (as measures by M2), interest rates, and industrial production (to proxy real output). The ratio of non-traded to traded prices is also added to capture the Balassa-Samuelson effect. All explanatory variables are defined relative to values for the euro area. The authors use monthly data over the time from September 1994 to March 2002 and employ a broad set of panel estimation procedures, such as fixed effects, FMOLS, PMG, and dynamic ordinary least squares (DOLS). The results deviate somewhat from other studies.

---

[49] The FMOLS estimation will be explained in more detail in chapter 4.

[50] As part of robustness checks, Kim and Korhonen (2002) also allow for heterogeneous intercepts in the transition economies.

The Slovenian tolar and the Czech koruna are found to have been overvalued by about 20 percent in March 2002. The Polish zloty is overvalued by 5 percent, whereas the Slovak koruna is roughly in equilibrium and the Hungarian forint even undervalued by about 5 percent.[51]

Égert and Lommatzsch (2004) apply several estimation techniques on the sample of five CEEC, i.e. Poland, Hungary, the Czech Republic, Slovenia, and Slovakia. The productivity differential, the real interest rate differential, a measure of regulated prices, foreign indebtness, openness, and government debt are used as explanatory variables in a number of specifications. Given the multitude of results, the authors identify ranges of misalignment. It turns out that the currencies of the Czech Republic and Slovakia are highly overvalued. While Poland and Slovenia exhibit slightly overvalued currencies, the Hungarian forint delivers inconclusive results.

While the previous two studies use "in-sample" estimations, *Maeso-Fernandez et al. (2004)* favour the "out-of-sample" approach. Rather than taking the real exchange rate as the explained variable, the authors opt for the exchange rate gap, which is defined as the ratio of the PPP exchange rate to the actual exchange rate. DOLS, FMOLS, and PMG estimators are used to regress the exchange rate gap on per capita GDP, openness and government consumption. The estimation is performed for 25 non-transition countries for the time period ranging from 1975 to 2002. The estimation proved to deliver a plausible and significant outcome. However, the authors encounter the problem that the results cannot be directly applied to the CEEC since the specific intercept for each of the CEEC cannot be observed and has to be either arbitrarily selected or somehow estimated. As a consequence equilibrium exchange rates and misalignments are not calculated and the shortcoming is left unanswered for future research.

A brief summary of panel studies and its most important characteristics is given in table 3.4.

---

[51] It should be noted that some of the assumptions of the model are not fulfilled in the investigated countries. The monetary model, for example, is built on the assumption of flexible exchange rate regimes, which is not consistent with the observation in the six countries over the entire period. Moreover, the inclusion of the Balassa-Samuelson effect is based on the assumption of purchasing power parity to hold for tradable goods, which according to the figures presented in chapter 3.2.2 is not true for all countries.

Table 3.4. Key elements of studies employing panel analysis

Authors	Countries	Period/ Frequency	Approach	Estimation technique	Explanatory variables
Halpern and Wyplosz (1997)	Poland Hungary Czech Rep. Slovenia Bulgaria Romania	1970-1990 Five years	Out-of-sample	Fixed effects	Govern. consumption (+) GDP per capita (+) School enrolment (+) Agriculture/industry (-)
Krajnyák and Zettelmeyer (1998)	CEEC	1990-1995 Annual	In-sample	Fixed and random effects	GDP per capita (+) School enrolment (-) Agriculture/GDP (-)
Begg et al. (1999)	CEEC	1970-1995 Five years	Out-of-sample	Generalised least squares	Net assets non-banks (+) Net assets banks (-) Govern. consumption (+) GDP per capita (+) Age dependency (+) Openness (+) Credit expansion (+)
Maurin (2001)	CEEC without Latvia and Lithuania	1990-1998 Annual	In-sample	Fixed effects	Govern. consumption (+) Net foreign assets (-)
De Broeck and Sløk's (2001)	CEEC	1993-198 Annual	In-sample	Fixed effects, PMG	Productivity (+) Government balance (+) Openness (-)
Deutsche Bundesbank (2002)	CEEC	1994:1-2000:4 Quarterly	In-sample	SUR, PMG	Productivity (+) Govern. consumption (+) Private consumption (+)
Kim and Korhonen (2002)	Poland Hungary Czech Rep. Slovenia Slovakia	1990-1999 Annual	Out-of-sample	PMG, FMOLS, MG	Govern. consumption (+) GDP per capita (+) Investment share (+) Openness (-)
Crespo-Cuaresma et al. (2003)	Poland Hungary Czech Rep. Slovenia Slovakia Romania	1994:9-2002:3 Monthly	In-sample	Fixed effects, PMG, FMOLS, DOLS	Productivity (+) Interest rate diff. (-) Money supply (-) Production (+)
Égert and Lommatzsch (2004)	Poland Hungary Czech Rep. Slovenia Slovakia	1993:1-2002:4 Quarterly	In-sample	DOLS, FMOLS, PMG, MG	Productivity (+) Net foreign assets (+) Interest rate diff. (-) Regulated prices (-) Openness (+) Government debt (-)
Maeso-Fernandez et al. (2004)	CEEC	1994:1-2001:1 Quarterly	Out-of-sample	DOLS, FMOLS, PMG	Govern. consumption (+) GDP per capita (+) Openness (-)

This chapter has provided an overview of the concepts to calculate equilibrium exchange rates and its applications to the CEEC. In this survey, however, one paper is still missing. Some of the estimations presented in this study have previously been published as a Bank of Finland discussion paper, see Rahn (2003). Chapters 4 and 5 will build on the results of this paper and will add some further information and estimations.

4 The behavioural equilibrium exchange rates of central and eastern European countries

4.1 Data overview

4.1.1 Data selection

The following empirical analysis is designed to determine equilibrium exchange rates of the ten CEEC presented in chapter 2.[52] Since all results will essentially depend on the selected input, the analysis starts with a thorough discussion of data selection issues such as data requirements, the frequency of data, the time series dimension, and the data source.

As far as ***data requirements*** are concerned, time series data for each of the CEEC is needed. In addition, data from the CEEC's main trading partners are required to calculate effective rates and comparative indices. For the group of CEEC, the by far most important trading partners are the euro area, the United States, the United Kingdom, Japan, and Russia. Trade with these economies accounted together with intra-CEEC trade for percentages ranging from 65 to 87 percent of external trade for the respective CEEC in 1996.[53] This comprehensive coverage guarantees a high degree of consistency and accuracy of the calculated figures.

An important issue is to choose the ***frequency of data*** for the empirical analysis. In this case either annual or quarterly data are feasible options. Annual time series have the advantage of the greatest choice of variables because not all series are available in higher frequencies. This, however, would come at the expense of having only one fourth of usable observations. Given the rather short time series this is a serious disadvantage as it would leave less than ten observations in some cases. Furthermore, annual data cannot capture all distinctive co-movements of exchange rates with economic fundamentals, which means that valuable information cannot be exploited. Therefore, quarterly data has been favoured for the econometric analysis.

The ***time series dimension*** essentially depends on the introduction of the current convertible currency. The CEEC time series start between the first quarter of 1990

[52] Main parts of chapters 4 and 5 have been published as a Bank of Finland Discussion Paper, see Rahn (2003).

[53] External trade is defined as the volume of imports plus exports. Data is taken from the International Trade Statistics Yearbook.

and the first quarter of 1993 and end in the first quarter of 2002. A complete overview is given in table 4.1.

Table 4.1. Time series dimensions

Country	Start	End
Poland	1990:1	2002:1
Hungary	1990:1	2002:1
Czech Republic	1993:1	2002:1
Slovenia	1993:1	2002:1
Estonia	1993:1	2002:1
Latvia	1993:1	2002:1
Lithuania	1993:1	2002:1
Bulgaria	1991:1	2002:1
Romania	1991:1	2002:1
Slovakia	1993:1	2002:1

The main ***data source*** for the time series is the International Financial Statistics (IFS) database. However, the IFS series contain a number of gaps, which have been filled with data from various national statistics.[54] This is, of course, a necessary evil since different sources can exhibit different time series. However, all time series have been cross-checked for consistency and in many cases the time series match perfectly because the IFS data is often based on national statistics as well.

The key fundamentals - productivity differentials and net foreign asset positions - that influence the behaviour of the real exchange rate have been presented in chapter 3. In the following, the practical implementation of the variables is discussed in more detail. As in most empirical studies, data limitations have to be considered.

4.1.2 The real effective exchange rate

Exchange rates are defined as an index, where an increase reflects an appreciation for the home country's currency. Real exchange rates are given as CPI-deflated

---

[54] More than 80 percent of all data are based on the IFS database. A detailed overview is given in appendix 2.

nominal exchange rates and represent average values for the period. For the calculation of effective rates, trade weights based on cumulated export and import volumes from the 1996 International Trade Statistics Yearbook are used. Trade volumes from the year 1996 work best as compromise between the earliest periods of transition and the recent time since trade patterns of CEEC's have changed significantly over the observed period.[55] The alternative of working with changing trade weights would have been inferior as such alterations could have led to structural breaks in the time series. The trade weights are presented in table 4.2.

Table 4.2. Trade weights for the determination of effective rates

	Pol	Hun	Cze	Sln	Est	Lat	Lit	Bul	Rom	Slk	UK	USA	Jap	Rus	Euro
Poland		2.8	4.7	1.4	1.5	2.8	5.7	1.0	1.0	4.0	0.8	0.0	0.0	4.8	4.7
Hungary	1.5		1.5	2.5	0.6	0.6	1.3	0.9	3.4	3.6	0.3	0.0	0.0	3.7	2.9
Czech Rep.	4.1	3.2		2.8	0.5	0.9	1.6	1.4	0.7	31.3	0.5	0.0	0.0	3.5	3.7
Slovenia	0.4	1.3	0.9		0.0	0.0	0.0	0.2	0.3	0.8	0.1	0.0	0.0	0.6	1.6
Estonia	0.1	0.1	0.1	0.0		6.6	3.1	0.0	0.0	0.0	0.0	0.0	0.0	0.9	0.2
Latvia	0.3	0.1	0.1	0.0	5.9		7.7	0.0	0.0	0.0	0.0	0.0	0.0	1.8	0.0
Lithuania	0.7	0.2	0.2	0.1	4.3	9.1		0.0	0.0	0.1	0.0	0.0	0.0	2.0	0.0
Bulgaria	0.2	0.2	0.2	0.1	0.0	0.3	0.4		1.1	0.2	0.1	0.0	0.0	1.9	0.5
Romania	0.3	1.7	0.3	0.3	0.0	0.0	0.0	2.3		0.4	0.2	0.0	0.0	1.5	1.3
Slovakia	1.5	2.6	13.4	1.1	0.1	0.4	0.4	0.4	0.7		0.1	0.0	0.0	3.0	1.2
UK	6.5	3.7	3.7	2.7	4.5	8.0	4.6	3.8	4.2	2.0		13.4	6.5	6.6	36.8
USA	4.6	4.2	3.3	4.1	3.0	2.1	2.3	3.5	4.5	2.4	17.9		63.5	11.3	28.6
Japan	1.4	1.9	1.3	1.3	2.0	0.4	0.5	0.9	1.1	1.2	5.5	41.0		6.2	12.1
Russia	8.7	11.4	6.4	3.7	19.6	28.5	33.5	33.7	11.8	12.9	0.9	1.6	1.6		6.4
Euro-area	69.8	66.7	64.1	80.0	58.0	40.3	38.9	51.9	71.3	41.1	73.7	44.1	28.3	52.3	

Note: The numbers are in percentages. The countries in rows are the trading partners of the countries in columns. Source: Own calculations based on 1996 data from the International Trade Statistics Yearbook.

The real effective exchange rate for country i (q_i) is thus the trade-weighted average of the bilateral real exchange rates (e_{ij}) vis-á-vis its trading partners

[55] More precisely, the weight of Russia and other former Soviet Union member countries has declined, whereas trade with the euro area has increased over-proportionally.

$$(4.1) \qquad q_i = \sum_j w_{ij}\, e_{ij},$$

where the trade weights w_{ij} add up to one, $\sum_j w_{ij} = 1$.[56] The resulting time series is then transformed to logs.

Figures for the euro do not exist prior to its introduction in 1999. Still, the European Central Bank (ECB) has published a synthetic value for the nominal euro/dollar exchange rate preceding its introduction, which is based on the exchange rates of the twelve participating countries with each country weighted by its share of manufacturing trade of the euro area. However, for this research project an own value is constructed. The reason is that own calculations guarantee more consistency with other variables such as the productivity differential since this value is not available from other sources. The synthetic euro time series in this study is based on the real exchange rates of the twelve participating countries with each country weighted by the 1996 share of trade with economies outside the European Union.

Table 4.3. Cross correlations of calculated real effective exchange rates with officially published time series

Country	Source	Correlation coefficient
Poland	IFS	0.98
Hungary	IFS	0.85
Czech Republic	IFS	0.96
Slovenia	n.a.	n.a.
Estonia	Bank of Estonia	0.97
Latvia	Bank of Latvia	0.96
Lithuania	Bank of Lithuania	0.99
Bulgaria	IFS	0.91
Romania	IFS	0.96
Slovakia	IFS	0.77

To cross-check the results, the calculated real effective exchange rates of all CEEC are compared with real effective exchange rates from other sources. Table

56 Since not all time series are available prior to 1993, the trade matrix for the period ranging from 1990 to 1992 has to be adjusted to control for the missing values.

4.3 shows that these figures match very well; correlation coefficients turn out to range from 0.77 to 0.98 over the respective sample period for the CEEC. This outcome serves to improve the confidence that the real effective exchange rate measures used are plausible.

4.1.3 The relative productivity differential

In order to capture the Balassa-Samuelson effect directly, productivity measures for the traded goods sector and the non-traded goods sector are required. However, such data is essentially unavailable. Traded and non-traded goods sectors naturally overlap, so that productivity measures are difficult to isolate. Instead, proxies have to be considered. A proxy frequently used is the relative price ratio between at home and abroad.[57] Relative price ratios have two desirable features. First, in most CEEC they are available on a quarterly basis and second, this proxy is homogenous across countries, which is important for such a broad range of economies.

Studies from de Gregorio et al. (1994) and Canzoneri et al. (1999) support the suitability of this proxy since they testify to a close link between productivity differentials and relative price ratios in developed countries. Furthermore, Lane and Milesi-Ferretti (2000) emphasize the role of relative price ratios as the primary component for the real exchange rate.

In practice, the relative productivity differential is calculated as the ratio of the domestic CPI to the domestic PPI relative to the corresponding foreign ratio. Taking logs gives

$$(4.2) \qquad prod_{i,t} = \log\left(\frac{cpi_{i,t} / ppi_{i,t}}{\prod_{\forall j \neq i} (cpi_{j,t} / ppi_{j,t})^{w_j}} \right).$$

The idea of this comparative index, suggested by Kakkar and Ogaki (1999), is that the CPI contains a high proportion of non-tradable goods like services, whereas the producer price index contains mostly tradable goods. The trade weights used here are the same as used for the real effective exchange rate determination. This

---

[57] Examples include Alberola et al. (1999), Chinn (2000), Clark and MacDonald (1999), as well as Clostermann and Schnatz (2000). Other potential proxies include a comparative index of labor productivity in the manufacturing sector, see e.g. Faruqee (1995) or Feyzioglu (1997), or the ratio of GDP to employed persons, see e.g. Clostermann and Friedmann (1998).

feature guarantees consistency between the time series. Consistency applies to the euro time series as well. The euro price index is based on the price indices of the twelve participating countries with each country weighted by the share of its trade with economies outside the European Union.

4.1.4 The net foreign asset position

According to the balance of payments definition the net foreign asset position is calculated as the sum of the net foreign direct investment position, the net portfolio equity stock position, the net debt position and the foreign exchange reserves. In principle, these data are available from the IMF's Balance of Payments Statistics. However, not all of these figures have been recorded in all countries at all times. In fact, time series of a reasonable length only exist for a few industrialised countries. Moreover, quarterly figures have only been published in very recent years. In the CEEC, collecting reliable data was almost impossible in the first years of transition, so that they are no positive exception. Therefore, alternative ways to generate figures on net foreign assets have to be considered.

Lane and Milesi-Ferretti (2001) suggest two alternatives to determine net foreign asset values, which make use of more frequently available flow data. Both methods start with an initial stock value (or if even this is not obtainable an estimate of an initial stock) and then flow data is added up to calculate past and future values. The first approach is directly connected to the balance of payments definition and uses flow data of all the components listed above. The second approach consists in cumulating current account balances, adjusted by the capital account balance. This link between the net foreign asset position and the current account balance is straightforward and the analytical derivation is provided by Lane and Milesi-Ferretti (2001).

Although in principle all three methods ought to deliver the same numbers there are certain valuation deficits, which have to be kept in mind. One possible cause for deviations comes from price and exchange rate fluctuations as these have direct effects on the value of asset and liability stocks as well as foreign exchange reserves, which are not captured in the flow dynamics. Another reason for divergences is due to changes in the value of equity and FDI, e.g. movements in the stock exchange.[58]

---

[58] See Lane and Milesi-Ferretti (2001) for a detailed discussion of possible reasons for divergence.

In the following empirical analysis the current account approach is utilized since current account balance data is most readily available on a quarterly basis. The adjustment for the capital account balance, which reflects mainly net capital transfers, plays a minor role in most economies compared to the current account balance. Thus, the capital account balance is omitted from the calculations for practical reasons.

For all countries taken into consideration stock of net foreign asset values for the end of 1998 exist, so that it is taken as the initial value from where quarterly current account data are used to calculate past and future periods.[59] For the euro area figures on current accounts of all twelve member countries are summed up.[60] The calculated net foreign assets are then normalised by nominal GDP (in US Dollars) to account for the size of each country.[61, 62] Some of the resulting time series revealed seasonal patterns, which are rather typical for net foreign asset time series. Therefore, the time series are seasonally adjusted using the additive *X-12* method when tests approved seasonality.[63]

---

[59] For very few periods and countries only annual current account time series are available. These time series are transformed from low frequency (annual data) to high frequency (quarterly data) using an optimal interpolation procedure. Very briefly, the quarterly data are derived by solving a quadratic optimization problem. For details on the dynamic programming algorithm see Bertsekas (1976), pp. 70-72. One must keep in mind that interpolated data is no substitute for actual data since the greater detail is fictitious. However, interpolation is very useful if most of the data in a multivariate analysis are at a higher frequency and if one would have to compact them all in order to use them together with just a few low frequency series.

[60] For Greece, Ireland and Luxemburg no data on stocks of net foreign assets are available. In this case current account data are added up historically.

[61] Please note that GDP data is denominated in national currency, whereas net foreign assets are denominated in US dollars. Consequently, GDP data must be converted with the prevailing exchange rate. Hansen and Roeger (2000) point out that this conversion could lead to spurious correlation between real effective exchange rates and net foreign assets. Countries most likely to be affected are those with large fluctuations in the nominal US dollar exchange rate. For the CEEC with a peg to the US dollar or to a basket containing a large US dollar share the effect is of minor importance. Nevertheless, this issue must be borne in mind.

[62] For some CEEC only annual GDP data are available for the early years of transition. These data are transformed as described above. GDP data for the euro area countries without quarterly IFS figures (Ireland, Greece, Luxemburg) are simply divided by four since the impact of these countries on the overall value is very small.

[63] The *X-12* method comes from the Census Bureau, which provides a full documentation of the procedure.

4.2 Time series estimation of the behavioural equilibrium exchange rates

4.2.1 Unit root tests

Before estimations are carried out, it is necessary to test for the degree of integration of the individual time series, because the choice of the appropriate estimation technique essentially depends on the presence of unit roots. A standard tool to test for unit roots in the time series is the augmented Dickey Fuller (ADF) test. Consider the equation

$$(4.3) \qquad y_t = \eta + \delta t + \rho y_{t-1} + \sum_{j=1}^{p} \varphi_j \Delta y_{t-j} + \varepsilon_t \ ,$$

where the time series y is regressed on a constant η, a deterministic time trend t with coefficient δ, the lagged time series y_{t-1} with autoregressive coefficient ρ, p lagged first differences of y with coefficients φ_j,[64] and the error term ε. The ADF test hypothesis is

H_0: $\rho = 1$

H_1: $\rho < 1$.

If the autoregressive coefficient ρ equals one the series contains a unit root, i.e. is integrated of order I(1).[65] If ρ is smaller than one, the series is assumed to be stationary, i.e. I(0).

Dickey and Fuller (1979) showed that the distribution under the null hypothesis is nonstandard, and simulated the critical values for selected sample sizes. The critical values, however, are not independent of the inclusion of intercept and deterministic trend. Moreover, the power of the test is reduced if irrelevant lags are included in equation (4.3). A standard procedure to control for these issues is to determine the equation form with the general-to-specific method. Starting with a maximum number of lags (in this case five) and a time trend, the number of lags is reduced as long as the last lag is insignificant. If then the last lag is significant the time trend is assessed for its significance and eventually omitted.

[64] Δ denotes the difference operator and p reflects the lag length.

[65] More accurately, the series is at least I(1) as it may also be integrated of higher grade, e.g. I(2).

Application of this procedure on the CEEC time series delivers the results in table 4.4. The outcome is mixed. Countries with purely non-stationary time series comprise Hungary, the Czech Republic, Slovenia, and Estonia. Other countries exhibit one or more stationary time series. This result is not surprising. The issue if time series like real exchange rates are stationary or non-stationary has filled the literature and there is no definite answer. In general, however, non-stationarity is more likely for short time spans as given in this sample than for long time spans.[66]

Table 4.4. Augmented Dickey-Fuller unit root test results

Country	RER	PROD	NFA
Poland	-5.56 (2,T) **	-6.24 (0,T) **	-1.57 (1)
Hungary	-2.52 (0)	-0.98 (0)	-1.07 (1)
Czech Republic	-3.34 (1,T)	-2.42 (0)	-1.58 (1)
Slovenia	-1.63 (4)	-3.53 (4,T)	-2.58 (4,T)
Estonia	-2.24 (0)	-2.75 (4)	-3.29 (0,T)
Latvia	-2.31 (0)	-3.24 (1) *	-2.62 (2,T)
Lithuania	-3.40 (0) *	-3.63 (4,T) *	-1.79 (2)
Bulgaria	-3.52 (0) *	-3,18 (4) *	-3.05 (0) *
Romania	-4.12 (4,T) *	-4.58 (4) **	-4.38 (3,T) *
Slovakia	-3.74 (0,T) *	-1.73 (1)	-4.98 (3,T) **

Note: Number of lags and inclusion of time trend for ADF test in parentheses. Critical values (with/without time trend): 5 % critical value: -2.96 / -3.56 (* denotes significance at this level); 1 % critical value: -3.55 / -4.27 (** denotes significance at this level).

As stated before, the ADF test is a standard procedure to test for unit roots. Perron (1989), however, has shown that discontinuities in macroeconomic time series may bias the test statistic. A failure to take account of a structural break in the slope or intercept will be mistaken by the usual ADF unit root test as a persistent innovation to a stochastic trend. That is, a unit root test which does not take into account a break in the series will have very low power. If the breaks in the series are known, the ADF test can be adjusted relatively simple by including dummy

[66] It is worth mentioning that all series exhibit stationary behaviour at the second order of integration, i.e. ADF tests of the first difference reject the unit root hypothesis.

variables. However, it is unlikely that the break date is known a priori. For this reason, Perron (1997) suggests a unit root test where the timing of the break point is determined endogenously. More precisely, Perron (1997) offers three different tests depending on assumptions regarding the type of the structural break. The first test allows for a change in the intercept, the second allows for a switch in the intercept and the slope, and under the third model a change in the slope is allowed but both segments of the trend function are joined at the break point.

In the following it is assumed that both a change in the intercept and the slope may occur at time T_b. This assumption is rather flexible and it is the best way to capture all possible breaks in the period of transition. Sudden revaluations, for example, are associated with changes in the intercept. Modifications of the crawling peg rate, on the other hand, are most likely associated with changes in the slope. And a switch of the exchange rate regime can have impacts on both intercept and slope. The unit root test is performed by testing for $\rho = 1$ in the regression

$$(4.4) \qquad y_t = \eta + \theta DA_t + \delta t + \tau DT_t + \psi D(T_b)_t + \rho y_{t-1} + \sum_{j=1}^{p} \varphi_j \Delta y_{t-j} + \varepsilon_t$$

where $DA_t = 1(t > T_b)$, $DT_t = 1(t > T_b)t$, and $D(T_b)_t = 1(t = T_b + 1)$ with $1(\cdot)$ as the indicator function. θ, τ, and ψ are parameters for the respective equation term.

In consistency with the ADF test, the lag length is selected with the general-to-specific procedure. Table 4.5 shows the results of the unit root test of all three time series as well as the corresponding break points.

In the majority of cases the null hypothesis of a unit root cannot be rejected at the 5 percent level of significance. This result refers to all three variables, showing only two or three exceptions for each variable. This outcome tends to support the assumption of predominantly non-stationary time series. Looking at the break date, the structural shift for the real exchange rate is most evident in the third quarter of 1998. Five countries exhibit a structural break at this point of time and two others have break dates close by. Moreover, the productivity and net foreign assets time series also show clusters around this date. This timing is not a coincidence, but the result of the Russian exchange rate crisis in August 1998. Further investigations revealed that the Russian crisis indeed caused structural break points for most real exchange rate and productivity time series. Therefore, its impact must be considered carefully.

Table 4.5. Perron unit root test results with endogenous structural breakpoints

Country	RER		PROD		NFA	
	Test statistic	Break date	Test Statistic	Break date	Test statistic	Break date
Poland	-5.48 (2)	1998:3	-6.33 (0)**	1998:1	-6.29 (0)*	1994:2
Hungary	-4.76 (4)	1992:2	-3.62 (1)	1995:4	-3.81 (0)	1999:3
Czech Republic	-5.85 (0)*	1998:3	-6.37 (4)**	1998:1	-4.61 (1)	1995:4
Slovenia	-5.82 (3)*	1998:3	-5.05 (5)	1998:1	-2.86 (4)	1993:4
Estonia	-5.80 (5)*	1998:3	-4.81 (3)	1994:4	-3.98 (0)	1994:2
Latvia	-5.05 (2)	1998:2	-3.31 (1)	1995:2	-6.95 (1)**	1998:1
Lithuania	-5.42 (2)	1998:3	-4.48 (2)	1998:4	-1.43 (1)	1994:3
Bulgaria	-4.20 (1)	1992:3	-4.55 (4)	1994:2	-4.74 (4)	1998:2
Romania	-4.92 (2)	1992:2	-4.19 (3)	1992:3	-8.33 (5)**	1998:3
Slovakia	-5.57 (2)	1999:1	-4.29 (0)	1999:3	-5.14 (3)	2000:3

Note: 5 % critical value: -5.59 (* denotes significance at this level). 1 % critical value: -6.32 (** denotes significance at this level). Number of optimal lags in parentheses.

4.2.2 The Russian financial crisis and its consequences for the estimations

Russia's role as one of the main trading partners leads to a specific problem for the analysis, which appears as a consequence of the Russian financial crisis. In August 1998 the Russian government was forced to abandon the US dollar peg of the rouble, default on its domestic debt and declare a moratorium of payments by commercial banks to foreign investors. Poor fiscal management combined with negative external factors had led to panic-driven capital outflows and speculations against the Russian currency.[67] In the following weeks the rouble fell sharply by more than 60 percent against the US dollar and inflation rates rose quickly to hyperinflationary levels (figures 4.1 and 4.2 show the evolution of monthly nominal and real effective exchange as well as monthly inflation rates). When the Russian economy recovered from the turmoil at the beginning of 1999, the nominal exchange rate stabilized at a low level. Then, high inflation rates brought about a slowly appreciating real exchange rate.

[67] For a thorough discussion about the history and causes of the Russian exchange rate crisis see Desai (2000) and Kharas et al. (2001).

Figure 4.1. Russian monthly nominal and real effective exchange rates during the financial crisis

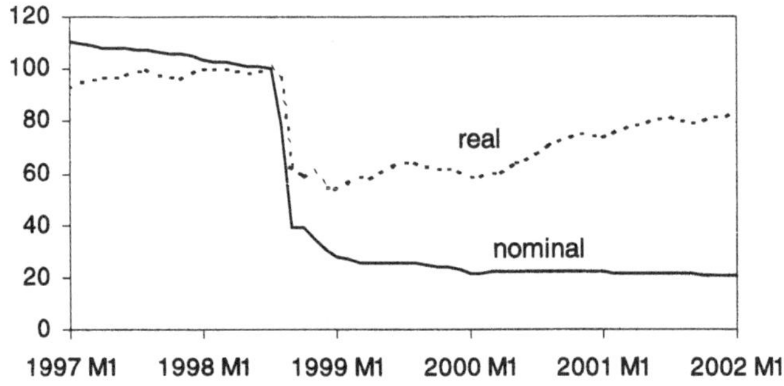

Data source: International Financial Statistics.

Figure 4.2. Russian monthly inflation rates during the financial crisis

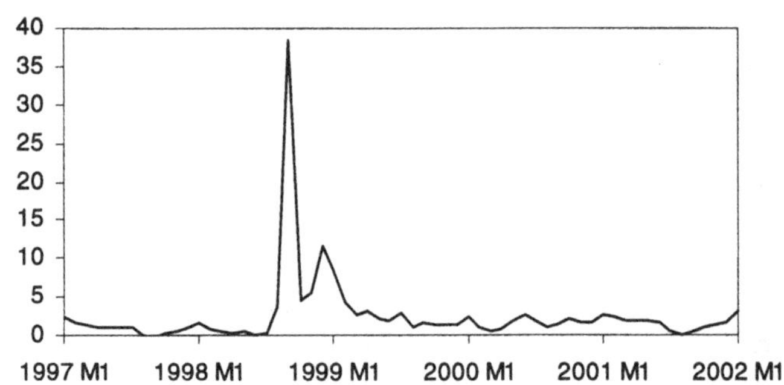

Data source: International Financial Statistics.

The Russian crisis severely affected the CEEC and caused an economic slowdown in these countries. Apart from the recessionary effect, the sharp decline of the rouble had direct and indirect impacts on the CEEC countries. The direct impact was a sudden appreciation of the CEEC's real exchange rates. Due to Russia's high trade share the devaluation of the Russian rouble leads directly to a rise in the real effective exchange rate index. The indirect effect stems from the price effects of the devaluation. Imports to Russia became more expensive and led to higher inflation in Russia. On the other hand, imports from Russia to the CEEC became cheaper and thus lowered the price level in these countries. Hence, the CEEC's relative price index vis-á-vis the rest of the world declined. Once the situation in Russia stabilized, both impacts reversed since the Russian rouble recovered and the import prices from Russia adjusted to a higher level. Given the short time series this period induces a negative link between the real exchange rate and the Balassa-Samuelson effect, which contradicts the theoretical relationship. This could lead to incorrect outputs and interpretations if no adjustments are made. Hence, an exogenous Russian crisis variable is introduced to account for the overall impact.

The question is how this variable could be designed to depict not only the one time shock of the devaluation but also the subsequent adjustment process including both direct and indirect effects. The idea is to extract the average effect on the CEEC from the given data. Hence, deviations from the normal level of both effective exchange rate and productivity differential indices are calculated. Evidently, other factors have influenced the time series as well, so that it is difficult to separate the Russian crisis impact from other influences in countries, where Russia plays a minor role as trading partner. Thus, only the effect on the three CEEC with the highest share of trade with Russia is selected.[68] The absolute deviation of each of these three CEEC is weighted by the trade share of Russia to form an index. The resulting Russian crisis variable is shown in figure 4.3.

Figure 4.3. Russian crisis variable

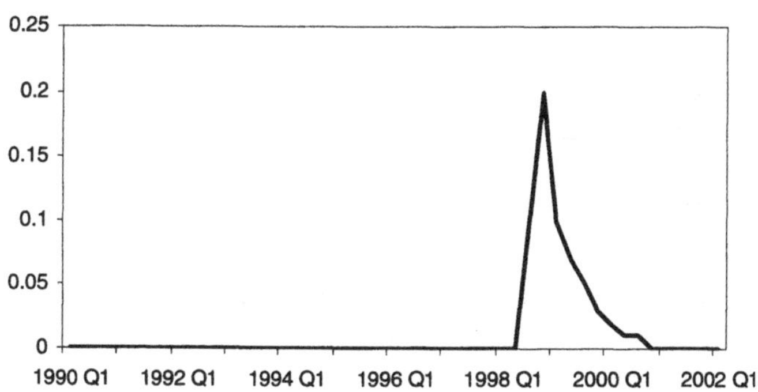

[68] The three CEEC with the highest trade share are Latvia, Lithuania and Bulgaria.

4.2.3 Econometric representation of the behavioural equilibrium exchange rates

Given the three time series and the Russian crisis variable, the appropriate estimation technique must be selected. As a first step, Granger causality tests have been conducted to control for the interrelation of the three relevant variables. Granger causality means that past values of one variable help explain another variable. Since each of the three variables is tested against all others and for all countries, the number of Granger causality tests is large. Therefore, not all test results are presented in detail. Instead, table 4.6 displays, for which countries the test for no Granger causality has been rejected. The explained variables are listed in the columns, the explanatory variables in the rows.

Table 4.6. Rejections of tests for Granger causality

	RER	PROD	NFA
RER		Czech Republic/ Estonia/Latvia	Poland/Hungary/ Slovenia/Estonia/Latvia/ Lithuania/ Romania
PROD	Poland/Czech Republic/ Estonia/Lithuania/ Slovakia		Poland/Hungary/ Slovenia/ Estonia/Latvia
NFA	Czech Republic/Slovenia/ Bulgaria/Romania/ Slovakia	Poland	

The output indicates a high degree of interrelation among the variables. Not only do productivity differential and net foreign assets influence real exchange rates, but other forces are present as well. Therefore, none of the variables should be considered exogenous a priori.

When time series variables are interrelated with each other and when it is not clear whether certain variables are exogenous, the standard econometric representation is a vector autoregressive system (VAR), where each variable depends on the lagged values of all endogenous time series

$$x_t = \eta + \sum_{i=1}^{p} A_i x_{t-i} + \varepsilon_t . \qquad (4.5)$$

In the equation, η is a $k \times 1$ vector of constants, ε represents a $k \times 1$ vector of white noise residuals and $\boldsymbol{A}$ denotes a $k \times p$ coefficient matrix, where k reflects the number of variables. In this analysis $\boldsymbol{x}_t$ is a vector of three variables, namely real effective exchange rates, the productivity differential, and the net foreign asset position:

(4.6) $$\boldsymbol{x}_t = [q_t, prod_t, nfa_t].$$

Direct estimation of VARs requires all time series to be stationary. Unit root tests, however, have indicated mostly non-stationary behaviours. Moreover, the "atheoretical" VAR model cannot be considered as the appropriate estimation method for the BEER concept. The BEER approach presumes a long-run relationship amongst the relevant variables, where deviations (or errors) from this long-run equilibrium are corrected over time. Such a relationship may be interpreted as a linear combination of variables, i.e. the variables are assumed to be cointegrated. Thus, they are best represented with a vector error correction model (VECM), where an error correction term is added to the VAR system. Under the null hypothesis of one cointegration the VAR may be rewritten as the VECM

(4.7) $$\Delta \boldsymbol{x}_t = \eta + \sum_{i=1}^{p-1} \Phi_i \Delta \boldsymbol{x}_{t-i} + \Pi \boldsymbol{x}_{t-1} + \varepsilon_t ,$$

where Φ denotes a $k \times (p-1)$ matrix of short-run coefficients and Π is a $k \times k$ coefficient matrix. If Π has a reduced rank $r < k$, then two $k \times r$ matrices α and β exist, such that $\Pi = \alpha\beta'$, where α is interpreted as the adjustment matrix and the columns of β are the linearly independent cointegrating vectors of the VECM. These cointegrating vectors finally determine the BEER.

4.2.4 Cointegration tests

The hypothesis that there is such a long-run relationship between the variables can be tested with cointegration tests. In the following the maximum-likelihood method of Johansen (1995) is used to determine the existence of cointegration. The Johansen procedure is particularly appropriate for this research since the results can be directly used to extract not only BEER but also PEER estimates.

Two different cointegration tests are suggested by Johansen (1995) and employed in this study. Both tests exploit the information contained in the matrix Π. More precisely, the number of nonzero characteristic roots in Π determines the rank of the matrix and thus the number of cointegrating equations. If, however, the rank of Π is zero the variables are not cointegrated. Let $\hat{\lambda}_i$ denote the *i*'s estimated characteristic root, where the $\hat{\lambda}_i$'s have been ordered such that $\hat{\lambda}_1 > \hat{\lambda}_2 > \ldots > \hat{\lambda}_k$. Then the first cointegration test, the trace statistic, is defined as

$$(4.8) \qquad \lambda_{trace}(r) = -N^* \sum_{i=r+1}^{k} log(1-\hat{\lambda}_i),$$

where N^* denotes the number of usable observations and *r* denotes the rank of the matrix. The statistic tests the null hypothesis that the number of cointegrating vectors is less than or equal to *r* against a general alternative.

The second test, the max-eigen statistic, tests the null hypothesis that the number of cointegrating vectors is equal to *r* against the alternative of *r + 1* cointegrating vectors. The statistic is given as

$$(4.9) \qquad \lambda_{max}(r, r+1) = -T \sum_{i=r+1}^{k} log(1-\hat{\lambda}_{r+1}),$$

where *T* denotes the time series dimension.

Critical values for both test statistics are provided by Johansen and Juselius (1990). However, Reimers (1992) as well as Cheung and Lai (1993) have found evidence that these test statistics are subject to size distortions when small samples are used. More precisely, small samples may cause spurious rejection of the null hypothesis of no cointegration. To correct for such a possibility, the more restrictive procedure suggested by Reimers (1992) is employed in this study. Reimers (1992) proposes to adjust for the scaling factor by replacing N^* with (N^*-kp).

The test results depend on the number of lags for the underlying VAR system. The lag length ought to be selected carefully. Any additional lag improves the goodness of fit, reducing the unexplained variances. However, this improvement comes at the cost of more parameters to be estimated, thus reducing the number of observations, which are "free" to be used for the estimation. Therefore, the choice of the lag length may be thought of as a compromise between goodness of fit and degrees of freedom.

Table 4.7. Cointegration test results

Country	No. of Lags	Null hypothesis	Eigenvalue	Trace statistic: Statistic	Trace statistic: 5 % critical values	Trace statistic: 1 % critical values	Max-Eigen statistic: Statistic	Max-Eigen statistic: 5 % critical values	Max-Eigen statistic: 1 % critical values
Poland	2	at most 1	0.45	**50.70	29.68	35.65	**39.09	20.97	25.52
		at most 2	0.12	11.61	15.41	20.04	8.64	14.07	18.63
		at most 3	0.06	2.96	3.76	6.65	2.96	3.76	6.65
Hungary	1	at most 1	0.44	*35.53	29.68	35.65	*25.33	20.97	25.52
		at most 2	0.17	10.20	15.41	20.04	8.33	14.07	18.63
		at most 3	0.04	1.87	3.76	6.65	1.87	3.76	6.65
Czech Republic	2	at most 1	0.60	*32.64	29.68	35.65	*24.43	20.97	25.52
		at most 2	0.17	8.21	15.41	20.04	5.14	14.07	18.63
		at most 3	0.11	3.07	3.76	6.65	3.07	3.76	6.65
Slovenia	1	at most 1	0.64	**50.49	29.68	35.65	**36.22	20.97	25.52
		at most 2	0.32	14.27	15.41	20.04	13.74	14.07	18.63
		at most 3	0.01	0.53	3.76	6.65	0.53	3.76	6.65
Estonia	2	at most 1	0.57	**36.78	29.68	35.65	*24.91	20.97	25.52
		at most 2	0.29	11.87	15.41	20.04	10.00	14.07	18.63
		at most 3	0.06	1.87	3.76	6.65	1.87	3.76	6.65
Latvia	2	at most 1	0.81	**57.83	29.68	35.65	**46.82	20.97	25.52
		at most 2	0.31	11.01	15.41	20.04	10.52	14.07	18.63
		at most 3	0.02	0.49	3.76	6.65	0.49	3.76	6.65
Lithuania	2	at most 1	0.45	28.49	29.68	35.65	19.36	20.97	25.52
		at most 2	0.29	10.84	15.41	20.04	9.89	14.07	18.63
		at most 3	0.03	0.94	3.76	6.65	0.94	3.76	6.65
Bulgaria	1	at most 1	0.26	25.31	29.68	35.65	12.21	20.97	25.52
		at most 2	0.19	13.10	15.41	20.04	8.23	14.07	18.63
		at most 3	0.11	4.87	3.76	6.65	4.87	3.76	6.65
Romania	1	at most 1	0.34	26.48	29.68	35.65	16.89	20.97	25.52
		at most 2	0.20	9.59	15.41	20.04	9.02	14.07	18.63
		at most 3	0.01	0.57	3.76	6.65	0.57	3.76	6.65
Slovakia	1	at most 1	0.76	**57.22	29.68	35.65	**42.37	20.97	25.52
		at most 2	0.35	14.15	15.41	20.04	14.01	14.07	18.63
		at most 3	0.01	0.24	3.76	6.65	0.24	3.76	6.65

Note: * Means rejection at the 5 % critical value. ** Means rejection at the 1 % critical value. The maximum lag length was restricted to two since otherwise the number of free observations would be too low.

A commonly used information criterion, which incorporates both effects is the Akaike information criterion (AIC)

(4.10) $$AIC(p) = \log\left|\sum(p)\right| + \frac{2}{N^*}(number\ of\ parameters),$$

where $\left|\sum(p)\right|$ is the determinant of the variance-covariance matrix of the residuals. The first term of the AIC displays unexplained variances, whereas the second term penalizes additional parameters to be estimated. The optimal lag length is given as the lag length p that minimizes the AIC.

The output of the cointegration tests is displayed in table 4.7. Yet, before these results are examined in detail a warning note is useful, because the inclusion of an exogenous Russian crisis variable in the cointegration relationship can lead to slightly different critical values than the ones presented in this table. The direction of deviation cannot be anticipated, so that simulations would be needed. Since most of the findings presented here are not "at the edge", such a simulation has not been conducted.

The null hypothesis of no cointegration can be rejected for seven countries, which are Poland, Hungary, the Czech Republic, Slovenia, Estonia, Latvia, and Slovakia. In all these cases exactly one cointegration relationship has been identified. For Lithuania, Bulgaria and Romania there is no cointegration relationship evident. Since these countries are the least developed in terms of economic development and transition, this finding is not at all surprising. It is most likely that there will evolve a stable cointegration link once these economies have gone through economic stability for a longer period. For now, the outcome does not support the cointegrating assumption. Therefore the countries are not taken into account for the further analysis.

4.2.5 Estimation of the behavioural equilibrium exchange rates

Moving to the estimation of the cointegration relationship, table 4.8 presents the normalised cointegrating vectors, as well as the corresponding α adjustment coefficients from the Johansen (1995) methodology. Looking at the cointegrating vectors first, results denote a positive and significant impact of the productivity differential on the real exchange rate in all countries as theory suggests.[69] The

[69] The results are presented as estimated vectors. Reformulation in equation form with the exchange rate on one side changes the sign of the other variables.

magnitude of the calculated numbers varies between 0.41 and 2.19. Theoretically, the value ought to be close to one. However, empirical studies from Alberola et al. (1999), Clark and MacDonald (1999) and Maeso-Fernandez et al. (2001) have found coefficients between 0.6 and 3.0 for the same variable in studies on industrialised countries. Leaving the low coefficient for Slovakia aside, the estimated numbers are well in line with the findings in these papers.

The impact of the net foreign asset position is positive in Poland, Hungary, the Czech Republic, Slovenia, and Estonia, but negative for Latvia and Slovakia. This means, that in Latvia and Slovakia an improvement in the net foreign asset position results in a depreciation, which contradicts the theory. One reason for this finding may be that the sample period is too short or the transition process not advanced enough. This can be explained as follows. In the first phase strong investment in the traded goods sector is financed with capital inflows, which is reflected in a decline in net foreign assets. If this leads to productivity growth the real exchange rate appreciates. In the second phase, when investment in the traded goods sector is thriving, the trade balance improves, resulting in an increase in net foreign assets, combined with the appreciation of the real exchange rate. If this assumption holds for Latvia and Slovakia, it is not reasonable to expect the estimated cointegration relationship to persist for the future. Thus, it is most consequent to omit these two countries from any further analysis as otherwise results could lead to wrong conclusions. The magnitude of the coefficients for the other five nations corresponds to the estimated figures from the OECD studies, which have obtained values between 0.01 and 1.33.

Comparing the influence of both variables, the lower absolute value of the net foreign asset coefficients does not mean that its influence is necessarily less intense. On one hand the absolute values of the net foreign asset position may be higher and on the other hand volatilities of the variables must be considered as well. Taking the time series standard deviations of each fundamental variable and multiplying them with the respective coefficients reveals that in Poland and Estonia the productivity effect clearly dominates, while in Slovenia the net foreign asset position plays the major role. In the Czech Republic and Hungary, the impacts of both fundamentals are of similar importance. The significantly negative α coefficient in all countries indicates that the real exchange rate adjusts to close the gap to equilibrium. However, the speed of adjustment varies among transition economies. In Hungary, the Czech Republic, Slovenia and Estonia between 32 and 77 percent of the quarterly change of the real exchange rate can be attributed to the deviation between actual and equilibrium exchange rates. In the case of Poland any deviation is more than offset within one period.[70]

Table 4.8. Resulting vectors of BEER estimation

Country	Variable	RER	PROD	NFA
Poland	Coefficient	1	-1.29 (-19.93)	-0.05 (-2.14)
	α	-1.33 (-3.52)	-0.25 (-1.83)	0.26 (0.48)
Hungary	Coefficient	1	-1.84 (-7.15)	-0.18 (-4.74)
	α	-0.32 (-2.55)	0.11 (2.76)	-0.33 (-1.85)
Czech Republic	Coefficient	1	-1.03 (-2.53)	-0.04 (-2.08)
	α	-0.77 (-3.53)	-0.02 (-1.70)	-0.23 (-1.89)
Slovenia	Coefficient	1	-0.79 (-1.97)	-0.53 (-5.62)
	α	-0.53 (-2.17)	-0.18 (-2.31)	0.4 (1.75)
Estonia	Coefficient	1	-2.19 (-14.84)	-0.08 (-3.79)
	α	-0.34 (-6.25)	0.14 (1.62)	0.07 (0.52)
Latvia	Coefficient	1	-0.86 (-6.90)	0.16 (17.47)
	α	-0.45 (-0.42)	0.34 (5.79)	0.36 (3.19)
Slovakia	Coefficient	1	-0.41 (-2.08)	0.05 (5.19)
	α	-0.69 (-7.02)	0.07 (0.69)	0.32 (1.36)

Note: The numbers in brackets are t-values for the estimated coefficients.

The α coefficient also reveals information about the exogeneity of variables. Or more accurately, an insignificant α coefficient means weak exogeneity of the

[70] Sardà-Pons and Pérez-Lacasta (2003) also find rather fast adjustments of the Polish zloty real exchange rate to equilibrium.

variable. The results indicate that the real exchange rate is endogenously determined by the other two variables as the α is highly significant for all five countries. On the other hand, the net foreign asset position mostly exhibits weak exogeneity. The results for the α of the productivity differential are mixed, indicating interrelations among variables. Overall, there is strong support that despite some interrelations, the real exchange rate is determined by the two fundamentals in the equation and not the other way round.

In sum, the results for the majority of countries are plausible and the test statistics clearly confirm the adequacy of the chosen model. Nevertheless, in the next chapter stability tests for the cointegration relationship are performed. Instability could originate from exchange rate regime switches or exchange rate crises, or alternatively from the capital inflow effect described above as observed in Latvia and Slovakia.

4.2.6 Test for structural change in the cointegration relationships

Just like the time series, the cointegration relationship can also be exposed to structural change. In this context, Hansen (1992) proposes a SupF test statistic to control for parameter instability in the cointegration relationship, when the timing of the break point is unknown a priori. The test is particularly appropriate to check for swift shifts in the cointegration relationship such as a change in the exchange rate regime. The test involves a subdivision of the sample into two groups. Define $\boldsymbol{A_1}$ as the set of parameters for the regression of the first l observations and $\boldsymbol{A_2}$ as the set of parameters for the regression of the other observations as in

(4.11) $$y_t = \boldsymbol{A_1 x_t} + \varepsilon_t \text{ for } t \leq l,$$

(4.12) $$y_t = \boldsymbol{A_2 x_t} + \varepsilon_t \text{ for } t > l.$$

The null hypothesis

H_0: $\boldsymbol{A_1} = \boldsymbol{A_2}$

is tested versus the alternative

H_1: $\boldsymbol{A_1} \neq \boldsymbol{A_2}$.

If l is known the test statistic is simply given by a generalisation of the classical Chow test, which is based on the difference in the residual sum of squares between the estimates obtained from the two subsamples. Let $F_{T,t}$ denote the general version of the Chow test statistic. If the structural break point is now treated as unknown the Hansen's test statistic is

$$(4.13) \qquad SupF = \underset{\frac{s}{T} \in \tau}{Sup} F_{T,t},$$

where τ is a compact subset of (0,1), called the trimming region, and $s = 1,\ldots,T$. The definition of a trimming region is required as otherwise the test statistic would diverge to infinity at the endpoints of the time series. The choice of the trimming region is rather arbitrary, but Andrews (1990) suggests to cut off 15 percent of the observations at the beginning and at the end of the time period. This recommendation is applied in the following empirical analysis.

Employing the fully modified estimator from Phillips and Hansen (1990), Hansen (1992) derives the asymptotic distribution theory and provides critical values for the SupF statistic. The critical values depend on the number of regressors as well as on the inclusion or exclusion of deterministic trends. Figure 4.4 presents the sequences of the SupF tests for the five CEEC under consideration (normal line) and the respective critical values for the 5 percent level (dashed line).

The null hypothesis of constant coefficients cannot be rejected for Poland, Hungary, Slovenia and the Czech Republic, since the critical value exceeds the test statistics in all time periods. The exception is Estonia, which displays structural breakpoints near the end of the observed time period. The reasons for this outcome can be manifold. Possible explanations are the Russian crisis, a strong worsening of the net foreign asset position in recent periods, or the depreciation of the euro vis-á-vis most major currencies since Estonia is connected to the euro through a currency board. Overall, there is a relatively high stability in the cointegration relationship, so that reliable BEER estimates can be presented.

4.2.7 The estimated real effective behavioural equilibrium exchange rates

Taking the cointegrating vectors from table 4.8, BEERs are computed and compared with the real exchange rates. Figure 4.5 shows the real exchange rates (solid lines), the BEERs (dashed lines) and the deviations from equilibrium for each country (right panels) for all five CEEC.

Figure 4.4. SupF tests for parameter instability in the cointegration relationship

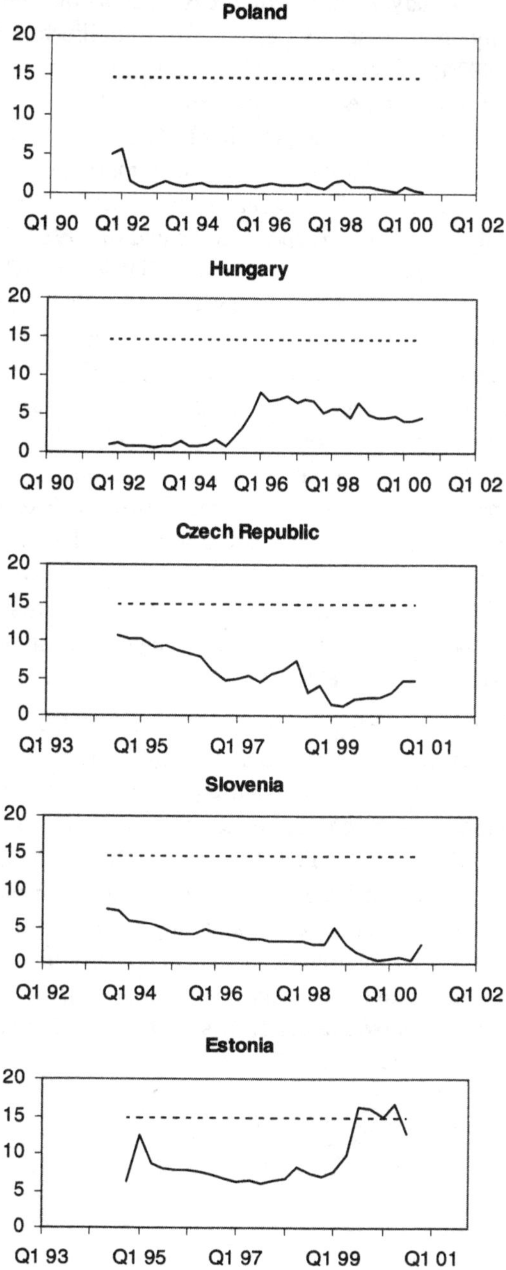

The strong appreciation of the exchange rate in ***Poland*** can partly be attributed to an initially undervalued currency when the BEER is taken as the benchmark. The Polish zloty deviated by more than 25 percent from equilibrium in the early 1990s. From 1994 to 1997 the exchange rate stayed near or even in equilibrium, but since 1998 the zloty has been persistently overvalued. With its overvaluation of about 8.6 percent in 2002, it is approaching dangerous magnitudes. The appreciation of the ***Hungarian*** forint has been of much more modest size, and so has been the initial undervaluation. The exchange rate mostly fluctuated around the equilibrium, with only one major exception at the end of 1998. This temporary peak in mid 1998 coincides with Russia's financial crisis. Currently, the Hungarian currency is neither significantly overvalued nor undervalued. The ***Czech Republic*** is an interesting case as it is the only country that was hit by a major exchange rate crisis during the observed time period. When investors speculated against the Czech koruna they argued that the currency was highly overvalued. According to the BEER approach, however, overvaluation prior to the crisis was moderate and the devaluation even resulted in an undervalued currency. When speculation on the exchange rate market abated, the Czech koruna surged to a level of overvaluation higher than prior to the crisis, provoking a second major correction. These results confirm the study from Frait and Komárek (1999) who find the same exchange rate behaviour despite using different explanatory variables. Since 2001 the koruna's real value is again on an upswing, and currently the Czech currency is overvalued by almost 10 percent.

Given ***Slovenia***'s flexible exchange rate regime, one would assume that misalignments are less severe since the nominal exchange rate can easily adjust. In fact, the figure shows that deviations from equilibrium have been moderate, seldom exceeding 5 percent. At the end of the inspected time series, the Slovenian tolar turns out to be slightly overvalued by 2.6 percent. During the first two years after its introduction the ***Estonian*** kroon saw large deviations from equilibrium. This can be attributed to high uncertainty and large fluctuation in economic fundamentals in the first phase of Estonia's independence. Beginning in mid 1998 Estonia experienced a critical overvaluation, which was caused by the Russian exchange rate crisis. While this overvaluation has been reduced in recent years, it has yet to be eliminated completely.

Figure 4.5. The real effective BEERs and misalignments

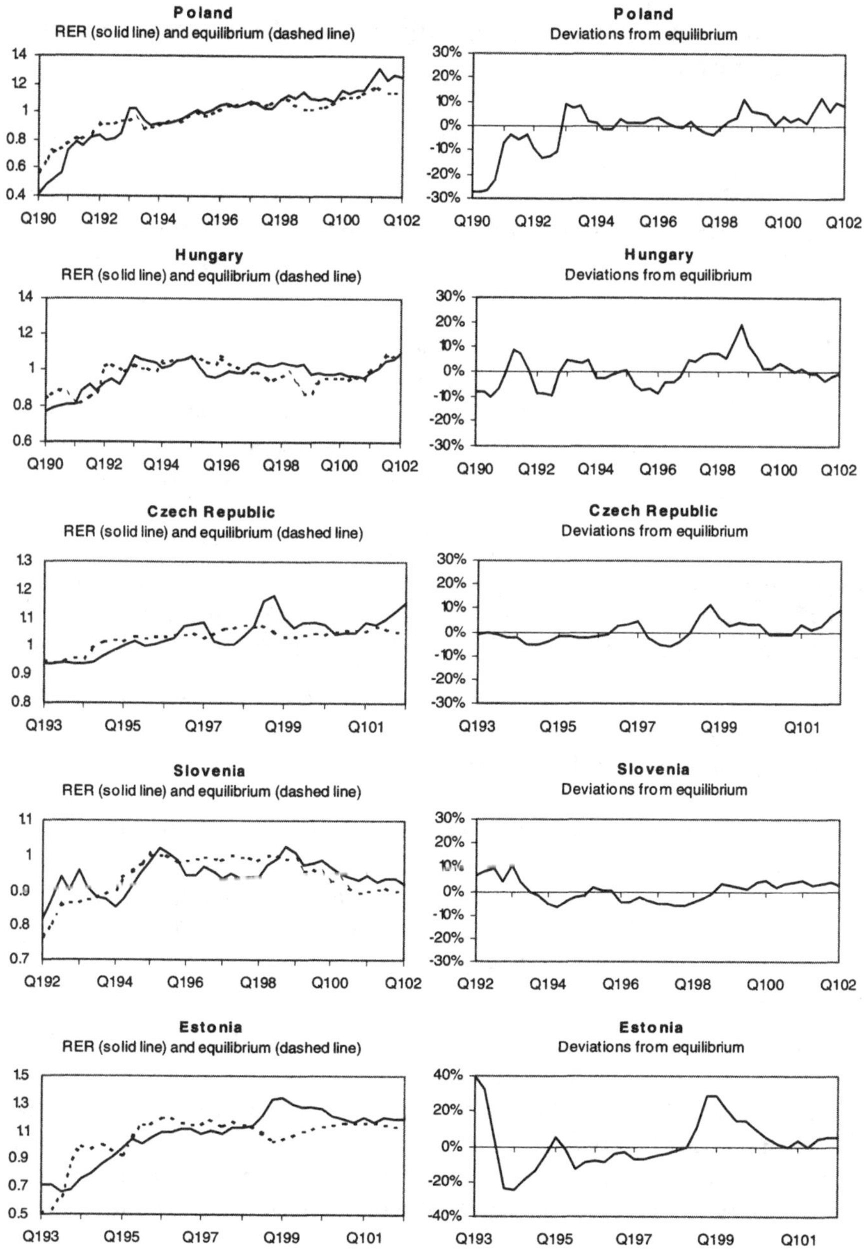

4.3 Bilateral equilibrium exchange rates against the euro

4.3.1 Motivation for the determination of bilateral equilibrium exchange rates

So far, multilateral real equilibrium exchange rates have been calculated. The outcome has given an indication if a currency is over- or undervalued against a trade-weighted basket of the country's trading partners. Obviously, this result is an important benchmark to assess the overall value of the currency. Yet, it can also lead to misguided policies if it is interpreted alone. The reason is that multilateral exchange rates can be rather ambiguous.

The ambiguity of multilateral exchange rate deviations can best be explained by means of a simple example. Assume two countries, a small country A and a large country B, with equal trade weights against the rest of the world. Say country A's currency is undervalued by 5 percent in effective terms and country B's is undervalued by 10 percent. Hence, despite its overall undervaluation country A's currency is overvalued against B's currency. Assume now, that country A fixes its exchange rate against country B's currency at the current level. For the moment this does not have economic implications for country A. However, it bears strong risks of overvaluation for the future since there is the expectation that country B's exchange rate will eventually move back to equilibrium.

With respect to the CEEC, any judgement exclusively determined on effective rates could result in future misalignment and its economic consequences. The forthcoming entry into the ERM2 system puts the value against the euro in the focus of policymakers, since any ERM2 reference rate will be selected in relation to the euro and not against a basket of currencies. Moreover, while the exchange rates against other trading partners will continue to fluctuate, the nominal exchange rate against the euro will be fixed, hence determining the terms of trade with the euro area. It is thus pivotal not only to consider the effective exchange rate equilibrium, but also to include the nominal bilateral equilibrium exchange rate against the euro in a general judgement.

However, this debate does not mean that equilibrium exchange rates should be determined on a country-to-country basis. Neglecting third country effects would most likely lead to biased results. In the case of the CEEC, any determination of exchange rate equilibrium would be incomplete and possibly misleading without incorporating the effects of countries like Russia and the United States. Fortunately, there is a way to extract bilateral nominal exchange rates without losing the information obtained from the above determined multilateral rates. The analytical procedure to do so will be presented in the next chapter.

4.3.2 Analytical derivation of bilateral nominal exchange rates

The underlying idea of deriving bilateral exchange rates is that in a whole world set-up cross rates between countries can be used to exactly identify each bilateral exchange rate. Up to now, however, the trade matrix from above does not cover the whole world and such an intention would be rather idealistic. Yet, the simple assumption that the "rest of the world" (ROW), a country to be defined, enters the analysis neutrally makes the system operational. The algebraic procedure to generate bilateral rates has been formalized by Alberola et al. (1999) and is presented in modified form here.

Consider the exchange rate (in logs) e_{ij} of country i against country j and split it up into two components, such that it is expressed in terms of an arbitrary numeraire currency (n)

(4.14) $$e_{ij} = e_{jn} - e_{in} .$$

Substituting this equation in the definition of the real effective exchange rate

(4.15) $$q_i = \sum_j w_{ij}\, e_{ij} ,$$

and doing so for all countries $i = 1, \ldots, n$ yields

(4.16) $$\boldsymbol{q} = (\boldsymbol{W}\text{-}\boldsymbol{I})\boldsymbol{e}$$

with $\boldsymbol{q} = (q_1, q_2, \ldots, q_n)'$ and $\boldsymbol{e} = (e_1, e_2, \ldots, e_n)'$. $\boldsymbol{W}$ is the $n \times n$ trade matrix and $\boldsymbol{I}$ is the identity matrix of order n. One exchange rate is redundant to solve the linear system in (4.16) and can be discarded without losing information. Define $\bar{\boldsymbol{q}} = (q_1, q_2, \ldots, q_{n-1})'$ as the $(n\text{-}1) \times 1$ vector where the numeraire real multilateral exchange rate has been discarded and $\bar{\boldsymbol{q}}_{num} = (q_n, q_n, \ldots, q_n)'$ as the $(n\text{-}1) \times 1$ vector, which consists of the real multilateral exchange rate of the numeraire. Expressing the multilateral exchange rates relative to the numeraire currency gives

(4.17) $$\bar{\boldsymbol{q}} - \bar{\boldsymbol{q}}_{num} = (\bar{\boldsymbol{W}} - \bar{\boldsymbol{I}})\bar{\boldsymbol{e}} - \bar{\boldsymbol{q}}_{num} ,$$

where a line on top of matrices means that the nth row and column have been deleted and where $\bar{e} = (e_1, e_2, ..., e_{n-1})'$ is a $(n-1) \times 1$ vector. With the use of (4.15) one obtains

$$\bar{q} - \bar{q}_{num} = [(\bar{W} - \bar{I}) - \bar{W}_{num}]\, \bar{e} \quad (4.18)$$

where $\bar{W}_{num}$ consists of the vectors $q = (q_{n1}, q_{n2}, ..., q_{nn-1})'$ as the rows of the matrix. Pre-multiplying both sides by the inverse of the $(n-1) \times (n-1)$ matrix $Z \equiv [(\bar{W} - \bar{I}) - \bar{W}_{num}]$ yields the derivation of bilateral equilibrium exchange rates

$$\bar{e} = Z^{-1} (\bar{q} - \bar{q}_{num}). \quad (4.19)$$

It is important to mention that this method only works if the exchange rate vector encompasses the whole world. This means the ROW must be included in the analysis, i.e. the trade matrix must be adjusted, so that it includes the trade share of the ROW. Since there is no information available about the ROW an assumption regarding its value has to be made. Rather than making a postulation about the absolute value, deviations from equilibrium of the ROW are considered. The most plausible assumption is that the multilateral real exchange rate of the ROW is constantly in equilibrium. If the trade share of the ROW is relatively small, the impact of violations to this hypothesis is negligible. Simulations for the transition economies with deviations of 10 percent in both directions have confirmed the robustness of the findings. To utilize this hypothesis equation (4.19) must be rewritten in terms of deviations from equilibrium

$$\hat{\bar{e}} = Z^{-1} (\hat{\bar{q}} - \hat{\bar{q}}_{num}). \quad (4.20)$$

All values on the right hand side in equation (4.20) are known since Z^{-1} can be computed from the trade matrix and $\hat{\bar{q}}$ and $\hat{\bar{q}}_{num}$ are deviations from the estimated real BEERs, respectively PEERs. Thus, the left hand side of equation (4.20), i.e. the deviations from the bilateral nominal equilibrium exchange rate, can be calculated directly. The corresponding nominal bilateral BEERs, respectively PEERs are then determined from the nominal exchange rates.

4.3.3 The estimated bilateral behavioural equilibrium exchange rates against the euro

The inclusion of the ROW trade share leads to a new trade matrix, which is presented in table 4.9. The figures show that for the CEEC between 65 percent and 87 percent of the trade share is covered by the economies included in the sample, so that the ROW plays a minor role in the determination of bilateral equilibrium exchange rates. The comparatively higher trade share of the ROW for the five main trade partners has only indirect impact.

Table 4.9. Trade matrix for the determination of bilateral equilibrium exchange rates

	Pol	Hun	Cze	Sln	Est	Lat	Lit	Bul	Rom	Slk	UK	USA	Jap	Rus	Row	Eur
Poland		2.3	4.1	1.1	1.1	2.1	4.3	0.6	0.7	3.5	0.6	0.0	0.0	2.3	0.5	2.2
Hungary	1.2		1.3	1.9	0.4	0.5	1.0	0.6	2.4	3.1	0.2	0.0	0.0	1.8	0.2	1.3
Czech Rep.	3.2	2.6		2.2	0.4	0.7	1.2	0.9	0.5	27.4	0.3	0.0	0.0	1.7	0.3	1.7
Slovenia	0.3	1.1	0.8		0.0	0.0	0.0	0.1	0.2	0.7	0.1	0.0	0.0	0.3	0.1	0.7
Estonia	0.1	0.1	0.0	0.0		4.9	2.4	0.0	0.0	0.0	0.0	0.0	0.0	0.4	0.1	0.1
Latvia	0.2	0.1	0.1	0.0	4.4		5.8	0.0	0.0	0.0	0.0	0.0	0.0	0.9	0.0	0.0
Lithuania	0.6	0.2	0.2	0.1	3.2	6.7		0.0	0.0	0.1	0.0	0.0	0.0	0.9	0.1	0.0
Bulgaria	0.1	0.2	0.2	0.1	0.0	0.2	0.3		0.7	0.1	0.0	0.0	0.0	0.9	0.1	0.2
Romania	0.2	1.4	0.2	0.3	0.0	0.0	0.0	1.5		0.4	0.1	0.0	0.0	0.7	0.2	0.6
Slovakia	1.2	2.2	11.6	0.8	0.1	0.3	0.3	0.3	0.5		0.1	0.0	0.0	1.4	0.1	0.5
UK	5.1	3.1	3.2	2.1	3.4	6.0	3.4	2.5	2.9	1.7		4.2	2.6	3.1	6.4	17.1
USA	3.6	3.5	2.8	3.2	2.3	1.6	1.7	2.3	3.1	2.1	12.4		25.4	5.3	38.1	13.2
Japan	1.1	1.6	1.1	1.0	1.5	0.3	0.3	0.6	0.7	1.1	3.8	12.9		2.9	17.6	5.6
Russia	6.8	9.5	5.5	2.9	14.7	21.2	25.1	21.8	8.2	11.3	0.7	0.5	0.7		3.0	3.0
ROW	21.4	16.1	13.2	21.8	25.1	25.6	25.1	35.3	30.5	12.3	30.6	68.6	60.1	52.7		53.7
Euro-area	54.8	56.0	55.6	62.6	43.4	30.0	29.1	33.6	49.5	36.0	51.1	13.9	11.3	24.7	33.2	

Note: The numbers are in percentages. The countries in rows are the trading partners of the countries in columns. Source: Own calculations based on 1996 data from the International Trade Statistics Yearbook.

Since not all countries are included in the BEER analysis the trade matrix must be adjusted.[71] This increases the share of the ROW, but it still remains at around one third for Poland, Hungary, the Czech Republic and Slovenia. The only exception is Estonia, where it accounts for more than 50 percent of the trade due to the elimination of Russia. Figure 4.6 presents the computed nominal bilateral exchange rates against the euro and the deviations from equilibrium for all five countries. It is worth comparing the findings with respect to the results of the real effective rates.

In the case of ***Poland***, the increasing and persistent divergence of the nominal zloty exchange rate from equilibrium since beginning of 1998 is most obvious. Misalignment against the euro is more pronounced than in real effective terms and the equilibrium level was above four zloty for one euro at the beginning of 2002.

The outcome for ***Hungary*** does not differ qualitatively from the multilateral case. Until 1997 the forint was predominantly undervalued, but since 1997 above equilibrium. Nevertheless, there is no sign for serious misalignment. A level of 250 forint for one euro seems to have been appropriate at the beginning of 2002.

For the ***Czech Republic*** there are major differences to observe. After the exchange rate crisis the value of the Czech koruna returned quickly to equilibrium against the euro, but then appreciated strongly, resulting in persistent overvaluation above 5 percent. At the beginning of 2002 misalignment approached peak values close to 14 percent.

Looking at ***Slovenia***, it seems as if the equilibrium exchange rate outpaced the nominal; while the nominal euro exchange rate had long been mostly below equilibrium the picture reversed in 1998. Nevertheless, misalignment stayed at moderate levels, not exceeding 10 percent.

While the nominal exchange rate of the ***Estonian*** kroon against the euro (or prior to the introduction of the euro against the German mark) has been fixed, the equilibrium rate fluctuated considerably over time. Having been mostly below the value of 15.66 kroon per euro prior to 1998, a large swing resulted in a dangerous overvaluation of above 20 percent. Since this shift was caused by the Russian crisis, misalignment decreased when the Russian economy recovered, though still exceeding 10 percent in 2002.

---

[71] Japan and Russia are also excluded from the BEER estimations since no reasonable cointegration relationship could be found.

Figure 4.6. The nominal bilateral BEERs against the euro and misalignments

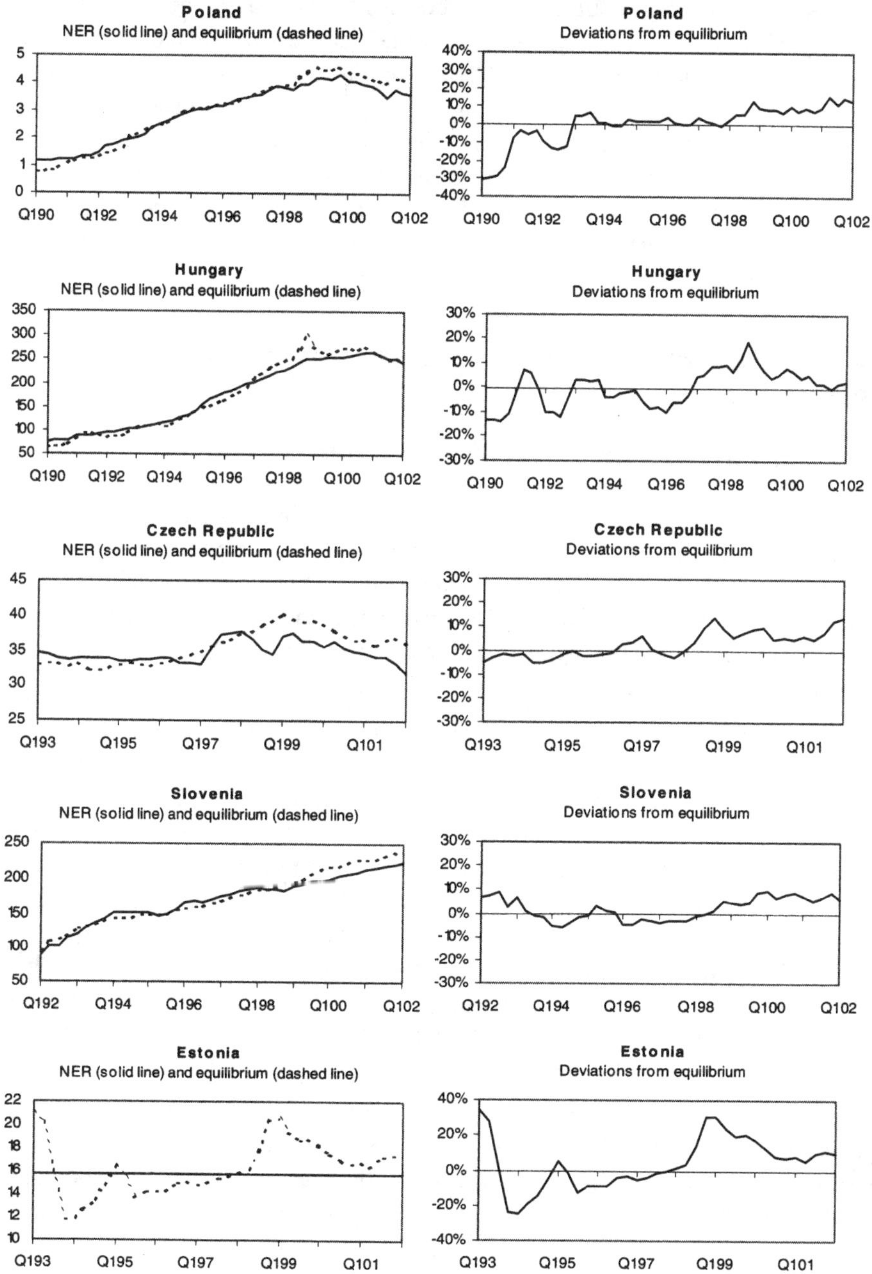

Overall, overvaluation is much higher when compared to the euro, particularly the period since 1999 shows substantial differences in the magnitude of deviations from equilibrium. This observation reflects the weakness of the euro against all other major currencies during this time. Recently, the euro has appreciated strongly against the US dollar, UK pound and Japanese yen, whereas the nominal exchange rates of most eastern European currencies have remained fairly stable. This applies particularly to Estonia, Hungary and the Czech Republic. The exchange rates of Poland and Slovenia depreciated slightly against the euro during this period. Overall, this development increases the burden on CEEC as their real effective exchange rates have tended to appreciate.

4.4 Panel estimation of the behavioural equilibrium exchange rates

4.4.1 The advantages of panel estimations

Tests for single time series have the disadvantage that the power of these tests can become very low if the time series are very short or consist of few observations. One solution to this shortcoming is to add a cross-sectional dimension to the time series data. In a panel, the number of observations is multiplied, so that the power of tests can be augmented significantly if the time series of the cross-sectional units share common features.

The selection of a panel involves the question which time series should be included in the panel. On one hand, it is favourable to add as many cross-sections as available. On the other hand, the panel should guarantee a reasonable degree of homogeneity across the cross-sectional dimension. Referring to the sample in this study it is questionable if countries on a different stage of economic development should be grouped together. Particularly, countries like Bulgaria and Romania could produce a misleading outcome if included in the panel. Since the accuracy of the calculated equilibrium exchange rates is an important issue, a smaller but more homogeneous sample is preferable. Therefore, the following analysis is restricted to the five CEEC, for which reliable time series BEER estimates have been found, i.e. Poland, Hungary, the Czech Republic, Slovenia, and Estonia.

Since some of the tests and estimation procedures require the panel to be balanced, data from the first quarter of 1993 is considered only. A few observations are lost for Poland, Hungary and Slovenia, but this loss is more than matched by the increase of observations through pooling the data.

Before panel data tests and estimations are carried out, it is necessary to control for the problem of cross-sectional dependence in the data. Hakkio (1984) demonstrate that in particular exchange rate time series are likely candidates for cross-sectional correlation. O'Connell (1998) shows that failure to control for heterogeneous correlation may induce significant size distortion in panel tests. O'Connell (1998) specifically reveals that panel data PPP evidence disappears once test procedures are modified to accommodate for cross-sectional dependence. Therefore, in this study the cross-sectional mean for each time period has been subtracted to eliminate cross-sectional dependence. The cross-sectional demeaned series have been used for all tests and estimation procedures.

4.4.2 Panel unit root tests

Panel based unit root tests have been advanced since the early 1990s, see e.g. Quah (1994), Im, Pesaran and Shin (2003), Harris and Tzavalis (1999), Maddala and Wu (1999) and Hadri (2000). In empirical work, the two most widely applied tests are from Levin et al. (2002) and Im, Pesaran and Shin (2003), henceforth IPS. Both tests allow for heterogeneity across groups such as country individual effects, i.e. different intercepts for each cross-section. The IPS test, however, has the further advantage to also allow for heterogeneity of the dynamics and different patterns of residual serial correlations across cross-sectional units. The results of the unit root tests for each individual country indicate that a higher degree of flexibility is favourable, so that the IPS test has been selected for this study.

Consider the panel model

$$(4.21) \qquad y_{it} = \eta_i + \delta_i t + \rho_i y_{it-1} + \sum_{j=1}^{p_i} \varphi_{ij} \Delta y_{it-j} + \varepsilon_{it} \quad , i = 1, \ldots, n \text{ and } t = 1, \ldots, T$$

where ε_{it} is white noise, η_i is the country specific intercept, δ_i is the country specific deterministic trend, ρ_i is the country specific autoregressive coefficient, and p_i is the country's individual number of lags.[72]

The null hypothesis of the IPS test is

H_0: $\rho_i = 1$ for all i,

[72] The inclusion of country specific intercepts and deterministic trends will affect the asymptotic distribution and the corresponding critical values, just as in the conventional time series case.

which is tested versus the alternative

H$_1$: $\rho_i < 1$ for at least one i.

The IPS t-bar statistic is basically defined as the average of the individual augmented Dickey-Fuller statistics

(4.22) $$\bar{t} = \frac{1}{n}\sum_{i=1}^{n} t_{\rho_i} ,$$

where t_{ρ_i} is the individual t-statistic for testing $\rho_i = 1$ in equation (4.21).

Using the asymptotic properties of the individual unit root test, IPS derive the asymptotic distribution for a test statistic t_{IPS}, which converges to the standard normal distribution as T and $n \to \infty$. Consequently, critical values for the standard normal distribution apply for the t_{IPS} test statistic.

Table 4.10 presents the output of the IPS panel unit root tests for the five CEEC. All three test statistics are not lower than the critical value, so that the unit root null hypothesis cannot be rejected in any of the cases. Thus, the panel can be considered non-stationary. This outcome also confirms the results from the single country analysis.

Table 4.10. Panel unit root test results

Series	Test statistic	Critical values
RER	-1.48	-1.69
PROD	-1.49	-1.69
NFA	0.32	-1.69

Note: The critical levels are given for the 5 percent level. The tests are without time trends.

4.4.3 Panel cointegration tests

Not only unit root tests have been extended to panels but also tests to control for cointegration in the panel. Pedroni (1999) proposes seven different test statistics, which compared to some other tests have the advantage that they do not only allow the dynamics and fixed effects to differ across groups, but also allow for heterogeneity of the cointegrating vector.[73] This flexibility seems to be a valuable feature for this work since the results from the country-individual analysis suggest significant deviations between the cointegrating vectors.

The tests from Pedroni (1999) are computed as follows. First, the regression residuals are obtained from the hypothesized cointegrating relationship

(4.23) $$y_{it} = \eta_i + \delta_i t + \sum_{j=1}^{k} \varphi_{ij} x_{ijt} + \varepsilon_{it} \quad , i = 1, \ldots, n \text{ and } t = 1, \ldots, T,$$

where k refers to the number of regression variables.[74]

Since all variables have the index i the above equation can be thought of as n different equations. The residuals of these equations are then tested for unit roots.[75] For this test Pedroni (1999) suggests seven different test statistics. These statistics can be classified into two categories. The first four tests are constructed by computing the average of both numerator and denominator terms over the n dimension separately, which means that they are based on estimators that effectively pool the autoregressive coefficients across different countries for the unit root tests on the estimated residuals. The three other tests are constructed by first dividing the numerator by the denominator prior to computing the average over n, which means that they are based on estimators that simply average the individually estimated coefficients for each country. The first category will be referred to as panel statistics and the second category as group statistics.

The two concepts imply different test hypotheses on the autoregressive coefficients γ_i of the residuals ($\hat{e}_{it}$) estimated from equation (4.23)

(4.24) $$\hat{e}_{it} = \hat{\gamma}_i \hat{e}_{it-1} + \hat{\mu}_{it} \quad , i = 1, \ldots, n.$$

In the case of the panel statistic the null hypothesis

H_0: $\gamma_i = 1$ for all i

---

[73] Alternative tests are from Kao (1999), McCoskey and Kao (1998), Kao and Chiang (2000), Larsson et al. (1998), Hall et al. (1999), and Groen and Kleibergen (2003) among others.

[74] Again, the inclusion of intercepts and deterministic trends affects the asymptotic distribution and the corresponding critical values.

[75] This two step procedure is similar to the Engle-Granger method to test for cointegration in a single time series.

is tested versus the alternative

H$_1$: $\gamma = \gamma_i < 1$ for all i,

so that it assumes a common value γ for all equations. In the case of the group statistics the null hypothesis

H$_0$: $\gamma_i = 1$ for all i

is tested versus

H$_1$: $\gamma_i < 1$ for all i,

so that it does not presume a common value under the alternative. Table 4.11 presents the seven test statistics.

Table 4.11. Panel cointegration tests

Statistic	Specification
Panel V-statistic	$Z_{v_{N,T}} = \dfrac{1}{\sum_{i=1}^{N}\sum_{t=1}^{T}\hat{L}_{11i}^{-2}\hat{e}_{it-1}^{2}}$
Panel ρ-statistic	$Z_{\rho_{N,T}} = \dfrac{\sum_{i=1}^{N}\sum_{t=1}^{T}\hat{L}_{11i}^{-2}(\hat{e}_{it-1}\Delta\hat{e}_{it} - \hat{\omega}_i)}{\sum_{i=1}^{N}\sum_{t=1}^{T}\hat{L}_{11i}^{-2}\hat{e}_{it-1}^{2}}$
Panel PP t-statistic	$Z_{t_{N,T}} = \dfrac{\sum_{i=1}^{N}\sum_{t=1}^{T}\hat{L}_{11i}^{-2}(\hat{e}_{it-1}\Delta\hat{e}_{it} - \hat{\omega}_i)}{\left(\tilde{\sigma}_{NT}^{2}\sum_{i=1}^{N}\sum_{t=1}^{T}\hat{L}_{11i}^{-2}\hat{e}_{it-1}^{2}\right)^{1/2}}$
Panel ADF t-statistic	$Z_{t_{N,T}} = \dfrac{\sum_{i=1}^{N}\sum_{t=1}^{T}\hat{L}_{11i}^{-2}\hat{e}_{it-1}^{*}\Delta\hat{e}_{it}^{*}}{\left(\tilde{s}_{NT}^{2}\sum_{i=1}^{N}\sum_{t=1}^{T}\hat{L}_{11i}^{-2}\hat{e}_{it-1}^{2}\right)^{1/2}}$

Group ρ-statistic	$\tilde{Z}_{\rho_{N,T}} = \sum_{i=1}^{N} \frac{\sum_{t=1}^{T}(\hat{e}_{it-1}\Delta\hat{e}_{it} - \hat{\omega}_i)}{\sum_{t=1}^{T}\hat{e}_{it-1}^2}$
Group PP t-statistic	$\tilde{Z}_{t_{N,T}} = \sum_{i=1}^{N} \frac{\sum_{t=1}^{T}(\hat{e}_{it-1}\Delta\hat{e}_{it} - \hat{\omega}_i)}{\tilde{\sigma}_i^2 \sum_{t=1}^{T}\hat{e}_{it-1}^2}$
Group ADF t-statistic	$\tilde{Z}^*_{t_{N,T}} = \sum_{i=1}^{N} \frac{\sum_{t=1}^{T}\hat{e}^*_{it-1}\Delta\hat{e}^*_{it}}{\left(\sum_{t=1}^{T}\hat{s}_i^{*2}\hat{e}_{it-1}^{*2}\right)^{1/2}}$
where $\hat{\omega}_i = \frac{1}{T}\sum_{s=1}^{k_i}\left(1-\frac{s}{k_i+1}\right)\sum_{t=s+1}^{T}\hat{\mu}_{it}\hat{\mu}_{it-s}$, $\hat{s}_i^2 \equiv \frac{1}{T}\sum_{t=1}^{T}\hat{\mu}_{it}^2$, $\hat{\sigma}_i^2 = \hat{s}_i^2 + 2\hat{\omega}_i$, $\tilde{\sigma}_{NT}^2 \equiv \frac{1}{T}\sum_{i=1}^{N}\hat{L}_{11i}^{-2}\hat{\sigma}_i^2$, $\hat{s}_i^{*2} \equiv \frac{1}{T}\sum_{t=1}^{T}\hat{\mu}_{it}^*$, $\tilde{s}_{NT}^{*2} \equiv \frac{1}{N}\sum_{t=1}^{N}\hat{s}_i^{*2}$, $\hat{L}_{11i}^2 = \frac{1}{T}\sum_{t=1}^{T}\tilde{\mu}_{it}^2 + \frac{2}{T}\sum_{s=1}^{k_i}\left(1-\frac{s}{k_i+1}\right)\sum_{t=s+1}^{T}\tilde{\mu}_{it}\tilde{\mu}_{it-s}$, and where the residuals $\hat{\mu}_{it}$, $\hat{\mu}_{it}^*$, and $\tilde{\mu}_{it}$ are obtained from the following regressions: $\hat{e}_{it} = \hat{\gamma}_i\hat{e}_{it-1} + \hat{\mu}_{it}$, $\hat{e}_{it} = \hat{\gamma}_i\hat{e}_{it-1} + \sum_{k=1}^{K_i}\hat{\gamma}_{ik}\Delta\hat{e}_{it-k} + \hat{\mu}_{it}^*$, $\Delta y_{it} = \sum_{m=1}^{M}\hat{b}_{mi}\Delta x_{mit} + \tilde{\mu}_{it}$	

Source: Pedroni (1999).

It is interesting to note that these panel statistics are based on well-known unit root tests. The second and fifth statistic are panel and group statistics analogous to the familiar non-parametric Phillips and Perron ρ-statistic. The third and sixth statistic can be regarded as panel and group statistics analogous to the non-parametric Phillips and Perron t-statistic. The fourth and seventh statistic have their counterpart in the parametric augmented Dickey-Fuller t-statistic. To complete the list, the first statistic is a non-parametric variance ratio t-statistic.

The statistics can be standardized so that critical values of the standard normal distribution apply.[76] In the case of the variance ratio statistic the null hypothesis is rejected if the test statistic is larger than the appropriate positive critical value, which means that the right tail of the normal distribution is used to reject the null hypothesis. In all other six cases the null hypothesis is rejected if the test statistic is smaller than the appropriate negative critical value, which means that the left tail of the normal distribution is used to reject the null hypothesis.

Table 4.12 shows that the null hypothesis is rejected in five out of the seven cases in our sample. Only the panel and the group ρ-statistics do not reject the null hypothesis. Although this result does not give a definitive answer, there is good reason to conclude that a cointegration relationship in the panel exists.

Table 4.12. Panel cointegration test results

Test	Test statistics	Critical values
Panel V-statistic	2.23*	1.69
Panel ρ-statistic	-1.35	-1.69
Panel PP t-statistic	-1.78*	-1.69
Panel ADF t-statistic	-2.69*	-1.69
Group ρ-statistic	-1.51	-1.69
Group PP t-statistic	-1.93*	-1.69
Group ADF t-statistic	-3.09*	-1.69

Note: * Means rejection at the 5 % critical value. Two lags have been imposed for all tests. The tests are without time trends.

4.4.4 Panel estimation techniques

Panel cointegration tests have given support to the existence of cointegration relationships, so that panel estimation techniques can be applied to obtain the

[76] See Pedroni (1997) for details.

cointegrating vectors. In the following, two different estimators are presented and employed to compute coefficient estimates for the cointegrating vectors. These are the Pooled Mean Group (PMG) estimator from Pesaran et al. (1999) and the Fully Modified Ordinary Least Squares (FMOLS) estimator from Pedroni (2000).

For the estimation of dynamic panels the Mean Group (MG) estimator suggested by Pesaran and Smith (1995) is often used as a standard tool. The MG estimator is simply based on averaging country individual coefficient estimates and does not impose any restrictions on homogeneity of coefficients across countries. This estimator, however, does not pay attention to the fact that certain parameters may be the same across countries. An estimator that assumes common long-run parameters across the panel, while still allowing for country specific short-run responses, is the PMG estimator from Pesaran et al. (1999). This specification is most appropriate for the panel estimation of BEERs. On one hand it means that the long-run relationship between real exchange rates and a set of fundamentals is assumed to be similar for the five CEEC, so that the additional information of pooling the data is used. On the other hand the speed of adjustment to equilibrium may differ from country to country. Imposing equal adjustment speeds would be too restrictive since estimation results have revealed large differences for the five economies.[77]

Both approaches, MG and PMG estimations, assume exogeneity of the fundamentals, which means that exchange rates do not feed back to the productivity differential or the net foreign asset position. The basic model is given as the following error correction representation

$$(4.25) \qquad \Delta y_{it} = \eta_i + \phi_i (y_{it-1} - \pi_i \boldsymbol{x}_{it-1}) + \sum_{j=1}^{p} \gamma_{ij} \Delta y_{it-j} + \sum_{j=1}^{q} \varphi_{ij} \Delta \boldsymbol{x}_{it-j} + \varepsilon_{it} \quad ,$$

$i = 1, \ldots, n$ and $t = 1, \ldots, T$,

where π_i are the long-run parameters of the cointegration relationship, γ_{ij} and φ_{ij} are the short-run parameters, ϕ_i are the error correction parameters, and $\boldsymbol{x}_{it-j}$ is the $k \times 1$ vector of explanatory variables. The lag parameters p and q may vary for the variables in the sample. Equation (4.25) constitutes the unrestrictive model for the MG estimator, where the long-run parameters π_i may vary across countries. Imposing the restriction that the π_i's are equal for all countries i, one obtains the underlying model for the PMG estimation

[77] Assuming common short-run responses and allowing only intercepts to differ across countries would lead to standard dynamic fixed effects estimators.

(4.26) $$\Delta y_{it} = \eta_i + \phi_i(y_{it-1} - \pi \boldsymbol{x}_{it-1}) + \sum_{j=1}^{p} \gamma_{ij} \Delta y_{it-j} + \sum_{j=1}^{q} \varphi_{ij} \Delta \boldsymbol{x}_{it-j} + \varepsilon_{it} ,$$

$i = 1, \ldots, n$ and $t = 1, \ldots, T$.

For the estimation of the PMG estimator the maximum likelihood method is adopted. The restriction of common long-run coefficients can be tested with a Joint Hausman test. The test can be employed to distinguish between two estimators that differ with respect to their use of information on homogeneity.[78] Under the null hypothesis the parameters are homogeneous and the PMG estimates are more efficient than MG estimates. Rejecting the null hypothesis would mean that the sample is too heterogeneous to be pooled. The Hausman test statistic is given as

(4.27) $$\mathrm{H} = \hat{q}' \left[var(\hat{q}) \right] \hat{q} \sim \chi^2 (k) ,$$

where $\hat{q}$ is the k x 1 vector of the differences between the MG and PMG estimates and $var(\hat{q})$ is the corresponding estimated covariance matrix. Under the null hypothesis that the two estimators are consistent but the PMG is efficient, $var(\hat{q})$ is calculated as the difference between the covariance matrices of the two underlying parameter vectors. H is asymptotically χ^2 - distributed with k degrees of freedom.

Table 4.13. Long-run coefficients of PMG and MG panel estimation

Series	PMG panel coefficients (t-values)	MG panel coefficients (t-values)
RER	1	1
PROD	-1.57 (-6.23)	-1.03 (-2.40)
NFA	-0.12 (-2.53)	-0.12 (-1.93)
Joint Hausman test (p-value)	3.61 (0.16)	

Note: The lag order was chosen with the Akaike information criterion. The maximum number of lags was set to two.

78 The original test has been derived by Hausman (1978). For details on this application of the Hausman test refer to Im et al. (1996).

Table 4.13 presents the results of the PMG estimator; MG estimates are reported for comparison.[79] The coefficients are as predicted since both productivity differential and net foreign assets have a positive and significant impact on the real exchange rate. A comparison of PMG and MG results reveals that the coefficient of the Balassa-Samuelson effect of the PMG estimator is to some extent larger than for the MG estimator. The magnitude of the estimated coefficient of the net foreign asset position does not alter whether the MG or PMG estimator is employed. The findings also indicate that imposing common long-run homogeneity significantly reduces the standard errors of the long-run coefficients.

The Hausman test statistic of 3.61 and the associated p-value of 0.16 imply that the restriction of long-run homogeneity of common long-run coefficients cannot be rejected. This confirms the hypothesis that the long-run relationship is equal across the five CEEC under consideration.

Pedroni (2000) suggests an alternative estimator, which builds upon the FMOLS estimation technique as advanced by Phillips and Hansen (1990). For the estimation of cointegrated panels, standard OLS is not applicable since it leads to asymptotically biased estimators (see Kao and Chen (1995)). Moreover, Chen et al. (1999) find that the bias corrected OLS estimator does not improve over the OLS estimator in general. The FMOLS techniques, however, have proven to be successful in dealing with problems of asymptotic biases in cointegrating vectors.[80]

As the PMG estimator, the FMOLS panel estimator from Pedroni (2000) allows for cross-sectional heterogeneity in short-run responses and intercepts, while long-run relationships are set to be common across the panel. The FMOLS estimator, however, employs the semi-parametric correction to the OLS estimator suggested by Phillips and Hansen (1990). Estimation is based on the following cointegrated system for panels

(4.28) $$y_{it} = \eta_i + \sum_{j=1}^{k} \beta_j x_{ijt} + \varepsilon_{it}$$

[79] Both estimation procedures are implemented in a GAUSS procedure, downloadable as JASA.EXE from http://www.econ.cam.ac.uk/faculty/pesaran/index.htm.

[80] Alternatively, Kao and Chiang (2000) suggest a panel Dynamic Ordinary Least Squares (DOLS) estimator to overcome the asymptotic bias of OLS. The DOLS estimator is based upon work of Saikkonen (1991) and Stock and Watson (1993).

(4.29) $x_{ijt} = \vartheta_{ij} + x_{ijt-1} + \mu_{ijt}$, with $i = 1, \ldots, n$, $j = 1, \ldots, m$ and $t = 1, \ldots, T$,

where ε_{it} and μ_{ijt} are stationary disturbance terms. The variables $\boldsymbol{x}_i = (x_{i1}, \ldots, x_{im})$ and y_i are cointegrated for each member of the panel, with cointegrating vector $\beta = (\beta_1, \ldots, \beta_m)$, if y_i is integrated of order one. The FMOLS estimator from Pedroni (2000) is basically the average of the individual FMOLS estimate for each country. He shows that an adjustment term which captures the potential contribution of heterogeneity from the dynamics of the panel produces minimal size distortions. The resulting estimator is asymptotically normal.

Table 4.14 presents the cointegration vector for the panel. Again, both the productivity differential and the net foreign asset position have a positive and significant impact on the real exchange rate. The magnitude of the parameters is comparable with the estimated coefficients in the BEER analysis. The t-statistics in parentheses indicate strong significance and, hence, confirm the adequacy of the chosen model.

Table 4.14. Long-run coefficients of FMOLS panel estimation

Series	**FMOLS panel coefficients (t-value)**
RER	1
PROD	-0.88 (-4.15)
NFA	-0.08 (-5.13)

Note: A common lag order of two was used.

4.4.5 The resulting behavioural equilibrium exchange rates of the panel estimation

Taking the estimated long-run coefficients, panel BEERs have been computed for the five CEEC under consideration. Since the PMG and FMOLS panel estimation techniques have produced different long-run coefficients of the fundamental variables, deviating BEER estimates are to be expected. For comparison, results from both procedures are investigated together. Figures 4.7 and 4.8 present the BEERs and misalignments from the PMG and FMOLS panel estimates for the five CEEC.

For ***Poland*** both panel estimation procedures reveal a substantial and persistent overvaluation of the zloty since 1993, which is different from the time series case, where the period of overvaluation commenced only in 1998. However, the outcome of the two panel approaches differs with respect to the evolution of overvaluation. While the PMG estimates disclose a rather stable overvaluation from 1993 to 2002, the FMOLS estimates show an upward trend in terms of misalignment. Panel estimation reveals an overvalued currency for ***Hungary***. The magnitude of misalignment is considerably high. According to the PMG estimator the overvaluation is in the range of 10 to 25 percent. The FMOLS estimates are more moderate in terms of misalignment with values between 5 and 20 percent. This result stands in contrast to the time series estimates. The patterns of the BEER estimates from panel and time series analysis are all very similar for the ***Czech Republic***, hence indicating a high degree of robustness. All estimates reveal only moderate overvaluation prior to the exchange rate crisis. Misalignment peaks at the end of the observed period. Contrary to the other countries, the currency of ***Slovenia*** exhibits periods of considerable undervaluation according to the panel estimates. Three periods of undervaluation are evident, the first one in 1993/1994, the second from 1996 to 1998, and the last since 1999. While during the first two periods misalignment was still relatively modest, it has reached values of up to 15 percent (FMOLS) and 20 percent (PMG) during the most recent period. According to the PMG and FMOLS estimates the real exchange rate of ***Estonia*** was not substantially overvalued until the Russian crisis hit the Estonian economy. At the peak of the Russian crisis misalignment approached 45 percent. This level of overvaluation is more pronounced than indicated by the time series estimates. Relatively high misalignment in a range of 20 to 30 percent is still notable at the beginning of 2002.

Overall, the results from the panel estimation techniques largely confirm the time series estimates for most countries. Notable exceptions are Hungary and Slovenia, where the FMOLS and PMG estimates lead to reinterpretations of the real exchange rate values. It is useful to note that panel estimations should not be regarded as inferior or superior to time series estimates. They should rather be interpreted as a new perspective, where the additional information of cross-country comparisons with other transition economies is incorporated. Qualitatively seen, the results are an important indicator of the exchange rate position. The quantitative figures, however, ought to be interpreted cautiously since the panel estimation techniques may ignore certain country-specific factors of exchange rate determination. The following chapter now turns from the BEER to an alternative equilibrium exchange rate concept, i.e. the PEER.

Figure 4.7. Pooled Mean Group real effective BEERs and misalignments

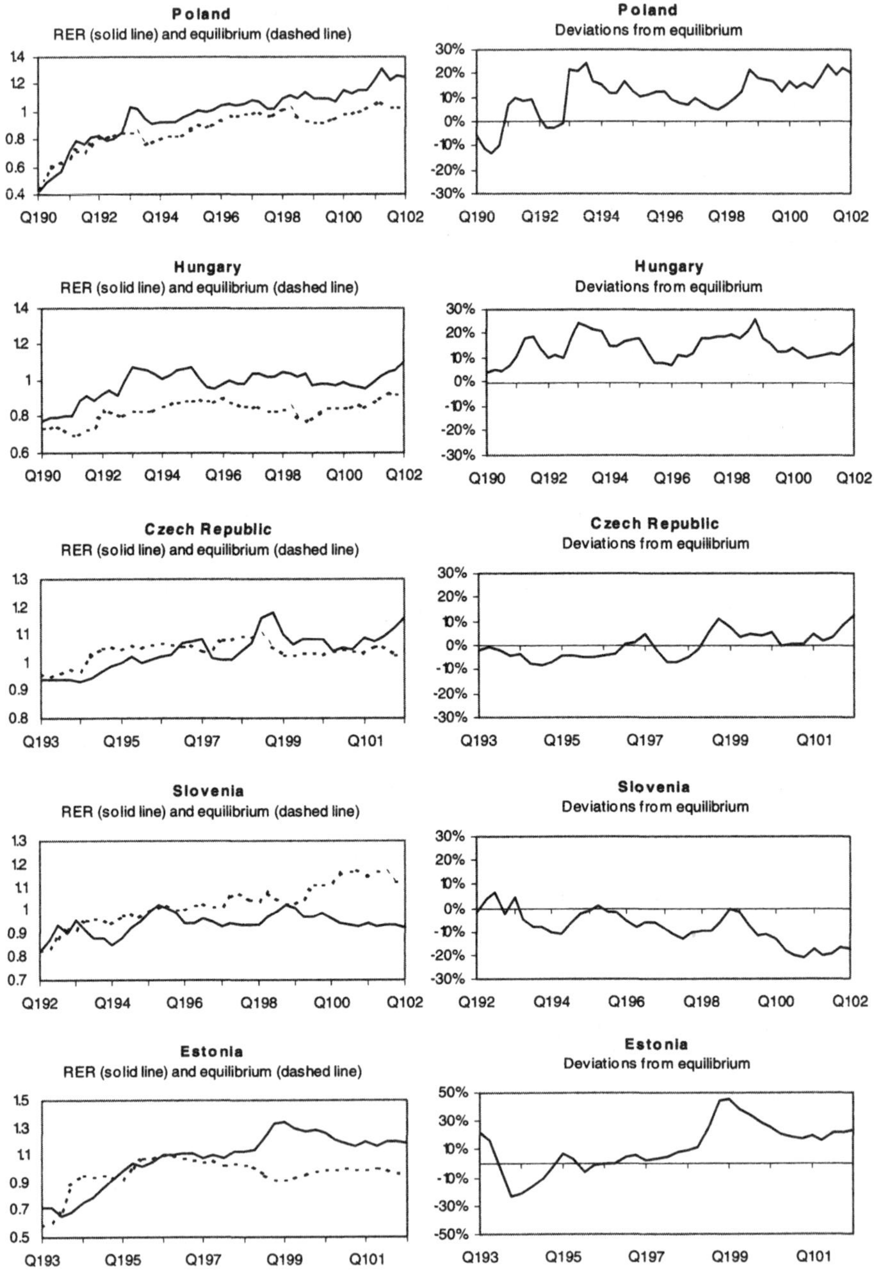

Figure 4.8. Fully Modified Ordinary Least Squares real effective BEERs and misalignments

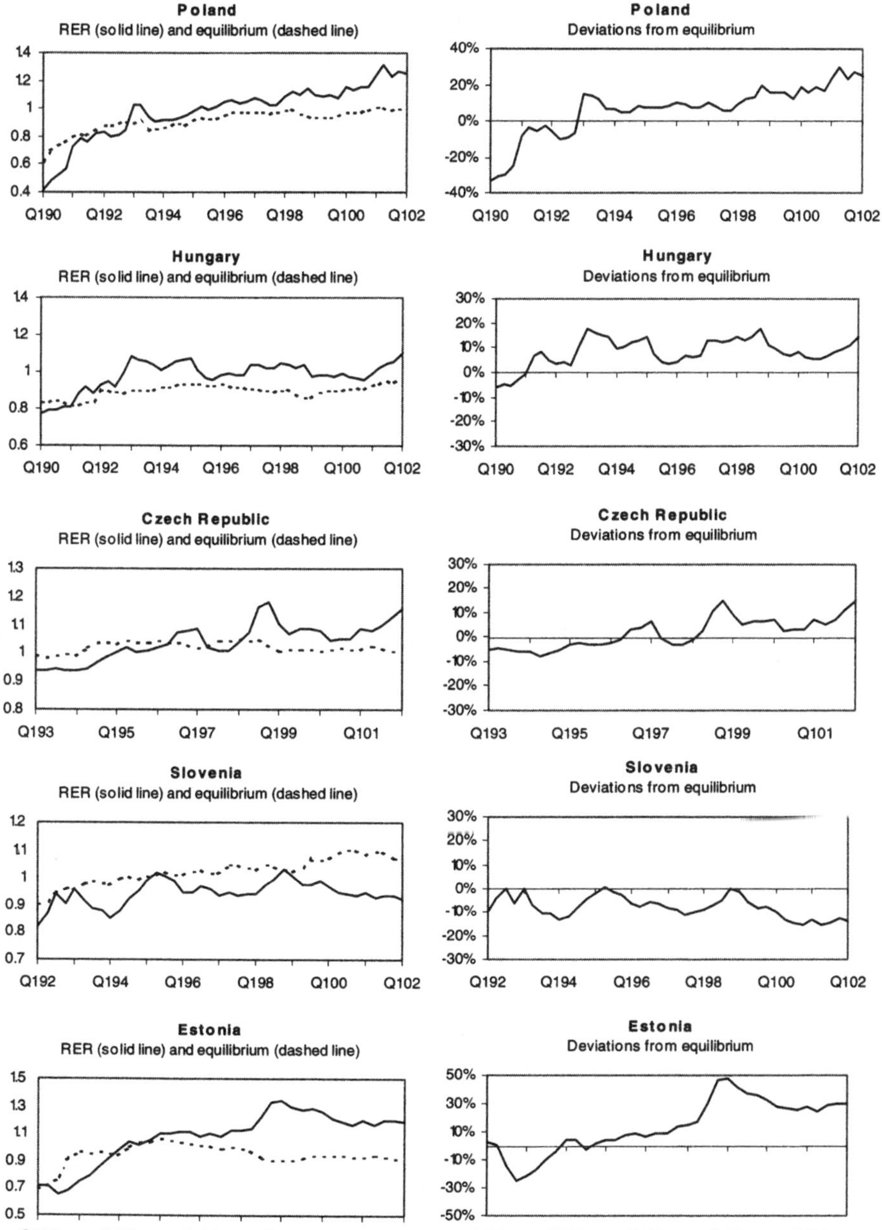

5 The permanent equilibrium exchange rates of central and eastern European countries

5.1 Decomposition of permanent equilibrium exchange rates

In the theoretical discussion of the PEER, different procedures for decomposing time series have been studied. For the following empirical analysis the procedure of Gonzalo and Granger (1995) is selected. This method shares two desirable features for the determination of both components. First, it explicitly considers the cointegration relationship among the variables and thus exploits all available information. Second, this decomposition guarantees that transitory components do not Granger-cause the permanent component. That means, a change in the transitory component does not have an impact on the long-run values of the variables, so that the resulting permanent time series may be considered as independent of the transitory component in all periods.

Analytically, Gonzalo and Granger (1995) make use of the results from the VECM

(5.1) $$\Delta \boldsymbol{x}_t = \boldsymbol{\eta} + \sum_{i=1}^{p-1} \boldsymbol{\Phi}_i \Delta \boldsymbol{x}_{t-i} + \boldsymbol{\Pi x}_{t-1} + \varepsilon_t$$

to identify the permanent and transitory components. Cointegration among the time series $\boldsymbol{x}_t$ means that the matrix Π is of reduced rank $r < k$. If this is the case, $\boldsymbol{x}_t$ may be explained in terms of $k - r$ non-stationary elements, called common factors $\boldsymbol{f}_t$, and r stationary elements. Gonzalo and Granger (1995) show that the common factors $\boldsymbol{f}_t$ can be identified under two rational assumptions. First, it is assumed that the common factors are linear combinations of the variables, and second it is assumed that the temporary component does not Granger-cause the permanent component. With this, the common factors are given as

(5.2) $$\boldsymbol{f}_t = \boldsymbol{\alpha}_{\perp} \boldsymbol{x}_t ,$$

where $\alpha_{\perp}$ denotes the orthogonal complement to the adjustment matrix α, such that the orthogonality condition $\boldsymbol{\alpha}_{\perp}' \boldsymbol{\alpha} = 0$ is satisfied.

This identification of the common factors makes it possible to decompose the time series x_t into permanent x_t^P and transitory x_t^T components

$$(5.3) \qquad \bar{x}_t^P = \beta_\perp(\alpha'_\perp\beta_\perp)^{-1}\alpha'_\perp x_t \text{ and}$$

$$(5.4) \qquad \bar{x}_t^T = \alpha(\beta'\alpha)^{-1}\beta' x_t,$$

where $\beta_\perp$ denotes the orthogonal complement to the cointegrating matrix β.

The PEER derivation also yields insights into the underlying forces of the system. The $\alpha_\perp$ vectors span the space of the common stochastic trends and thus identify the underlying driving forces. The $\beta_\perp$ give the loadings associated with $\alpha_\perp$, i.e. those variables driven by common trends. Another source of information is the matrix

$$(5.5) \qquad C = \beta_\perp(\alpha'_\perp(I - \sum_{i=1}^{p-1}\Phi_i)\beta_\perp)^{-1}\alpha'_\perp,$$

which measures the combined effects of the orthogonal components, i.e. the long-run effects of shocks to the system. This matrix is the same as in the moving average representation of the VECM as proposed by Johansen (1995)

$$(5.6) \qquad x_t = C\sum_{i=1}^{t}\varepsilon_t + C\eta + C(L)(\varepsilon_t + \eta),$$

where L constitutes the lag operator, such that $L(x_t) = x_{t-1}$.

5.2 The real effective permanent equilibrium exchange rates

The empirical PEER analysis is based on the results from the BEER analysis and is conducted for the five CEEC for which consistent cointegration relationships have been found, i.e. Poland, Hungary, the Czech Republic, Slovenia, and Estonia. The permanent and transitory components are derived from equations (5.3) and (5.4). The matrices α and β are known from the BEER approach, so that substituting the 3×1 vector $x_t = [q_t, prod_t, nfa_t]'$ into equations (5.3) and (5.4) delivers the permanent $\mathbf{x}_t^{\mathbf{P}} = \left[q_t^{perm}, prod_t^{perm}, nfa_t^{perm}\right]'$ and transitory vectors $\mathbf{x}_t^{\mathbf{T}} = \left[q_t^{trans}, prod_t^{trans}, nfa_t^{trans}\right]'$. Then q_t^{perm} constitutes the PEER.

Figure 5.1 presents the multilateral real PEER and deviations from equilibrium for the five CEEC. It is worth taking a closer look at the outcome since the PEER may reveal which part of misalignments stems from permanent factors and which part is only caused by transitory factors. In this context, the PEER estimates will also be compared with the time series BEER estimates.

According to the PEER concept undervaluation in ***Poland*** was very substantial at the beginning of the transition process. From 1994 to 1997 the real exchange rate was mostly in line with equilibrium. Overvaluation since 1998 was higher then indicated by the BEER approach. Looking at ***Hungary***, the peak overvaluation in 1998 that was revealed by the BEER approach seems to have been caused mainly by transitory influences; the PEER approach shows a much smaller hump. Serious misalignments cannot be observed over the entire period. In the ***Czech Republic***, overvaluation prior to the exchange rate crisis was slightly more pronounced when only permanent factors are considered. This result holds for the period since 2001 as well. The difference amounts to about 2 to 3 percent compared to the BEER. In ***Slovenia*** periods of serious misalignment are not observable. However, according to the PEER the Slovenian tolar was rather above than below equilibrium since 1998. For ***Estonia***, the PEER analysis reveals that the real exchange rate was overvalued by 20 percent during the Russian crisis. Contrary to the BEER results, the real exchange rate was still slightly overvalued in the first quarter of 2002.

Turning to the underlying forces of the system, table 5.1 displays the orthogonal components $\alpha_{\perp}$ and $\beta_{\perp}$, as well as values of matrix $\boldsymbol{C}$ from equation (5.4). Closer inspection of matrix $\alpha_{\perp}$ reveals which factors drive the common trends.[81] The variables associated with the highest value in each vector contribute most to the common trends. In all economies the first common trend is driven by the net foreign asset position. Although the picture is more ambiguous for the second trend, the productivity differential has the strongest influence in every case.

[81] Since there are no tests for the significance of the calculated values available, these results should be interpreted with prudence.

Figure 5.1. The real effective PEERs and misalignments

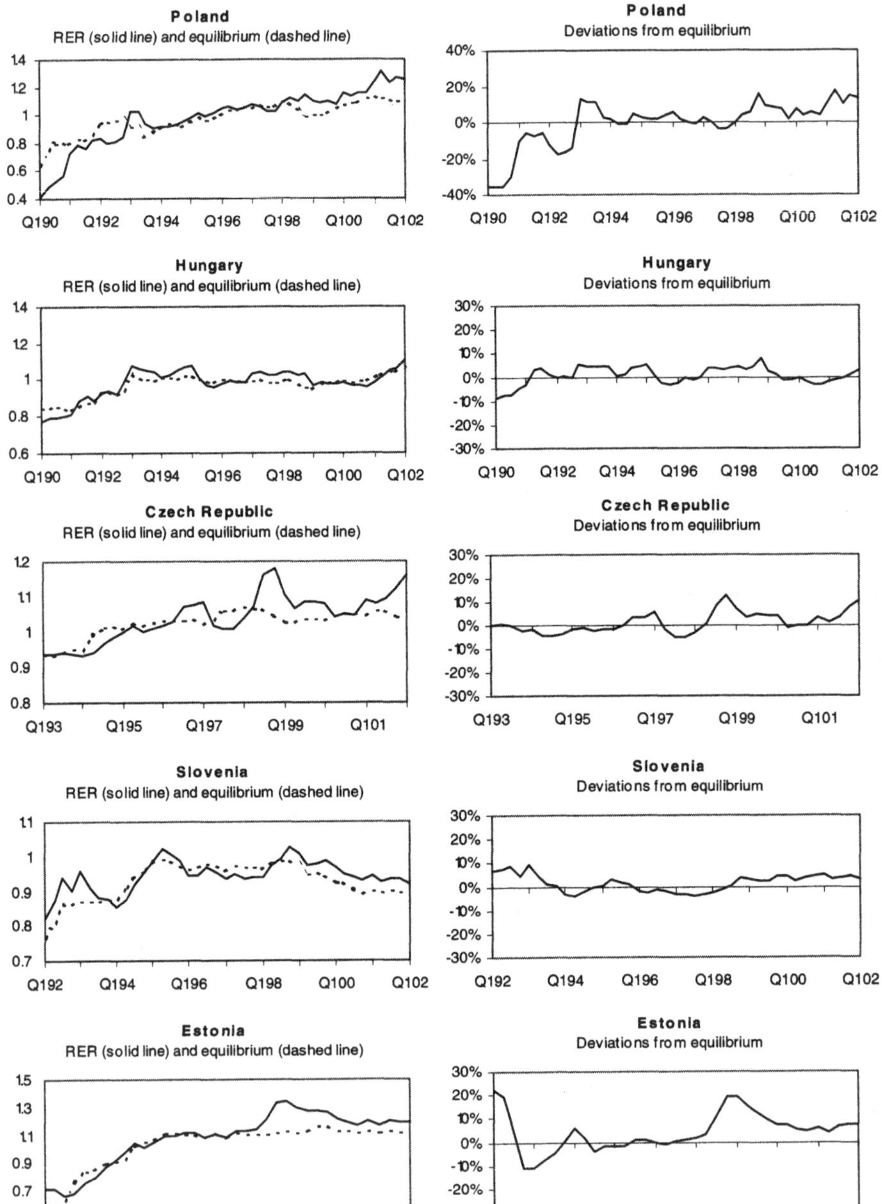

The highest values of the orthogonal component $\beta_\perp$ reveal, which common trend has the strongest impact on each factor. The estimates show that the exchange rate is mainly driven by the first common trend and only to a lesser extent by the second one. The influence of the trend related to the net foreign asset position is highest in the case of Slovenia.

The impact matrix $\boldsymbol{C}$ from equation (5.5) gives information about the reaction to shocks and may be used to check the consistency of the results. In all cases, the cumulative impact of a shock in the productivity differential and in the net foreign asset position is, as theory suggests, positive.

Table 5.1. Underlying forces of PEER results

Country	Variable	$\alpha_\perp^1$	$\alpha_\perp^2$	$\beta_\perp^1$	$\beta_\perp^2$	$\Sigma\,\varepsilon_{RER}$	$\Sigma\,\varepsilon_{PROD}$	$\Sigma\,\varepsilon_{NFA}$
Poland	RER	-0.2	0.14	0.79	0.03	-0.25	1.19	0.07
	PROD	0.98	0.01	0.61	-0.01	-0.24	1.03	-0.17
	NFA	0.01	0.99	-0.01	0.99	1.34	-2.90	5.22
Hungary	RER	0.25	-0.69	0.88	0.09	0.33	0.25	0.69
	PROD	0.96	0.10	0.48	-0.05	1.23	0.54	1.27
	NFA	0.10	0.71	-0.05	0.99	0.12	-0.04	1.12
Czech Republic	RER	-0.01	-0.29	0.72	0.03	-0.03	1.06	0.05
	PROD	0.99	-0.01	0.69	-0.01	-0.01	1.02	0.01
	NFA	-0.01	0.95	-0.01	0.99	-0.31	-2.90	1.01
Slovenia	RER	-0.26	0.58	0.57	0.39	0.12	0.34	0.73
	PROD	0.96	0.08	0.81	-0.12	0.59	0.46	0.42
	NFA	0.08	0.81	-0.13	0.91	0.42	-0.25	1.15
Estonia	RER	0.37	0.19	0.91	0.04	0.57	0.24	0.53
	PROD	0.93	-0.04	0.41	-0.02	1.21	0.53	0.56
	NFA	-0.04	0.98	-0.02	0.99	0.38	0.12	1.45

5.3 Bilateral permanent equilibrium exchange rates against the euro

As for the BEER, bilateral equilibrium exchange rates against the euro are calculated for the PEER. The procedure and the trade matrix are the same as documented for the BEER. Figure 5.2 depicts the bilateral rates for the five countries.

Figure 5.2. The nominal bilateral PEERs against the euro and misalignments

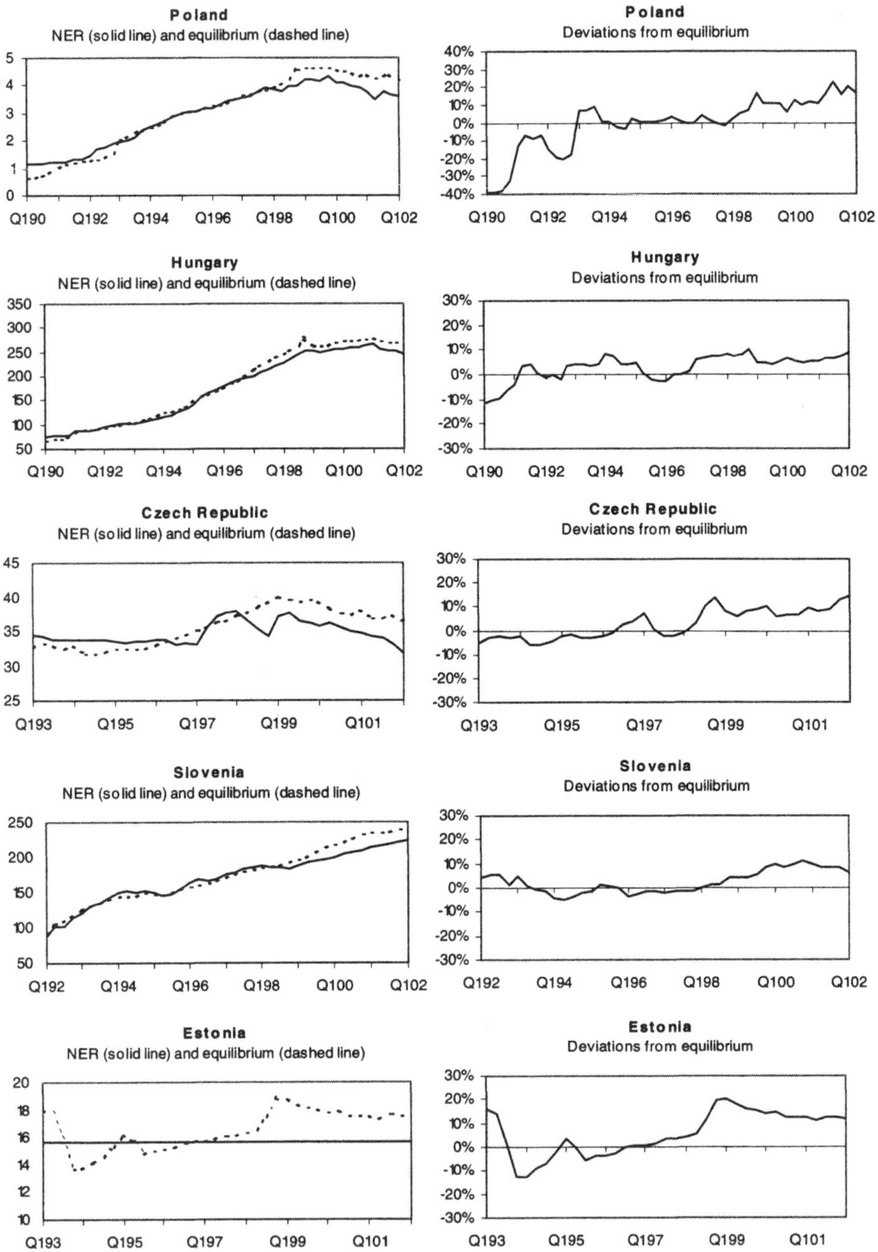

The nominal exchange rate against the euro of ***Poland*** deviated strongly from equilibrium at the beginning and at the end. While the Polish zloty was undervalued against the euro initially, it was overvalued by almost 17 percent in 2002. While the real PEER did not reveal any misalignment for ***Hungary***, the bilateral PEER indicates that the forint was overvalued against the euro since 1997. However, misalignment was of moderate size; according to the PEER approach, the equilibrium level was at about 260-270 forint per euro. The nominal exchange rate of the ***Czech Republic*** against the euro deviated notably from equilibrium since the beginning of 1998. While the equilibrium remained at levels between 36 and 40 euro, the nominal exchange rate declined to below 32. As a result, the Czech koruna was overvalued by almost 15 percent in the first quarter of 2002. The equilibrium euro exchange rate of ***Slovenia*** displayed a steady upward trend. The nominal euro exchange rate initially moved in line but has fallen behind this trend since 1998. However, misalignment was still at a moderate level at the end of the observed period. Beginning in 1995 the equilibrium exchange rate of ***Estonia*** displayed an upward drift. The Russian crisis induced a temporary shift above this trend, but the Estonian equilibrium exchange rate seems to have returned to this path by 2001. Since the nominal exchange rate against the euro had been fixed over the entire period, the Estonian currency was overvalued by almost 12 percent against the euro at the beginning of 2002.

Overall, the PEER results are qualitatively broadly in line with the BEER estimates. However, the discussion revealed some quantitative differences. Some of the misalignment has been caused mainly by transitory factors, but in the most recent period 2001/2002 misalignment was more pronounced in Poland, the Czech Republic and Estonia when permanent factor only are considered. Given the medium-run equilibrium values from the BEER approach and the medium to long-run values from the PEER, the analysis now turns to the long-run PPP concept, where a number of different aspects of PPP will be studied.

6 The purchasing power parity of central and eastern European countries

A study on equilibrium exchange rates cannot be comprehensive without assessing PPP values. For its simplicity and comprehensibility PPP is still widely used and commonly serves as a tool to determine a first reference value for equilibrium exchange rate levels. The PPP also acts as an indicator of the long-run direction of the real exchange rate and complements the BEER and PEER methods in this respect.

PPP may be expressed in two different ways, either in absolute or in relative terms. *Absolute PPP* is based on the assumption of strict equality between domestic and foreign price levels. This means that the real exchange rate ought to be equal to one. *Relative PPP* assumes that the exchange rate should equilibrate the inflation differential. This implies that the real exchange rate is constant, although it need not be unity. In the following both approaches are considered separately.

6.1 Absolute purchasing power parity

6.1.1 Absolute purchasing power parity for a basket of goods

The most reliable PPP data is available from the International Comparison Program (*ICP*). The *ICP* is a joint project of various organisations including the OECD and the World Bank. Its objective is to calculate PPPs based on a global survey of prices in order to make comparisons of GDPs and other economic aggregates between different countries. The program was first established in 1968 and since then the number of countries has continuously increased from initially ten countries to more than 130. The main objective of the *ICP* is to make price indices of different countries comparable, since consumption patterns and thus the underlying bundles of goods as well as the quality of products differ among the countries.

The PPP rates published by the *ICP* are expressed in comparison to the United States. For this study, the PPP conversion factors against the US dollar are transformed to determine effective rates as well as bilateral rates against the euro. These figures are more relevant for the evaluation of the current situation and the forthcoming adaptation of the euro currency since a simple comparison with the United States could give misleading results if the price levels in the euro area and in the other main trading partners deviate significantly from the US price level. The calculation of effective rates is based on the trade matrix presented in chapter 4.1.2 and comprises the ten CEEC, the United States, the United Kingdom, Japan, Russia, and the euro area.[82]

Figure 6.1 shows absolute PPP misalignment in effective terms of the CEEC from 1990 to 2001. The general observation is that the exchange rates of the CEEC are highly undervalued according to absolute PPP. The magnitude of undervaluation varies between the countries. While Slovenia, Latvia, and Lithuania, for example, exhibit undervaluation of below 30 percent at the end of the observed period, misalignment in Romania and Bulgaria is still close to 60 percent.[83] The currencies of the other countries are undervalued at around 40 to 50 percent. Concerning the evolution of deviation from PPP, visual inspection suggests a slow tendency to close the gap to PPP.[84]

Misalignment against the euro on a bilateral basis is depicted in figure 6.2. In this case, deviation from equilibrium is more pronounced for all countries compared to the effective PPP figures. The misalignment is the lowest for Slovenia at around 25 to 45 percent, whereas the other currencies are undervalued in a range of 50 to 80 percent. If there is adjustment to PPP at all, visual inspection suggests that it is slower than in the multilateral case.

The differences in magnitude emphasize the importance of examining both effective and bilateral rates. Since all CEEC exhibit low PPP values, misalignment is lower if these countries are included in the analysis as trading partners. That also means that in the current situation for each individual CEEC a price level close to the price level in the euro area cannot be considered as rational or realistic.

---

[82] A weighted average of the twelve members of the euro area served as an artificial value of the euro. The weights are the same as described in the data overview in chapter 4.1.2.

[83] From a first point of view, the relatively low undervaluation of Latvia and Lithuania may be surprising. However, one has to bear in mind that the trade share of Russia is comparatively high for these two countries and that the level of Russia's absolute PPP is very low.

[84] A statistical investigation is not conducted here. The usage of annual data only provides a limited number of observations, which are too low to give reasonably explainable results.

Figure 6.1. Absolute PPP misalignment in effective terms from 1990 to 2001

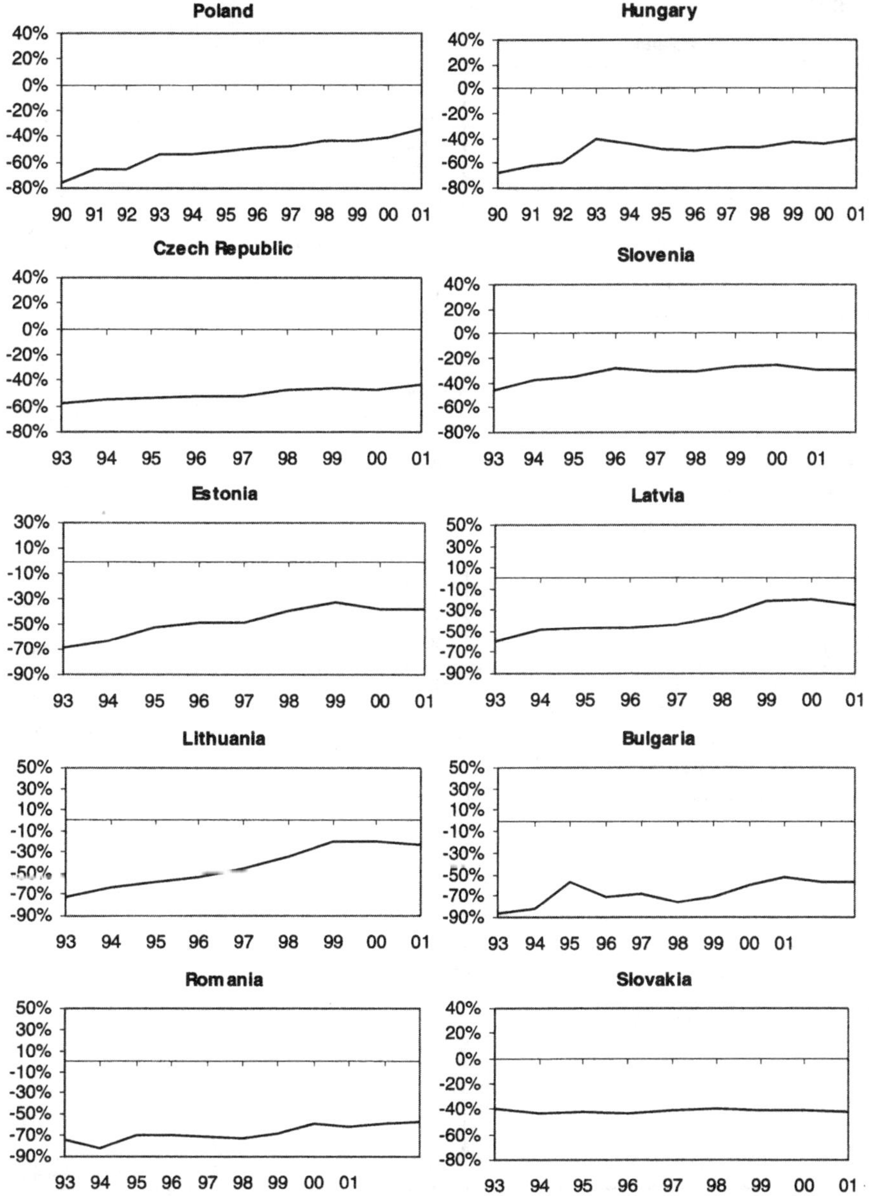

Note: The annual data comes from World Development Indicator CD-ROM 2003.

Figure 6.2. Absolute bilateral PPP misalignment against the euro from 1990 to 2001

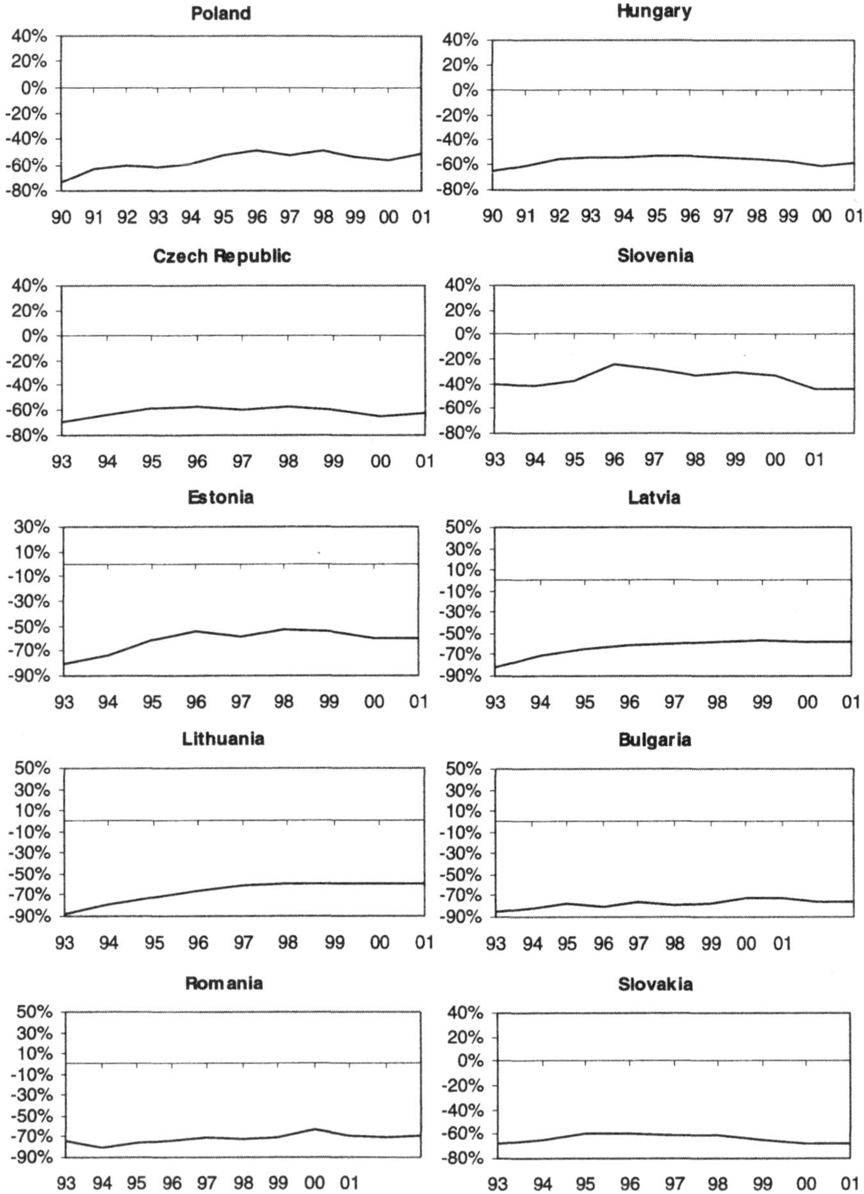

Note: The annual data comes from World Development Indicator CD-ROM 2003.

6.1.2 Absolute purchasing power parity for one single commodity – the Big Mac index

The *ICP* figures presented above are based on indices of a broad basket of goods and services. The composition of these baskets, however, varies across countries and the difficulties in comparing them have raised arguments over their usefulness. For example, Betton et al. (1995) note that when consumption bundles are not identical, price indices may behave differently even though the law of one price holds for each commodity. Furthermore, Kravis et al. (1975) use US weights to calculate price indices for foreign countries and show that these alternative indices far stronger support the PPP hypothesis than those indices based on local weights. The alternative to such baskets is to compare the price for one commodity that is homogenous and available in all countries under consideration. *The Economist* has applied the idea and since 1986 regularly publishes the local prices of a Big Mac. *The Economist* defines exchange rate equilibrium, or Big Mac parity, if under the prevailing exchange rate Big Mac prices are equal across countries when expressed in the same currency. The Big Mac has been selected since it is a standard product with the same ingredients and dimensions all over the world.

Although initially intended as a light-hearted measure only the so-called Big Mac index has gained considerable attention from economists and has been cited in respected economic journals. Cumby (1997) investigates how well the Big Mac performs as an indicator for exchange rate movements. He finds that the half-life of deviations from Big Mac parity is shorter than the half-life of PPP reported in the literature. Pakko and Pollard (1996) argue that the relatively good performance of the Big Mac index is not surprising as it is itself a composite of tradable goods and non-tradable services. The authors further note that the Big Mac index still has its limitations since barriers to trade, taxes or productivity biases are likely distortions not only for PPP, but also for the Big Mac parity. Ong (2003) confirms the existence of a productivity bias in the Big Mac index and suggests to extend the Big Mac index by adding a productivity bias proxy. Chen et al. (2003) employ panel unit root and cointegration tests to examine the validity of purchasing power parity. They find support for the Big Mac index in favour of a CPI-based basket. Parsley and Wei (2004) decompose the Big Mac index into its ingredients. The authors reveal that the speed of convergence of its tradable components is higher than for its non-traded components, and even sufficiently fast to be compatible with economic theories on purchasing power parity.

Unfortunately, *The Economist* publishes Big Mac prices only for a limited number of countries. From the group of CEEC, Hungary was the first to be included in

1991, followed by Poland and the Czech Republic in 1994. While *The Economist* traditionally compares the local Big Mac prices with the Big Mac prices in the United States, effective rates and price relationships against the euro are calculated for this study.

Figure 6.3 shows the deviations from Big Mac parity for the three CEEC in effective terms.[85] Misalignment is high in all three countries. In Poland, the magnitude of undervaluation lies in the range of 35 to 50 percent and in the Czech Republic between 25 and 35 percent. In Hungary, misalignment has more than halved from 50 to about 20 percent from 1991 to 2004. For Poland and the Czech Republic, the graph reveals no visible tendency to close the gap from PPP over the period of ten years. However, this outcome should be interpreted with caution and may not give a definite answer whether there is a mean reversion or not. Over relatively short time periods other influences such as changes in consumer behaviour, increasing competition, or different tax rates may have distorting implications on the evolution of Big Mac prices.

Figure 6.3. Big Mac index misalignment in effective terms from 1991 to 2004

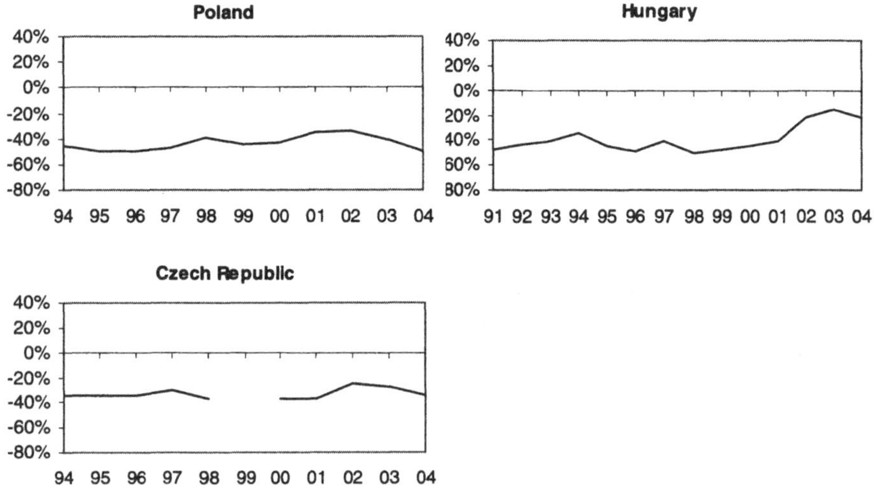

Note: Data comes from various issues of *The Economist*. In the case of the Czech Republic, data for 1999 is missing.

---

[85] The calculation of effective rates is once again based on the trade matrix from chapter 4.1.2. Prior to 1999 weighted averages of European countries served as an artificial value of the euro.

Comparing the Big Mac price levels in the three CEEC with the price level in the euro area does not alter the picture qualitatively. Figure 6.4 shows that undervaluation is high. Quantitatively, the gap to the euro price level is even larger than in effective terms. If there is a price adjustment process, it seems to be rather slow, particularly for Poland and the Czech Republic.

Figure 6.4. Misalignment of the bilateral Big Mac index against the euro from 1991 to 2004

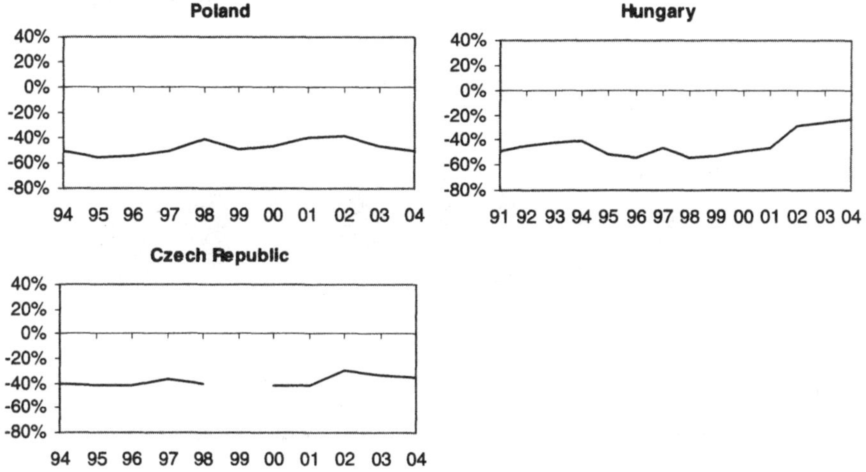

Note: Data comes from various issues of *The Economist*. In the case of the Czech Republic, data for 1999 is missing.

For the other CEEC time series data do not exist. However, in May 2004 *The Economist* published Big Mac prices for a number of additional countries.[86] Figure 6.5 presents misalignment of the Big Mac index in effective terms for nine CEEC. The situation is rather heterogeneous among the nine CEEC. While Poland, for example, displays misalignment of 40 percent, the currencies of Hungary, Estonia, and Latvia are only moderately undervalued at around 10

[86] The data has been published at www.economist.com on 27 May 2004. From the ten CEEC in this study Romania is the only country missing.

percent.[87] The Lithuanian currency is even slightly overvalued according to the Big Mac index. This result seems to be somewhat surprising, but it simply reflects the fact that the Big Mac price in Lithuania is relatively high compared to the weighted average price of its trading partners, of which Russia for example accounts for a high share.

Figure 6.5. Big Mac index misalignment in effective terms in 2004

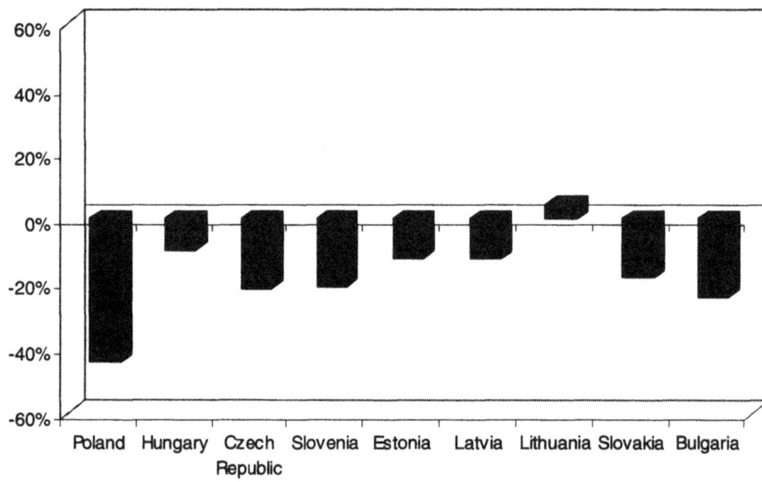

Note: Data comes from the internet version of *The Economist* at www.economist.com. Publication date is 27 May 2004.

The picture alters when bilateral misalignments against the euro are considered (see figure 6.6). Big Mac prices in CEEC are notably lower than in the euro area. The magnitude of price differences varies between 23 percent for Hungary and 50 percent for Poland.

In general, the results of the Big Mac index suggest somewhat lower misalignment than the results based on the *ICP* figures. However, the figures might be distorted because they just consider one single product. Different degrees of competition or deviating tax rates could have a strong impact on the

[87] Slightly deviating results compared to the time series analysis above for Poland, Hungary, and the Czech Republic occur as a result of different trade matrices.

price levels. In January 2004, *The Economist* introduced an alternative to the Big Mac index, the Tall Latte index. The idea is the same, except that the Big Mac is replaced by a cup of Starbucks coffee, acknowledging the global spread of that chain in recent years. The study revealed that though qualitative disparities are the exception, quantitative differences compared to the Big Mac index may be substantial.[88] This means that the magnitude of misalignment depends on the selected product and the Big Mac index should hence be considered with prudence.

Figure 6.6. Misalignment of the bilateral Big Mac index against the euro in 2004

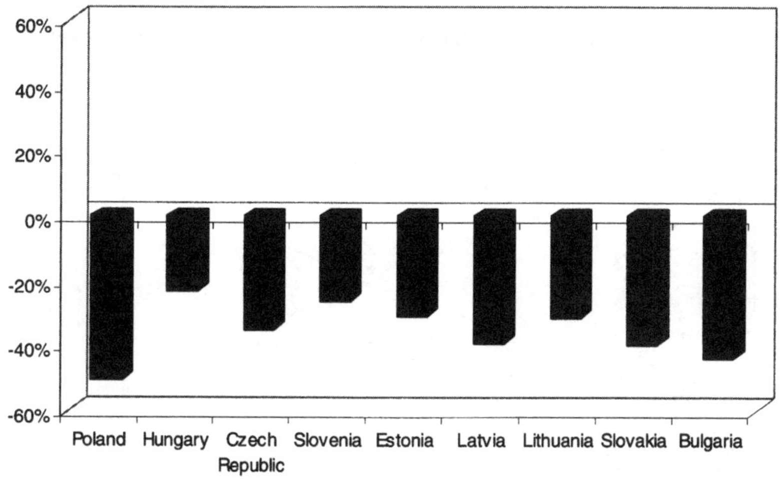

Note: Data comes from the internet version of *The Economist* at www.economist.com. Publication date is 27 May 2004.

6.1.3 Shortcomings of the absolute PPP approach in the application to the central and eastern European countries

Misalignment is large according to both the *ICP* figures and the Big Mac index. Although the interpretation of the latter result seems to be straight-forward, it is

[88] For example, the Chinese renminbi is undervalued by more than 50 percent according to the Big Mac index but only by 1 percent according to the Tall Latte index. Unfortunately, figures for eastern Europe are not available.

questionable to conclude that the currencies of the CEEC are in fact undervalued. It seems clear that in developing countries where the per capita income level is relatively low, the prices for goods are generally somewhat smaller. Particularly non-traded goods can be expected to be cheaper in low-income countries. Clements and Semudram (1983), for example, analyse the relationship between non-traded goods and per capita GDP. They find a strong positive association between prices for haircuts - as an example for a purely non-traded product - and GDP. Since services and other non-traded goods make up a high share of the Big Mac components and of consumer price indices in general, large deviations from parity are not at all surprising. If this is taken into account, the PPP conversion factors do not need to rise to a level of one.

Figure 6.7. PPP conversion factor to exchange rate ratio versus PPP per capita GNI in 2001

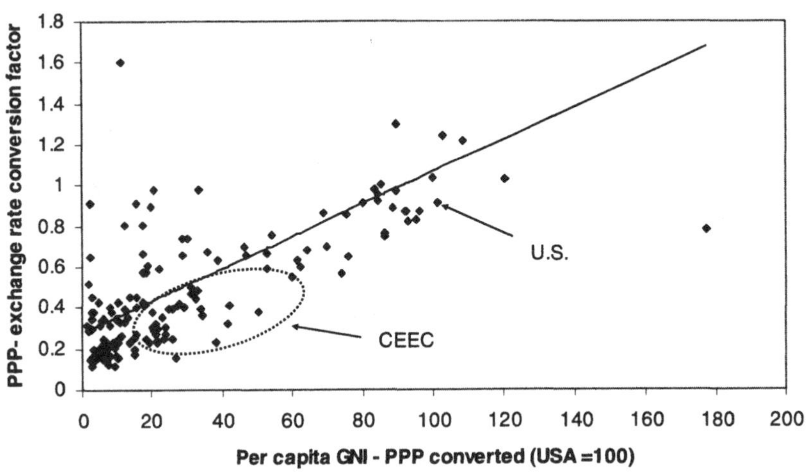

$R^2 = 0.51$ Adj. $R^2 = 0.50$

Note: PPP per capita GNI is per capita gross national income converted to US dollars. Data comes from *ICP* World Development Indicator CD-ROM 2003.

Figure 6.7 illustrates the above mentioned arguments in a scatter plot of 135 nations around the world for 2001.[89] The vertical axis shows the PPP conversion factor from the *ICP* database divided by the exchange rate and the horizontal axis shows PPP converted per capita gross national income (GNI). Running a regression reveals a significant and positive coefficient for the explanatory variable. Although the CEEC currencies still display misalignment, the degree of undervaluation shrinks when it is calculated relative to the regression line.

In this context, it might be useful to consider alternative ways to capture the deviations in PPP. One option that incorporates the level of economic development is presented in the next chapter.

6.2 GDP-adjusted relative purchasing power parity

6.2.1 Real exchange rates and GDP

The above mentioned arguments have already been considered in the literature of evaluating equilibrium exchange rate levels. In the case of the Big Mac index, Ong (2003) takes systematic relationships between departures from PPP and the level of GDP into account by introducing the No-Frills index. In the No-Frills index the nominal exchange rate is a function of relative prices and relative per capita GDP between home and abroad. Algebraically and in logs this means

(6.1) $$s_t = \gamma + p_t - p_t^* + \delta(yc_t - yc_t^*) + \varepsilon_t ,$$

where p and p^* represent home and foreign Big Mac prices and yc and yc^* are home and foreign per capita GDP in logs. Ong (2003) finds that the No-Frills index performs better than the Big Mac index in the way that the No-Frills index does not deviate significantly from the actual exchange rates anymore.

As an alternative to the explanation of the nominal exchange rate through price and GDP differences, Maeso-Fernandez et al. (2004) focus on (the log of) the exchange rate gap (*egap*), defined as the difference between (the log of) the PPP exchange rate (s^{PPP}) and (the log of) the actual exchange rate

(6.2) $$egap_t = s_t^{PPP} - s_t .$$

They consider the relationship between (the log of) the exchange rate gap and (the log of) per capita GDP in PPP terms (*ycppp*) and estimate the regression

[89] Funke and Rahn (2004) have presented this approach to evaluate the misalignment of the Chinese renminbi.

$$(6.3) \qquad egap_t = \gamma + \delta\, ycppp_t + \varepsilon_t$$

for a panel of 25 industrialised countries over the period from 1975 to 2002. In a BEER-type estimation model Maeso-Fernandez et al. (2004) find a positive link between the two variables and suggest to use this "out-of-sample" estimation to retrieve equilibrium exchange rate values for the CEEC. However, the problem of the approach is that the extrapolation requires to choose a dummy for the CEEC, which would introduce arbitrariness to the estimation. A further weakness is that the variable *egap* and *ycppp* are closely related by definition since an exchange rate appreciation raises both variables *egap* and *ycppp* simultaneously.

A somewhat different but straightforward idea to incorporate per capita GDP in the determination of the exchange rate equilibrium is employed in this study. In contrast to previous studies the approach will be related to the concept of relative PPP. Relative PPP is more likely to hold as it takes into consideration that transaction costs and price differences in non-traded goods may cause permanent deviations from absolute parity. However, the above mentioned objections against the validity of absolute PPP are to some extent also relevant for the case of relative PPP. Comparatively strong GDP growth rates in the CEEC should have appreciated the real exchange even in relative terms, so that the assumptions of constant real exchange rates might not be considered appropriate. Therefore, the question arises how then should one incorporate the economic development in the relative PPP analysis. In a study about the equilibrium PPP exchange rates of East Asian countries, Chinn (2000) uses a deterministic time trend in his regression, which could capture such an effect. However, the assumption of a constant rate may not reflect the development of GDP growth if it fluctuates significantly within the selected time period. Moreover, this may even yield misleading results if the appreciation is not or only in part related to GDP growth and reflects misalignment instead. Finally, there is no theoretical justification for including a deterministic time trend.

Therefore, an alternative idea is employed, where the equilibrium real exchange rate is directly related to the evolution of GDP. The following approach first attempts to capture the long-run relationship between real exchange rate and per capita GDP. Next, the estimated relationship is used to adjust the equilibrium level of a country's relative PPP depending on the evolution of relative GDP. Relative GDP means that a country's GDP is measured in comparison to the trade-weighted GDP of its trading partners. Finally, misalignment is determined as the deviation of the real exchange rate to the GDP-adjusted relative PPP rate.

6.2.2 GDP-adjusted relative purchasing power parity in a panel analysis

For the empirical analysis most of the required data, i.e. exchange rates, price indices, and GDP, is readily available from the analysis in chapter 4. The GDP data has been seasonally adjusted using the additive X-12 methodology. Population figures are obtained from the IFS database.[90]

The long-run connection between the real exchange rate and per capita GDP is estimated in a bivariate cointegration model which includes all ten CEEC. To make the development of GDP figures comparable, an index of per capita GDP (*capGDPI*) is calculated for each country. Relative GDP (*RelcapGDPI*) is then determined as the log of the ratio of a country's *capGDPI* and the trade-weighted index of its trading partners

$$(6.4) \qquad RelcapGDPI_{i,t} = log\left(\frac{capGDPI_{it}}{\prod_{\forall j \neq i} capGDPI_{jt}^{\ w_j}}\right).$$

The estimation will be carried out in a panel estimation framework. Panel estimation techniques are selected since the main focus of this analysis is the common effect of GDP on real exchange rates in CEEC and not the individual effect in each country. Furthermore, panel estimations have proven more successful in dealing with PPP. Given the relatively short time series the additional use of cross-sectional data is highly advisable. Panel unit root tests are conducted for the real exchange rate and the relative per capita GDP. The results are depicted in table 6.1.

Table 6.1. Panel unit root test results for the ten CEEC

Series	Test statistics	Critical values
RER	-1.71*	-1.69
GDP per capita	-0.68	-1.69

Note: * Means rejection at the 5 % critical value. Two lags have been imposed for all tests. The tests are without time trends.

The test indicates that relative GDP per capita is non-stationary, whereas the real exchange rate panel seems to be stationary. However, the result of the exchange

[90] Please note that population figures are only available at an annual frequency.

rate is very close to the critical value and further investigation revealed that the outcome varies with the specification of the unit root test. The ambiguity of the result does not allow a definite interpretation whether the exchange rate is stationary or non-stationary.

Although the following panel cointegration tests and estimation techniques are designed for unit root time series, they do not require all series to be non-stationary. At first, the panel cointegration tests from Pedroni (1999) are employed and the output is presented in table 6.2. There is strong evidence in favour of cointegration among the variables since the null hypothesis of no cointegration can be rejected in six out of seven cases. Therefore, the panel estimation techniques presented in chapter 4 may be used.

Table 6.2. Panel cointegration test results for the ten CEEC

Test	Test statistics	Critical values
Panel V-statistic	1.89*	1.69
Panel Rho-statistic	-1.71*	-1.69
Panel PP-statistic	-1.78*	-1.69
Panel ADF-statistic	-2.79*	-1.69
Group Rho-statistic	-1.41	-1.69
Group PP-statistic	-1.73*	-1.69
Group ADF-statistic	-3.25*	-1.69

Note: * Means rejection at the 5 % critical value. Two lags have been imposed for all tests. The tests are without time trends.

Table 6.3 presents the panel cointegration estimates of the PMG and MG estimators. The signs of the coefficients are as predicted. The test statistic for the MG estimator is not significant, but imposing common long-run homogeneity reduces the standard errors of the long-run coefficients, so that the coefficient of the PMG estimator is significantly different from zero. The Hausman test statistic indicates that the restriction of long-run homogeneity of common long-run coefficients cannot be rejected. This confirms the hypothesis that the long-run relationship is equal across the ten CEEC under consideration. Overall, the results are very robust. Modifications in lag length or estimations with different time periods do not alter the magnitude of the coefficients significantly.

Table 6.3. Long-run coefficients of PMG and MG panel cointegration estimation

Series	PMG panel coefficients (t-values)	MG panel coefficients (t-values)
RER	1	1
GDP per capita	-0.65 (-5.11)	-0.39 (-0.92)
Joint Hausman test (p-value)	0.42 (0.52)	

Note: The lag order was chosen with the Akaike information criterion. The maximum number of lags was set to two.

To further check the results, the FMOLS estimator is employed as well. Table 6.4 reveals that the FMOLS estimator largely confirms the previous figures. The magnitude of the coefficient is slightly smaller, but still significantly different from zero.

Table 6.4. Long-run coefficients of FMOLS panel estimation

Series	FMOLS panel coefficients (t-value)
RER	1
GDP per capita	-0.57 (-3.85)

Note: A common lag order of two was used.

Since the figures of both estimators do not deviate very much from each other, the results of the PMG estimator are used to determine equilibrium values exclusively.[91] The procedure is as follows. *First*, the equilibrium value of the real exchange rate is determined. For this, the real exchange rates are centered using a

[91] The resulting PPP equilibrium values do not differ significantly when the results from the FMOLS estimation procedure are used instead.

regression of the real exchange rate on a constant over the period 1995 to 2002.[92] The period prior to 1995 has been excluded from the determination of equilibrium in order to account for a possible undervaluation in the early years of transition since disregarding such a case could lead to biased results. *Second*, the deviations of GDP per capita from its mean are computed. Again, the mean level is based on the period from 1995 to 2002 to account for potential economic adjustments in the early period of transition. *Third*, the deviations of GDP per capita are multiplied by the estimated coefficient from the PMG estimation to determine their impact on the equilibrium level of the real exchange rate. *Fourth*, the relative PPP equilibrium values are adjusted to include the impact of GDP per capita on the real exchange rate.

The outcome for the ten CEEC is worth being examined in more detail since it deviates considerably from the BEER and PEER estimates presented in chapter 4 and 5, respectively.

6.2.3 Results of the GDP-adjusted relative purchasing power parity

The resulting equilibrium exchange rates and the misalignment of the actual exchange rate are presented in figures 6.8 and 6.9. According to the GDP-adjusted relative PPP concept, ***Poland*** started with a severely undervalued currency. However, already in 1993 the exchange rate touched the equilibrium level. This timing coincides with the point of time at which the economic downturn ended and the growth rates turned to positive numbers. From 1993 to 2000 the real exchange rate remained at parity to its equilibrium value. Only since 2001 the actual exchange rate has departed from equilibrium and has quickly risen to an overvaluation of more than 10 percent. The picture for ***Hungary*** is similar to the Polish. Until the end of 1992 the exchange rate had been undervalued. After a period of moderate overvaluation the exchange rate stabilised at parity to the equilibrium level until 1998. In the years 1999 and 2000 the Hungarian forint was somewhat undervalued, but returned to parity in 2001. Although the ***Czech Republic*** did not start with an undervalued currency in 1993, the exchange rate stayed below equilibrium from 1994 to 1996. At the timing of the exchange rate crisis, the exchange rate was at parity according to the GDP-adjusted relative PPP. Since 2000 the Czech krona has been overvalued, but the extent of misalignment

[92] Chinn (2000) has used the relative PPP to evaluate misalignment for a number of Asian currencies prior to the East Asian exchange rate crisis. He uses the same regression to compute forecasts of equilibrium values for each period.

is relatively low when the outcome is compared to the previous concepts. The equilibrium exchange rate level of ***Slovenia*** has slowly tended upward for most of the observed period and with it has the actual exchange rate, so that serious misalignments have not occurred. Only after 1999 the equilibrium rate has stabilised at the current level. As the real exchange rate had even declined since 1999 the Slovenian tolar was slightly undervalued in 2002. The currency of ***Estonia*** has not been significantly overvalued except for two short periods at the beginning of transition and during the Russian exchange rate crisis. Given the strong and persistent upward trend of the equilibrium rate the exchange rate of Estonia was even undervalued by 2002. This outcome deviates from the results of the previous applications in this paper.

The real exchange rates of ***Latvia*** and ***Lithuania*** display strong appreciation from 1993 to 2000. The sharp upward trend in the first years suggests that both countries started with an initially undervalued currency. However, the correction after the peak level at the beginning of 2000 might reveal that the adjustment process had been too rapid. In the year 2000, the real exchange rate of Latvia was 20 percent above parity, but the recent correction seems to have brought the exchange rate back to parity by 2002. In Lithuania, however, the exchange rate was still severely overvalued in 2002.

The development of the ***Bulgarian*** currency has to a great deal been influenced by periods of high inflation. The peak of the real exchange rate in mid 1993 was the consequence of such a period and the slump in 1996 was the result of hyperinflation. Until the introduction of the currency board and except for a short period in 1993 the exchange rate had been mostly undervalued. After the adoption of the currency board, the real exchange rate rose strongly while the equilibrium rate remained at a constant level. This led to a persistent overvaluation of about 20 percent since mid 1998. ***Romania***'s real exchange rate fluctuated heavily since 1991. Periods of strong misalignment were followed by sudden returns to parity. High inflation rates combined with partly administered exchange rates might have been the root for these fluctuations. Meanwhile, the equilibrium level of Romania's exchange rate has been fairly stable over the whole decade. Two periods of misalignment can be distinguished. The period of undervaluation lasted from 1991 to 1997 and the period of overvaluation lasted from 1998 to 2002. In 2002 overvaluation was at around 20 percent. The real effective exchange rate of ***Slovakia*** was relatively stable. Misalignment in Slovakia was moderate throughout the period. Since the beginning of 2000, however, the exchange rate seems to have been above parity by 7 to 12 percent.

Figure 6.8. The real effective, GDP-adjusted relative PPP equilibrium exchange rates (Part 1)

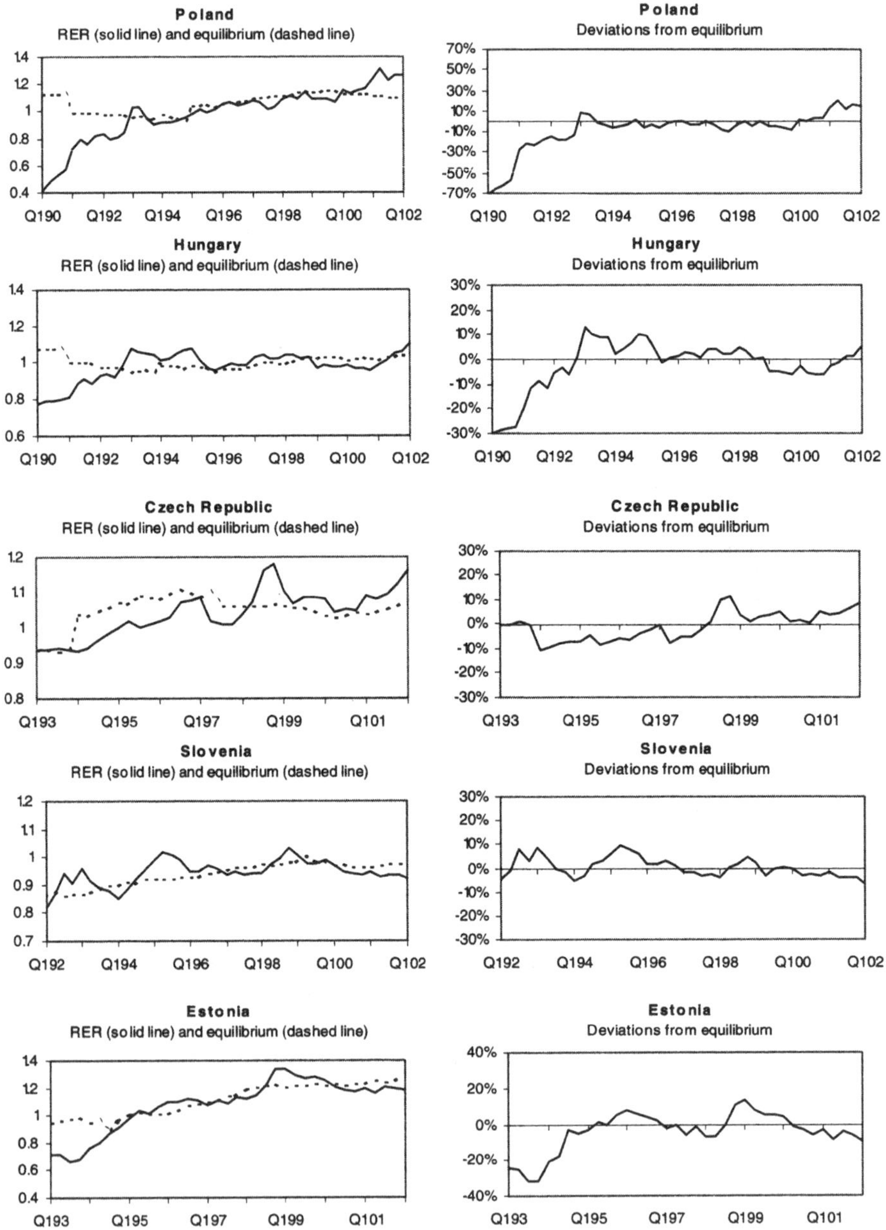

Figure 6.9. The real effective, GDP-adjusted relative PPP equilibrium exchange rates (Part 2)

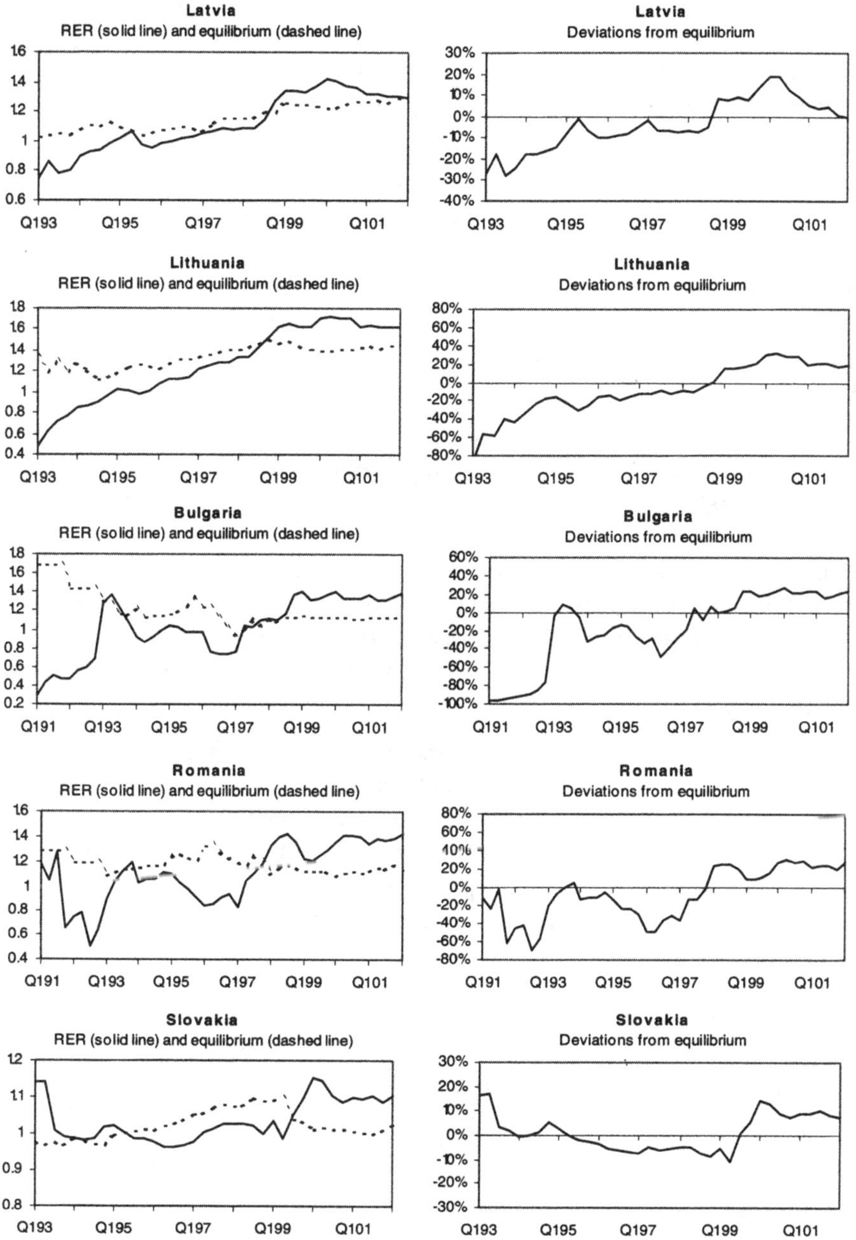

6.2.4 Nominal GDP-adjusted relative purchasing power parity against the euro

As for previous exchange rate concepts, nominal bilateral exchange rates against the euro are calculated through the algebraic transformation described in chapter 4.3. Figures 6.10 and 6.11 present the results of the transformation.

In 1999 the nominal exchange rate of ***Poland*** departed from the long-term trend of the equilibrium rate, which resulted in an overvalued currency. Overvaluation against the euro was about 5 percent higher than in effective terms at the end of the observed period. In the case of ***Hungary*** the picture does not alter very much irrespective whether the equilibrium exchange rate is considered in effective terms or against the euro. The only disparity to the real effective case is that the currency was not overvalued against the euro in the period ranging from 1993 to 1995.

The main difference between the effective and nominal exchange rate in the ***Czech Republic*** is that the exchange rate has been continuously overvalued since mid 1999. In 2002, misalignment peaked at almost 12 percent. If the ***Slovenian*** currency is compared to the euro the result does not change qualitatively. The Slovenian tolar was in equilibrium most of the time. The nominal GDP-adjusted relative PPP equilibrium exchange rate of ***Estonia*** has been relatively stable since 1995. Given the fixed parity against the euro periods of severe misalignment have not been encountered. However, the exchange rate was not significantly undervalued against the euro in 2002 as it was in real effective terms.

While the nominal exchange rate of ***Latvia*** slowly declined from 1993 to 2002, the equilibrium exchange rate against the euro steadily rose until 2000, before declining thereafter. The Latvian currency recovered from the peak overvaluation in 2000, but did not reach the equilibrium level against the euro by the beginning of 2002. ***Lithuania***'s development displays similarities to Latvia's. However, the Lithuanian currency was dangerously overvalued against the euro in 2002. The size of overvaluation approached 25 percent. The same result as for Lithuania applies to ***Bulgaria.*** The nominal exchange rate against the euro had been undervalued until the introduction of the currency board. However, the currency board put a high burden of overvaluation on the local economy. The magnitude of overvaluation against the euro is somewhat higher than in effective terms.

Figure 6.10. The nominal bilateral, GDP-adjusted relative PPP equilibrium exchange rates against the euro (Part 1)

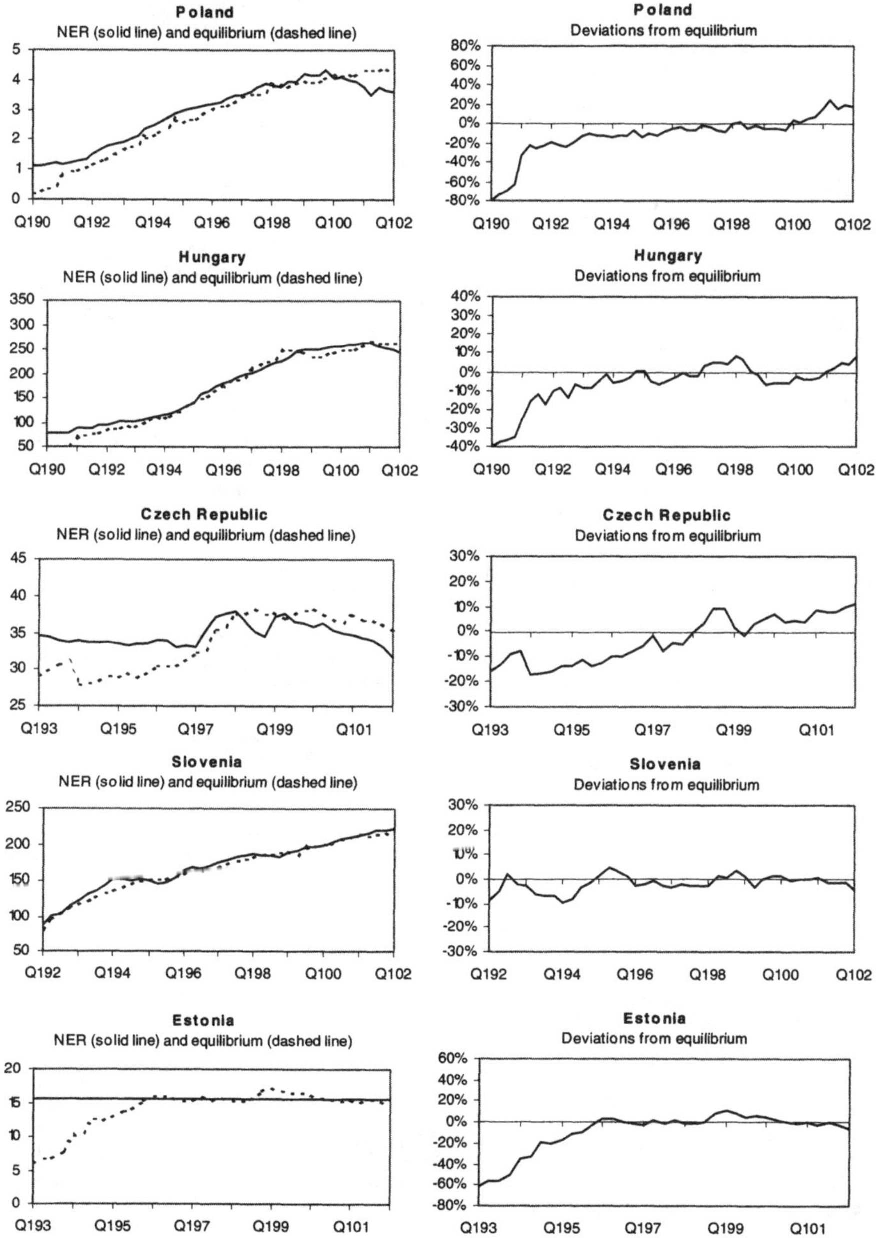

Figure 6.11. The nominal bilateral, GDP-adjusted relative PPP equilibrium exchange rates against the euro (Part 2)

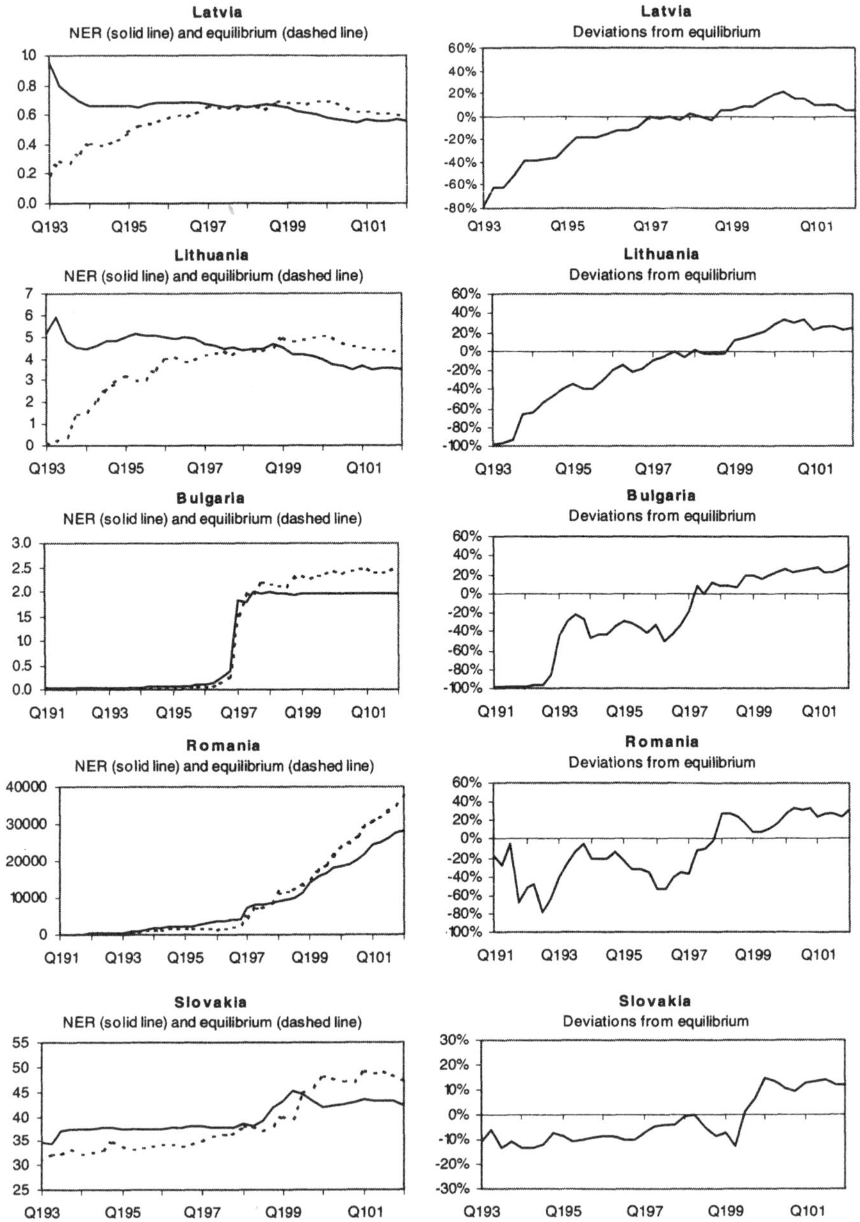

Romania has experienced a steady devaluation of its currency against the euro. However, over the entire period the equilibrium rate has outpaced the nominal exchange rate devaluation, so that the currency was misaligned by more than 30 percent against the euro in 2002. In the case of ***Slovakia*** misalignment against the euro is much more pronounced than in effective terms. Prior to 1997 the exchange rate had constantly been undervalued, but since mid 1999 it stayed overvalued by about 10 percent. The fluctuations of misalignment in 1998 and 1999 are closely related to the exchange rate development of the Czech Republic.

This analysis has provided equilibrium exchange rates for all ten CEEC based on the idea of relative PPP. However, it must be considered that the PPP is essentially a long-run concept, so that given the relatively short time series the outcome should be interpreted with prudence. Nevertheless, the use of panel data and the adjustment for economic development serve to increase the confidence that the calculated figures give new insights to the level of equilibrium exchange rates. In particular, the level of misalignment in comparison to other CEEC may reveal valuable information.

So far, a number of different concepts have been presented and a variety of different exchange rate evaluations have been made. Although the general direction of the calculated figures is apparent, a review of the results will be helpful, so that country-by-country judgements for the current exchange rate position can be given. The following chapter will thus review the main outcomes, address some interesting findings and consider the forthcoming path to EMU accession with respect to all of the estimates.

7 An evaluation of the results and the road to European Monetary Union accession

Different concepts and estimation techniques have led to a broad spectrum of outcomes. In the following the results of this study shall be used to address some specific questions concerning the transition economies of central and eastern Europe. In the first section, the question of whether the real exchange rate of transition countries were substantially undervalued at the beginning of transition, as some authors claimed in the mid 1990s, will be reviewed. The figures of this study may offer a new perception of this issue. The second section is concerned with the current situation. The focus will be on the question of whether the currencies are in fact critically overvalued as other papers suggest. The third section will examine the consequences of alternative exchange rate regimes. In the centre of the discussion will be whether certain exchange regimes systematically lead to serious misalignment. In the final section the strategy for achieving membership in the EMU will be discussed with respect to the calculated figures and the political guideline.

7.1 Were the exchange rates of central and eastern European countries undervalued at the beginning of the transition process?

Halpern and Wyplosz (1997) raised the argument that the real exchange rates at the beginning of the transition period were far from their equilibrium values and that a large share of the observed appreciation in transition economies could be attributed to a correction of an initially strong undervaluation. The authors provide four reasons that could have accounted for the undervaluation. First, the transition economies were confronted with a severe monetary overhang, which resulted from a shortage and hence a rationing of real goods as was common practise in planned economies. Second, the unavailability of foreign assets under the communist system led to excess demand for foreign goods. Third, the authorities' lack of credibility at the beginning of transition caused substantial risk premia, which would either be reflected in high interest rates or alternatively in an overly devalued exchange rate with room for future appreciation. Fourth, given the uncertainty about the equilibrium value of exchange rates and the fear of credibility losses from subsequent devaluations the authorities chose to err on the side of undervaluation rather than overvaluation. The outcome is what the authors considered to be undervalued currencies in the CEEC after the introduction of the new convertible currencies.

As part of the examination of equilibrium exchange rates, Halpern and Wyplosz (1997) attempt to determine the magnitude of the initial undervaluation of transition countries. Their empirical work and the related paper of Begg et al. (1999), however, both suffer from lack of data and the short length of time series at that point of time. As a consequence, the authors did not estimate real exchange rates directly, but selected US dollar wages instead.[93] The results, based on an "out-of-sample" analysis, suggest a substantial initial undervaluation, ranging from a negligible size, as in the case of Hungary, to almost 100 percent (Halpern and Wyplosz, 1997). Begg et al. (1999) improve the estimation and find massive undervaluation in the early years of transition. Although exact figures are not provided, the authors note that misalignment was highest in the Baltic countries and that Slovenia's exchange rate was even above equilibrium. By 1996 Poland, Hungary and Romania seemed to have more than offset the initial undervaluation.

The analysis of Halpern (1997) and Begg et al. (1998), however, exhibits a number of deficiencies. First, the time series dimensions of the studies appear to be too short for a thorough assessment since it comprises only five or six observations. Second, US dollar wages do not seem appropriate to determine exchange rate misalignment since its definition varies considerably among countries. In the case of transition countries this may be a serious problem since direct wages used to be only a small part of total labour costs given the social amenities granted by most firms. Third, the "out-of-sample" estimation leads to questionable results when mostly development indicators are considered as determinants of equilibrium exchange rate levels. In transition economies the level of social development was relatively high, therefore suggesting a relatively high equilibrium exchange rate value. However, the competitiveness of the economy was far lower than any social development indicator suggested. Production and services were highly inefficient and many firms and even countries were nearly bankrupt. Since the real exchange rate to a large extent reflects the competitiveness of the economy rather than the level of social development, development indicators as explanatory variables in the regression may well overestimate the equilibrium exchange rate level. Furthermore, the degree of economic breakdown differed substantially

[93] See chapter 3.2.4 for a detailed description of the estimations in the three papers.

among the CEEC, so that grouping all transition economies together does not overcome this problem.[94]

In view of these shortcomings, it is interesting to assess what indication the estimates of this study give as far as the situation at the beginning of the transition process is concerned. Table 7.1 illustrates the average misalignment of the real effective exchange rate in the first year of observation for all seven methodologies. As mentioned earlier, the PPP and Big Mac figures should be considered with caution since the *absolute* numbers can hardly display the true level of misalignment. Nevertheless, the numbers have been included as the *relative* magnitude of deviation can reveal additional information.

Substantial undervaluation can be observed in Poland. Although the magnitude of misalignment differs among the concepts, all methods clearly support this hypothesis. Hungary, the Czech Republic and Slovenia seem to have been roughly in equilibrium, with Hungary perhaps slightly undervalued and Slovenia somewhat overvalued.[95] The result for Estonia may be surprising at first glance if one expects an initial undervaluation of the Estonian kroon. A closer inspection, however, reveals that at the beginning of 1993 the kroon was in fact somewhat overvalued, but subsequently became strongly undervalued according to most equilibrium exchange rate concepts in 1994. This observation is largely confirmed by the study of Filipozzi (2000). According to his analysis the Estonian real exchange rate was only marginally undervalued in the second quarter of 1993, but strongly undervalued at the beginning of 1994.[96]

The interpretation of the remaining five countries must be considered with prudence since there are less data available. Nevertheless, the findings offer some interesting insights. In the case of the Baltic States misalignment was far more pronounced in Lithuania than in Estonia or Latvia. Elsewhere the Bulgarian currency was substantially undervalued, whereas Romania's misalignment was not as marked. Slovakia's currency exhibited overvaluation, which could have reflected the devaluation of 10 percent in mid 1993 and thus the strong terms of trade improvement against its main trading partner, the Czech Republic.

---

[94] Halpern and Wyplosz (1997) calculate values for Czechoslovakia and use data from Yugoslavia to determine values for Slovenia and Croatia.

[95] Darvas (2001) claims that the Hungarian forint was not undervalued at the beginning of the transition process.

[96] The magnitude of misalignment varied depending on the selected equilibrium exchange rate concept (see chapter 3.2.1).

Table 7.1. Real effective exchange rate misalignment (1990-1994)

Country	BEER	PMG	FMOLS	PEER	PPP	Big Mac	Rel. PPP
Poland	- 25.9 (1990)	- 9.9 (1990)	- 29.8 (1990)	- 33.8 (1990)	- 75.6 (1990)	- 46.1 (1994)	- 63.6 (1990)
Hungary	- 8.6 (1990)	+ 5.1 (1990)	- 4.9 (1990)	- 7.0 (1990)	- 67.3 (1990)	- 48.2 (1991)	- 28.4 (1990)
Czech Republic	- 1.2 (1993)	- 2.4 (1993)	- 5.2 (1993)	- 0.4 (1993)	- 58.4 (1993)	- 34.1 (1994)	+ 0.2 (1993)
Slovenia	+ 7.1 (1992)	+ 1.6 (1992)	- 5.0 (1992)	+ 6.9 (1992)	- 46.4 (1992)	-	+ 1.6 (1992)
Estonia	+ 13.1 (1993)	+ 2.8 (1993)	- 9.3 (1993)	+ 9.1 (1993)	- 68.6 (1993)	-	- 28.1 (1993)
Latvia	-	-	-	-	- 59.2 (1993)	-	- 24.2 (1993)
Lithuania	-	-	-	-	- 72.6 (1993)	-	- 60.5 (1993)
Bulgaria	-	-	-	-	- 86.1 (1991)	-	- 95.0 (1991)
Romania	-	-	-	-	- 74.4 (1991)	-	- 24.4 (1991)
Slovakia	-	-	-	-	- 39.3 (1993)	-	+ 9.8 (1993)

Note: Numbers are in percentages.

To summarize the results, undervaluation can hardly be considered a common phenomenon of transition countries.[97] The majority of exchange rates have not deviated significantly from equilibrium. Only Poland, Lithuania, and Bulgaria appear to have started with a severely undervalued currency. Misalignment should therefore rather be regarded as a temporary occurrence of only a few countries. The low exchange rate values at the beginning of the transition period seem to

[97] The results of this study may be open to criticism with respect to a possible bias of the estimated coefficients if the currencies were in fact undervalued at the beginning of the transition process since any estimated cointegration relationship will tend to account for the lower level at the beginning of the time frame. However, there are reasonable arguments against this claim. First, it is doubtful that exchange rates can remain severely misaligned for a long time span. Second, the panel studies (PMG, FMOLS) are based on the time period starting in 1993 and the reference period of the GDP-adjusted relative PPP even only begins in 1995, so that the early period of transition is essentially determined as an out-of-sample forecast. This should therefore lead to unbiased results.

have reflected the weak economic situation, which was characterized by a very weak level of productivity and a lack of competitiveness.

7.2 Are the currencies of central and eastern European economies overvalued?

The strong appreciation of the real exchange rates in transition economies has raised concern about dangerous overvaluation in a number of countries. Such a misalignment would not only have negative effects on economic growth through the loss of competitiveness, but also increase the risk of speculative attacks on the mostly pegged currencies. Kaminsky and Reinhart (1999) and Berg and Patillo (1999) among others have investigated the determinants of currency crises. One of their main results is that exchange rate overvaluation has proven to be a key determinant for the occurrence of currency crises. Brüggemann and Linne (2002) explicitly examine determinants of currency crises in CEEC and again exchange rate overvaluation significantly increases the risk of speculation against the currency. Obviously real exchange rate misalignment is only one piece of the puzzle for the determination of vulnerability since the studies have also revealed that a number of other factors also play an important role and that vulnerability can better be described with the help of a composite index of indicators. Nevertheless, the negative implications of misalignment should not be neglected and the development of real exchange rate should be monitored carefully.

A successful speculation against any of the CEEC's currencies would result in a loss of confidence for the entire region and could even lead to contagious effects spreading to other countries. The figures calculated in the previous chapters have given an indication of the seriousness of this threat. Tables 7.2 and 7.3 summarize misalignments in real effective terms and in nominal terms against the euro for the end of the observed period as determined by the various equilibrium exchange rate concepts in this study. The first five countries have been examined in great detail by applying five different concepts (plus absolute PPP and Big Mac values) including both real effective and nominal rates against the euro, so that fairly well-founded conclusions can be drawn. The results for the other five CEEC should be considered with caution. These five economies have lagged behind the others in terms of economic development, so that stable economic relationships between fundamental variables and the real exchange rate have not yet emerged. As a consequence the reliability of equilibrium values, which are based on one methodology, i.e. the long-term PPP concept, is clearly limited.

Table 7.2. Calculated real effective exchange rate misalignments (2001-2004)

Country	BEER (2002)	PMG (2002)	FMOLS (2002)	PEER (2002)	PPP (2001)	Big Mac (2004)	Rel. PPP (2002)
Poland	+ 8.6	+ 20.1	+ 24.9	+ 13.2	- 34.5	- 44.2	+ 14.3
Hungary	- 0.4	+ 16.4	+ 14.3	+ 3.4	- 40.9	- 9.6	+ 5.4
Czech Rep.	+ 9.7	+ 12.3	+ 14.9	+ 11.0	- 44.0	- 21.6	+ 8.4
Slovenia	+ 2.6	- 17.5	- 14.0	+ 3.4	- 29.2	- 21.0	- 6.4
Estonia	+ 5.3	+ 23.0	+ 30.1	+ 7.4	- 38.5	- 12.1	- 10.0
Latvia	-	-	-	-	- 25.0	- 12.5	- 0.3
Lithuania	-	-	-	-	- 22.8	+ 4.5	+ 19.0
Bulgaria	-	-	-	-	- 57.5	- 24.2	+ 23.7
Romania	-	-	-	-	- 57.9	-	+ 27.8
Slovakia	-	-	-	-	- 42.3	- 18.1	+ 7.5

Note: Numbers are in percentages.

Table 7.3. Calculated nominal exchange rate misalignments against the euro (2001-2004)

Country	BEER (2002)	PEER (2002)	PPP (2001)	Big Mac (2004)	Rel. PPP (2002)
Poland	+ 12.7	+ 16.9	-51.7	- 50.3	+ 17.4
Hungary	+ 2.5	- 8.6	-58.7	- 23.2	+ 8.5
Czech Republic	+ 13.7	+ 14.7	-62.3	- 35.1	+ 11.3
Slovenia	+ 6.0	+ 6.5	-44.9	- 26.2	- 4.2
Estonia	+ 10.2	+ 11.6	-60.4	- 30.8	- 5.7
Latvia	-	-	-58.6	- 39.0	+ 24.2
Lithuania	-	-	-59.4	- 31.1	+ 29.4
Bulgaria	-	-	-75.5	- 43.6	+ 23.7
Romania	-	-	-69.6	-	+ 31.6
Slovakia	-	-	-68.3	- 39.6	+ 12.3

Note: Numbers are in percentages.

Examining the estimated misalignments reveals that the currencies of Poland and the Czech Republic are clearly overvalued. The range of figures suggests a departure from equilibrium by at least 10 percent. The results of Hungary are more ambiguous. While the PMG and FMOLS estimates indicate a significant overvaluation, PEER and relative PPP only reveal marginal misalignment and the BEER even shows a slight undervaluation. The Slovenian tolar seems to reside below rather than above equilibrium. In particular, the outcome of the panel estimation suggests that Slovenia's currency is highly competitive compared to those of the other CEEC. Considering only the BEER and the PEER approach, Estonia's currency seems to be overvalued. However, the result of the relative PPP shows that this observation may not necessarily hold for the long run. As for the remaining five countries, their currencies tend to be overvalued as well. The misalignment seems to be more pronounced in Lithuania, Romania and Bulgaria than in the cases of Latvia or Slovakia.

Given the findings of this study, it is interesting to examine how these results compare to other work in this area. Table 7.4 lists calculated misalignments of the papers that have been investigated in chapter 3.2. In the case of Poland, all studies confirm the overvaluation of the zloty. The real exchange rates of the Czech Republic, Slovakia and Estonia are also found to be above the equilibrium value in the majority of papers, which is to a large extent consistent with this study. The outcomes for Hungary, Slovenia, Latvia and Lithuania are rather inconclusive. Different approaches lead to very diverse conclusions for these countries. In the case of Bulgaria only one alternative study exists, which indicates a slight overvaluation. In general, the results of this work are consistent with the outcomes of other empirical studies.

Table 7.4. Calculated misalignments of other studies (1999-2003)

Country	Authors	Concept	Date	Misalignment
Poland	Coudert and Couharde (2002)	FEER	2001	+
	Crespo-Cuaresma et al. (2003)	Monetary (panel)	2002:3 M	+
	Égert and Lahrèche-Révil (2003)	BEER	2001:2 Q	+++
	Égert and Lommatzsch (2004)	BEER (panel)	2002:4 Q	+
	Kemme and Teng (2000)	BEER	1999:5 M	++
	Kemme and Teng (2000)	Relative PPP	1999:5 M	++++
	Kim and Korhonen (2002)	BEER (panel)	1999	+++
	Rawdanowicz (2002)	BEER	2002:2 Q	+
	Rawdanowicz (2002)	FEER	2002	++
	Smidkova et al. (2002)	FEER	2002	++++
Hungary	Coudert and Couharde (2002)	FEER	2001	+
	Crespo-Cuaresma et al. (2003)	Monetary (panel)	2002:3 M	–
	Drummond et al. (2004)	BEER	2003:3 Q	o
	Égert and Lahrèche-Révil (2003)	BEER	2001:2 Q	o
	Égert and Lommatzsch (2004)	BEER (panel)	2002:4 Q	o
	Kim and Korhonen (2002)	BEER (panel)	1999	++++
	Smidkova et al. (2002)	FEER	2002	++++
Czech Republic	Coudert and Couharde (2002)	FEER	2001	–
	Crespo-Cuaresma et al. (2003)	Monetary (panel)	2002:3 M	++++
	Égert and Lahrèche-Révil (2002)	BEER	2001:2 Q	+++
	Égert and Lommatzsch (2004)	BEER (panel)	2002:4 Q	++++
	Kim and Korhonen (2002)	BEER (panel)	1999	+++
	Smidkova et al. (2002)	FEER	2002	++
Slovenia	Coudert and Couharde (2002)	FEER	2001	+
	Crespo-Cuaresma et al. (2003)	Monetary (panel)	2002:3 M	++++
	Égert and Lahrèche-Révil (2003)	BEER	2001:2 Q	o
	Égert and Lommatzsch (2004)	BEER (panel)	2002:4 Q	++
	Kim and Korhonen (2002)	BEER (panel)	1999	——
	Smidkova et al. (2002)	FEER	2002	–
Estonia	Burgess et al. (2003)	BEER	2002:4 Q	—
	Coudert and Couharde (2002)	FEER	2001	o
	Filipozzi (2000)	BEER	1999:2 Q	++
	Hristov (2002)	FEER	1999	+++
	Randveer and Rell (2002)	BEER	2000:4 Q	+
	Randveer and Rell (2002)	Relative PPP	2000:4 Q	++++
	Smidkova et al. (2002)	FEER	2002	++++
Latvia	Beguna (2002)	BEER	2001:4 Q	+
	Bitans (2002)	BEER	2001:2 Q	o
	Bitans (2002)	Relative PPP	2001:2 Q	++++
	Burgess et al. (2003)	BEER	2002:4 Q	–
	Kazaks (2000)	BEER	1999:6 M	o
Lithuania	Alonso-Gamo et al. (2002)	BEER	2001:3 Q	–
	Burgess et al. (2003)	BEER	2002:4 Q	–
	Vetlov (2002)	BEER	2001:2 Q	—

	Vetlov (2002)	Relative PPP	2001:6 M	++++
Bulgaria	Chobanov and Sorsa (2004)	BEER	2003:1 Q	+
Slovakia	Crespo-Cuaresma et al. (2003)	Monetary (panel)	2002:3 M	o
	Égert and Lahrèche-Révil (2003)	BEER	2001:2 Q	+++
	Égert and Lommatzsch (2004)	BEER (panel)	2002:4 Q	++++
	Kim and Korhonen (2002)	BEER (panel)	1999	+++

Explanation:

––––	more than 15 percent undervaluation	++++	more than 15 percent overvaluation
–––	11-15 percent undervaluation	+++	11-15 percent overvaluation
––	6-10 percent undervaluation	++	6-10 percent overvaluation
–	0-5 percent undervaluation	+	0-5 percent overvaluation
o	no misalignment		

7.3 Exchange rate regimes and misalignment

The choice of exchange rate regimes has been a vital decision for the CEEC on their transition path from planned to market economies. Faced with very high inflation rates and an economic downturn the exchange rate has had to serve as a stabiliser on the one hand and as a tool to promote export growth on the other hand. The overview in chapter 2 has shown that most CEEC opted for some kind of peg either against a well-established anchor currency or against a basket of currencies. The advantage of fixed exchange rates for transition countries is that they can support the stabilisation of the economy. In particular, pegging the exchange rate can increase the credibility of macroeconomic stabilisation since a fixed parity demands high commitment to monetary and fiscal discipline for the peg to be viable in the long run. Credibility can reduce inflation expectations more rapidly and thus can make deflation less costly. Such a peg can also facilitate the political implementation of indispensable but costly reforms if these are deemed necessary to secure the exchange rate stability (Gaspar, 1995).[98] The disadvantage of fixed exchange rates is that macroeconomic shocks cannot be absorbed as the automatic adjustment process of flexible exchange rates is ruled out and the options for monetary policy adjustment are limited.[99] Fixing the currency through a monetary union, dollarization, or a currency board would ultimately lead to a complete loss of independence in the monetary policy. Pegging the currency

98 Another advantage of fixed exchange rates for transition countries is that they can speed up the import of an international pricing structure (Borensztein and Masson, 1993). Furthermore, a fixed rate can reduce the risk premium and thus promote foreign investment (Fröhlich, 1992).

99 A missing exchange rate adjustment process often leads to persistent trade imbalances. High and continuous current account deficits proof that the CEEC are no exception from this rule.

without giving up independence, however, increases the risk of speculative attacks and exchange rate crises.

In the process of globalisation the danger of currency crises has increased substantially. According to the "bipolar view" in a world of free capital movement the only viable options are either absolutely fixed or completely free floating exchange rates (Fischer, 2001). Bubula and Otker-Robe (2002) focus on "de facto" exchange rate regimes and reveal that financially highly integrated countries have increasingly abandoned intermediate regimes in favour of corner solutions. On the other hand, Bofinger (2004) argues that the intermediate option of a managed float may be a viable option and that this strategy can also be compatible with inflation targeting. The author claims that a managed float could help avoid macroeconomic disequilibria as seen in some of the CEEC, and cites Slovenia as a successful example.

In this paper, the calculated misalignments are used to determine whether fixed or floating exchange rate regimes systematically exacerbate overvaluation.[100] Two issues shall be addressed. First, it shall be examined whether overvaluation *is* more pronounced under fixed or flexible regimes. Second, it shall be investigated whether an exchange rate regime type *tends* to produce higher overvaluation. For this, a dynamic panel approach is employed where misalignment is regressed on an exchange rate regime dummy variable D with zeros for flexible and ones for fixed regimes to capture the first issue and the product of D and a time trend t to capture the second issue

$$(7.1) \qquad Mis_{it} = \alpha_i + \beta_1 Mis_{it-1} + \beta_2 D_{it} + \beta_3 D_{it} * t + \varepsilon_{it}.$$

Time period-specific dummies are also included to control for exogenous effects. The classification of regimes is based on the overview in chapter 2 and summarized in table 7.5.

Due to the endogeneity of the lagged dependent variable in equation (7.1) the standard ordinary least squares estimator leads to biased and inconsistent coefficient estimates. Therefore, the generalized methods of moments (GMM) estimation procedure as suggested by Arellano and Bond (1991) is employed. This estimator is based on first differencing the regression to eliminate country-specific fixed effects. Since the error-term is correlated with the lagged dependent variable

---

[100] It would be even more informative to distinguish between hard and soft pegs as well as between managed and free float. However, the limited number of examples of free float and hard peg could lead to arbitrary results.

previous observations in levels are used as instruments for the endogenous variable.

Table 7.5. Classification of exchange rate regimes

Country	Fixed regime	Flexible regime
Poland	1990/1-2000/1	Since 2000/2
Hungary	Since 1990/1	
Czech Republic	1993/1-1997/1	Since 1997/2
Slovenia		Since 1992/1
Estonia	Since 1993/1	
Latvia	Since 1994/1	1993/1-1993/4
Lithuania	Since 1994/2	1993/1-1994/1
Bulgaria	Since 1997/3	1991/1-1997/2
Romania		Since 1991/1
Slovakia	1993/1-1998/3	Since 1998/4

Equation (7.1) is estimated for each of the five different equilibrium exchange rate approaches of this paper. The outcome of the one-step GMM estimator is presented in table 7.6. The second line of results shows whether overvaluation depends on the exchange rate regime. It turns out that the type of regime does not have a significant impact on the level of misalignment since all coefficients end up insignificant. This outcome is easily explained if one assumes that the initial peg is chosen to be at or at least close to the equilibrium value of the exchange rate. The third line of results determines whether fixed regimes tend to raise the difference between the real exchange rate and the equilibrium value. In the cases of the BEER, PEER and relative PPP the outcomes reveal that misalignment is appreciating faster by 0.20 to 0.31 percentage per quarter under fixed exchange rate regimes than under flexible regimes. This means pegged currencies tend to diverge to more overvalued exchange rates. The results for the PMG and FMOLS are also positive, but insignificant.

The propensity of fixed regimes to generate more overvalued currencies in the CEEC has a negative impact on competitiveness and vulnerability to currency crises. Nevertheless, overvaluation is only one factor, which cannot be isolated from other influences. For example, competitiveness is not only determined by the exchange rate; the development of productivity and the structure of production are also relevant. Vulnerability, on the other hand, also depends on the credibility of the exchange rate regime, which again relies on the commitment towards the chosen regime. As discussed above, each type of exchange rate regime has its advantages and disadvantages, from which this analysis has just focussed on a single issue. It should thus be emphasized that this examination cannot determine which exchange rate regime serves better for the CEEC in a general perspective.

Table 7.6. Estimation results of the relationship between misalignment and exchange rate regimes

	BEER (CEEC5)	PMG (CEEC5)	FMOLS (CEEC5)	PEER (CEEC5)	Rel. PPP (CEEC10)
Mis_{it-1}	0.75	0.81	0.39	0.83	0.20
(t-value)	(6.80)	(5.83)	(9.38)	(8.69)	(3.86)
D	0.15	-0.14	0.17	-0.05	0.13
(t-value)	(0.16)	(-0.12)	(1.15)	(-0.14)	(1.46)
D*t	0.0022	0.0054	0.0063	0.0031	0.0020
(t-value)	(2.11)	(0.37)	(0.87)	(2.31)	(1.99)

7.4 The road to the European Monetary Union

Three main objectives, in which the exchange rate plays a dominant role, have to be accomplished by the CEEC in order to secure EMU status. First, the convergence criteria for the accession to the EMU must be met.[101] Second, the authorities should retain the international competitiveness of the local economy because

[101] These criteria encompass an inflation rate, which must not exceed the average EU inflation rate by more than 1.5 percent, nominal long-run interest rates, which must not go beyond more than 2 percentage points above those for the three countries with the lowest inflation rates, a government budget deficit of less than 3 percent of the country's GDP, a gross debt to GDP ratio of below 60 percent, and the participation in the ERM2 system without revaluations for at least two years. It is noteworthy that not all of the criteria are definitely binding. The level of gross debt may exceed 60 percent if credible measures are taken to reduce this level in the future. Moreover, the recent experience has shown that a fiscal deficit above 3 percent does not necessarily have negative consequences.

exports are the main source of economic growth in these countries.[102] Third, during the adjustment process the risk of a currency crisis should be kept as low as possible since any forced revaluation would not only delay the accession to the EMU, but also have a negative impact on growth and thus prolong the adjustment to the level in the European Union. Figure 7.1 illustrates this trinity of objectives.

The three objectives can be viewed as either complementary or contradictory. For example, a devaluation of the exchange rate can (at least in the short run) improve competitiveness and at the same time reduce the risk of a currency crisis. However, such a step could also lead to a loss of credibility in the exchange rate system and thus increase rather than decrease the risk of speculation against the currency. Furthermore, a devaluation can on the one hand boost the economy and thus ease the meeting of the Maastricht criteria on fiscal balance and public debt. On the other hand, a devaluation tends to raise prices by making imports more costly, which could in turn make the meeting of the Maastricht criterion on inflation a more difficult task.

Figure 7.1. Exchange rate policy objectives for EMU candidates

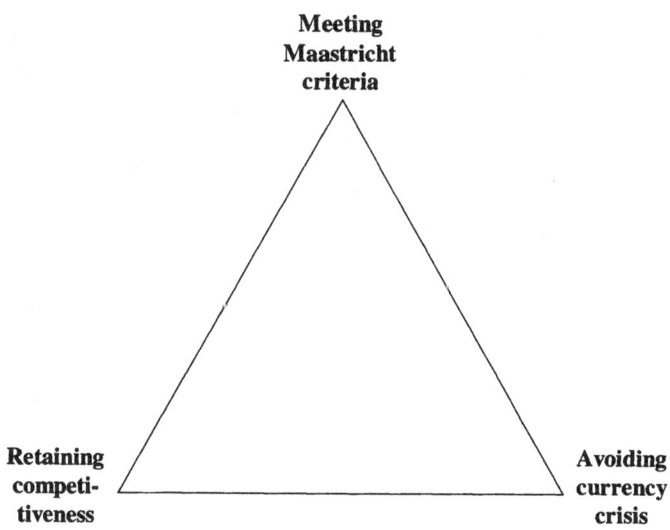

[102] Bénassy-Quéré et al. (2001) show that competitiveness is pivotal for the attraction of foreign direct investment. Foreign direct investment in turn is considered a key element of growth and convergence of the CEEC.

As the CEEC differ greatly in terms of their exchange rate regimes and economic structures, as well as in the degree of nominal and real convergence towards the EMU members, distinct paths towards EMU membership can be identified.[103] The anticipated EMU entry dates range from 2006 to about 2010 for the eight new central and eastern European EU members and somewhat later for Bulgaria and Romania.[104] Before joining the EMU the candidates are required to participate at the ERM2 for at least two years. The two main objectives of this rule are on the one hand to lend credibility to the exchange rate markets of the acceding countries and on the other hand to discipline the economic policies towards a stable macroeconomic environment. From the candidates' perspective, however, the ERM2 is merely an obligatory but questionable system. They argue that the ERM2 system does not serve to enhance the credibility, but rather increases the risk of speculative attacks. The current systems such as the currency boards or the flexible exchange rates seem to be more viable than an exchange rate band system with a corridor of ± 15 percent around a central parity. The disciplinary effect of the ERM2 in turn is considered marginal since the main policy challenges already arise from the Maastricht criteria and the Stability and Growth Pact (SGP). In view of these negative aspects most CEEC plan to keep the participation time at the ERM2 as short as possible.

Despite these reservations, on June 28, 2004 the first three countries joined the ERM2 system. For *Estonia* and *Lithuania* participation in the ERM2 system did not involve any significant policy alterations. Both countries have voluntarily maintained their currency boards and the reference rate of the ERM2 corridor was selected equivalent to the central parity of the peg. *Slovenia* in contrast had to adjust its exchange rate policy. The strategy of discretionary devaluation had been continued just before entering the ERM2. The new central parity of the exchange rate band was set at the reference rate of the last day before ERM2 accession. Since entering the ERM2 the Slovenian tolar remained very stable and close to the central parity. It is envisaged that these three economies will become members of the EMU relatively soon, possibly already at the beginning of 2007. Furthermore, these examples demonstrate that a sudden revaluation just before the entrance to the ERM2 system is most unlikely. If an exchange rate adjustment is considered

---

[103] The convergence report of the European Central Bank (2004) surveys the current situation and lists the criteria that still need to be accomplished.

[104] Backé et al. (2004) provide a detailed overview of official statements regarding the prospective ERM2 and EMU entry dates, which is based on the Preaccession Economic Programme (PEP) exercise.

appropriate to strengthen the competitiveness of the local economy, it should be realised sooner rather than later.

Before joining the ERM2, *Latvia* needs to revise its exchange rate peg and make the euro the sole reference currency. Since the euro's share in the currency basket is only at around 35 percent, any strengthening of the euro exchange rate against other currencies such as the US dollar can lift the burden of the lats' overvaluation against the euro and facilitate the step towards ERM2. For *Slovakia*, ERM2 participation is not such a big step. The exchange rate volatility against the euro has been relatively low since 2000 and the Slovak koruna has already remained within a much tighter band than the ± 15 percent corridor of the ERM2. Participation in the ERM2 system is expected for 2005, but EMU membership is unlikely to take place before 2008 (Backé et al., 2004).

On average, the smaller CEEC tend to envisage an EMU membership earlier than the larger economies like *Poland*, *Hungary*, or the *Czech Republic*. None of these three larger countries currently plans to join the EMU before 2008 (Backé et al., 2004).[105] Since ERM2 participation is not regarded as very tempting, it is most unlikely that these countries will enter the ERM2 prior to 2006. Until then the flexible character of the Polish and Czech exchange rate systems could help to reduce the high level of misalignment without administrative intervention. However, the prospects of financial transfers from the EU and the soaring direct investment could attract large capital inflows and thus further place appreciative pressure on the exchange rate. If, however, a time comes when the high expectations cannot be met or if an economic downturn sets in, the capital flow may suddenly revert and may even induce speculations against the currency. In this context, careful observation of the exchange rate movements is advisable. A deliberate intervention in the foreign exchange rate market before entry to ERM2 system may be advisable if the disequilibrium becomes severe.

The road to the EMU is still long for *Bulgaria* and *Romania*. First of all, both countries must qualify for EU membership. However, there is little doubt that these two economies will follow the other CEEC soon and the expected date of

[105] This incidence could be explained by the theory of optimum currency area since larger countries tend to be more prone to asymmetric shocks, less open, and less integrated in the common market. However, studies from Lättemäe (2003) and Backé et al. (2004) show that this assumption is not valid for the CEEC. More precisely, according to Lättemäe (2003) real shocks are asymmetric to the current EMU members in the case of Poland and Lithuania, but symmetric to Latvia, Estonia, Slovakia and Hungary. Backé et al. (2004) reveal that Poland, Hungary and the Czech Republic are the countries with the highest EU trade share. The degree of openness is found to be the lowest for Poland, Latvia and Lithuania.

EU accession is January 2007 (Commission of the European Communities, 2004). Despite a joint accession of both countries being the most likely scenario, the economic situation in Bulgaria and Romania is quite different. While Bulgaria has already successfully stabilised its currency through the adoption of a currency board, Romania's stabilisation process is still in progress. However, Bulgaria's drawback and disadvantage is its highly overvalued currency, which comes as a consequence of the currency board introduction. If productivity increases cannot match the inflation differential Bulgaria will face a severe loss of competitiveness and thus pressure will be exerted on its exchange rate.

This overview illustrates that each country faces individual challenges in terms of the trinity of objectives. Countries such as Estonia and Lithuania that have established a currency board are less vulnerable to currency crises, but competitiveness becomes an important issue. The example of Slovenia shows how joining the ERM2 system can be accomplished without having to bear an overvalued currency. In contrast, Poland and the Czech Republic in particular run the risk of economic distortions if they enter ERM2 at their current exchange rate levels. Meeting the Maastricht criteria will in any case demand strong efforts from all countries. It is therefore advisable to adopt a strategy that decreases the level of exchange rate misalignment in order to minimise the burden resulting from a loss of competitiveness. In order to limit the risk of currency crises, staying out of ERM2 until a convergence is most likely to be achieved within the minimum participation time of two years could prove to be a wise policy option.

8 Conclusion

In view of the forthcoming integration of CEEC in the EMU, this study has been concerned with the equilibrium exchange rate levels of eight new EU members and two accession candidates. Three different concepts have been applied to determine equilibrium exchange rates and real misalignment. First, time series as well as panel estimation techniques have been employed to establish a medium-run relationship between the real exchange rate and its fundamental determinants in the spirit of the BEER approach. The aim of the PEER has then been to filter out the long-run component of the relationship. Lastly, the PPP concept has been revisited. Since the direct application of the PPP concept does not lead to plausible results, the PPP has been adjusted by the level of GDP to account for the economic development of the transition countries over time.

This research differs from other studies not only in its wide range of applications, but also in its determination of nominal bilateral equilibrium exchange rates against the euro through algebraic transformation. For this purpose, a broad set of data has been collected that not only encompasses western industrialized countries but also Russia and other transition countries. Disregarding other CEEC or Russia would significantly bias the results since these countries still play a dominant role as trading partners.[106]

The outcome of the estimations provides a number of interesting insights. The presumption that all transition countries started with an exchange rate far below equilibrium could not be confirmed. On the contrary, most currencies seem to have been fairly valued at the beginning of the transition period. However, the strong appreciation over time appears to have led to overvalued exchange rates in a number of CEEC, particularly in Poland, the Czech Republic, Estonia, Latvia, Lithuania, and Bulgaria. These results are to a large extent supported by other empirical research. In all countries, overvaluation is accentuated when the nominal exchange rates against the euro are considered. The recent appreciation of the euro against major currencies such as the US dollar may exacerbate the overvaluation problem, as exchange rates of the CEEC against the euro have tended to be fairly stable. Furthermore, this study reveals that opting for fixed exchange rate regimes tends to increase the risk of overvaluation.

The findings emanating from the quantitative analysis immediately raise the issue of whether devaluation prior to joining ERM2 or EMU is a reasonable policy

[106] Russia, for example, is still the main supplier of raw materials.

option. Obviously, such a measure must be considered carefully. In the first place, such a move implies that the exchange rate is amenable to control by the central bank or government. Moreover, even if the central bank fixes the nominal exchange rate at a particular value, it would only determine the real exchange rate over the short run, since monetary policy actions feed back on domestic inflation. More specifically, devaluation tends to raise prices by making imports more costly. Any adjustment of the real exchange rate will eventually be offset by the inflationary feedback. Finally, a deliberate weakening of the exchange rate, which improves competitiveness, is a double-edged sword. Other factors, such as productivity and the structure of production seem to be relevant factors in the determination of the economic position in world comparisons. Nevertheless, substantial overvaluation, given the importance of external trade in these small open economies, could slow economic growth. Indeed, on the eve of EU accession the bright economic prospects of these countries may well attract high capital inflows, creating further upward pressure on real exchange rates. However, any economic downturn during the participation in ERM2 might alter the expectations of international financial investors, leading to speculative attacks and financial crises.

Appendices

Appendix 1: Macroeconomic developments in central and eastern European countries

Figure A1. Annual inflation rates of central and eastern European countries

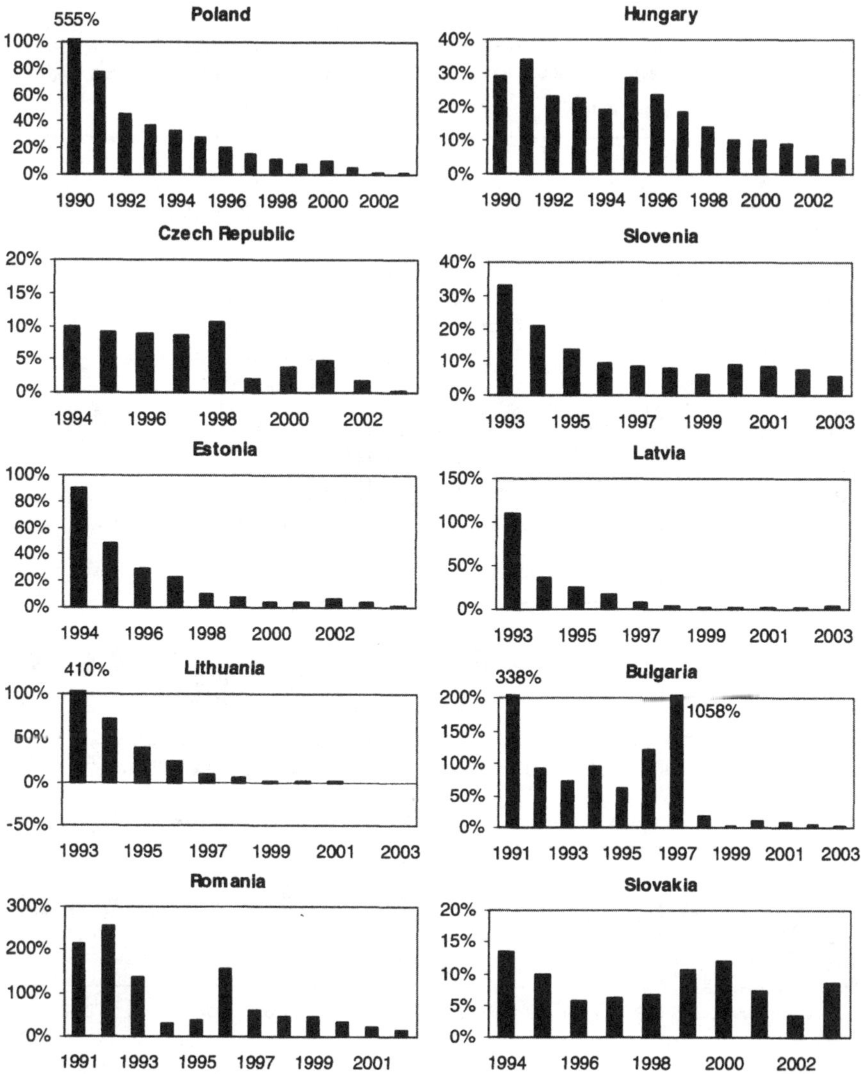

Data sources: IFS and WIIW.

Figure A2. Annual real GDP growth rates of central and eastern European countries

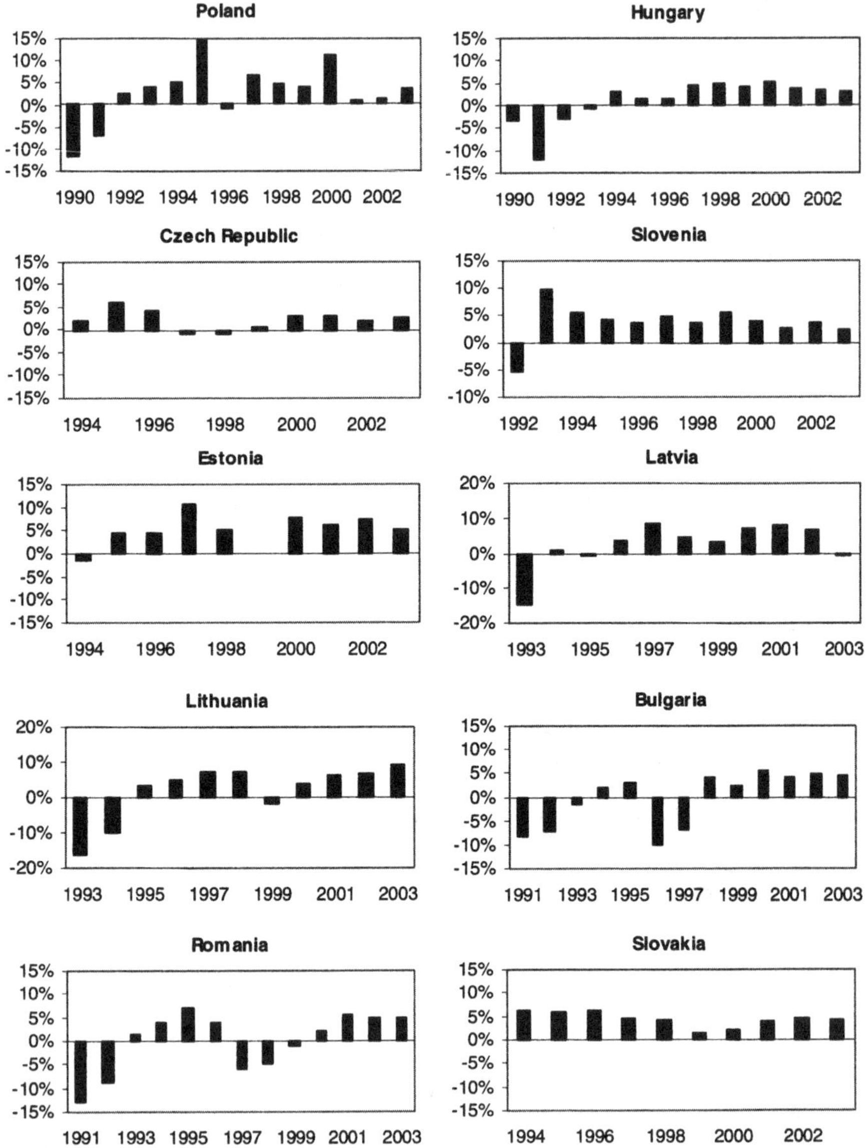

Data sources: IFS and BNB.

Appendix 2: Data sources for economic time series

Table A1. Data sources for central and eastern European countries

Country	Consumer Prices (CPI)	Producer Prices (PPI)	Nominal exchange rates	Nominal Gross Domestic Product (GDP)	Current Account (CA)	Stock of net foreign assets in 1998
Poland	IFS	IFS	IFS	IFS *(till 1994 only annual data)*	IFS *and* PCS *(for III/1995 till IV/1999)*	IFS
Hungary	IFS	IFS *(wholesale prices)*	IFS	IFS *(till 1995 only annual data)*	IFS	IFS
Czech Republic	IFS	IFS	IFS	CSO *(for 1993)* IFS *(since 1994)*	IFS	IFS
Slovenia	IFS	IFS	IFS	IFS	IFS	IFS
Estonia	IFS	BOE *(for 1993)* IFS *(since 1994)*	IFS	IFS	IFS	IFS
Latvia	IFS	IFS	IFS	IFS	IFS	IFS
Lithuania	IFS	IFS	IFS	IFS	IFS	IFS
Bulgaria	IFS	IFS *(annual data for 1991 and quarterly data since 1994)* WIIW *(monthly data for 1992 and 1993)*	IFS	IFS *(till 1993 only annual data)* NBB *(since 1998)*	IFS	IFS
Romania	IFS	IFS *(wholesale prices)*	IFS	IFS *(till 1997 only annual data)*	IFS	IFS
Slovakia	IFS	IFS	IFS	IFS	IFS	IFS

Data source information

BOE: Bank of Estonia at http://www.eestipank.info/frontpage/et/

CSO: Czech Statistical Office at http://www.czso.cz/eng/redakce.nsf/i/home

IFS: International Financial Statistics at http://ifs.apdi.net/imf/

NBB: National Bank of Bulgaria at http://www.bnb.bg/

PCS: Poland Central Statistical Office at http://www.stat.gov.pl/index.htm

WIIW: Wiener Institute for International Economic Studies, Handbook of Statistics, "Countries in Transition", various issues.

Table A2. Data sources for other countries

	Consumer Prices (CPI)	Producer Prices (PPI)	Nominal exchang e rates (NER)	Nominal Gross Domestic Product (GDP)	Current Account (CA)	Stock of net foreign assets in 1998 (NFA)
Germany	IFS	IFS	IFS	IFS	IFS	IFS
Netherlands	IFS	IFS	IFS	IFS	IFS	IFS
Belgium	IFS	IFS *(industrial production prices)*	IFS	IFS	IFS	IFS
Luxem-bourg	IFS	IFS	IFS	IFS *(only annual data since 1995)*	IFS *(only since 1995)*	*Not applicable*
France	IFS	IFS	IFS	IFS	IFS	IFS
Spain	IFS	IFS *(industrial prices)*	IFS	IFS	IFS	IFS
Portugal	IFS	IFS *(industrial production prices)*	IFS	IFS *(index numbers till 1998 only)*	IFS	IFS
Italy	IFS	IFS	IFS	IFS	IFS	IFS
Austria	IFS	IFS *(wholesale prices)*	IFS	IFS	IFS	IFS
Finland	IFS	IFS	IFS	IFS	IFS	IFS
Greece	IFS	IFS *(wholesale prices)*	IFS	IFS *(till 1994 an-nual data only)*	IFS	*Not applicable*
Ireland	IFS	IFS *(wholesale prices)*	IFS	IFS *(till 1996 an-nual data only)*	IFS	*Not applicable*
Euro-Area	ECB	ECB	ECB	ECB	IFS	*Not applicable*
UK	IFS	IFS	IFS	IFS	IFS	IFS
USA	IFS	IFS	IFS	IFS	IFS	IFS
Japan	IFS	IFS *(manufacturing output prices)*	IFS	IFS	IFS	IFS
Russia	IFS	IFS *(percentage change over previous period only)*	IFS	IFS *(since III/93)*	IFS *(since 1994 only; for 1993 trade balance from IFS)*	IFS

Data source information

ECB: European Central Bank at http://www.ecb.int/

IFS: International Financial Statistics at http://ifs.apdi.net/imf/

Other data

Population figures for all countries: International Financial Statistics at http://ifs.apdi.net/imf/

Trade Weights for all countries: International Trade Statistics Yearbook, International Monetary Fund, various issues.

References

Alberola, E., S. G. Cervero, H. Lopez, and A. Ubide, 1999, "Global Equilibrium Exchange Rates: Euro, Dollar, "Ins," "Outs" and Other Major Currencies in a Panel Cointegration Framework," IMF Working Paper, No. 175, Washington D.C.

Alonso-Gamo, P., S. Fabrizio, V. Kramarenko, and Q. Wang, 2002, "Lithuania: History and Future of the Currency Board Arrangement", IMF Working Paper, No. 127, Washington D.C.

Andrews, D. W. K., 1990, "Tests for Parameter Instability and Structural Change With Unknown Change Point", Yale University, Discussion Paper No. 943, Cowles Foundation for Research in Economics.

Arellano, M., and S. Bond, 1991, "Some Tests of Specification for Panel Data: Monte Carlo Evidence and an Application to Employment Equations", Review of Economic Studies, Vol. 58, pp. 29–51.

Artis, M., and M. Taylor, 1995, "The Effect of Misalignment on Desired Equilibrium Exchange Rates: Some Analytical Results", in Bordes, C., E. Girardin, and J. Mélitz (eds.), European Currency Crises and After, Manchester University Press.

Backé, P., C. Thimann, O. Arratibel, O. Calvo-Gonzalez, A. Mehl, and C. Nerlich, 2004, "The Acceding Countries' Strategies Towards ERM II and the Adoption of the Euro: An Analytical Review", European Central Bank Occasional Paper Series, No. 10, Frankfurt (Main).

Balassa, B., 1964, "The Purchasing-Power-Parity Doctrine: A Reappraisal", Journal of Political Economy, Vol. 72, No. 6, pp. 584–596.

Bank of Estonia, "Annual Report", Tallinn, various issues.

Bank of Estonia, 1992, "The Monetary Reform in Estonia", Tallinn.

Bank of Latvia, "Monetary Bulletin", Riga, various issues.

Bank of Latvia, 1994, "Monetary Review of the Bank of Latvia", No. 2, Riga.

Bank of Lithuania, "Quarterly Bulletin of the Bank of Lithuania", Vilnius, various issues.

Bank of Lithuania, 1992, "Annual Report", Vilnius.

Bank of Lithuania, 1994, "Law of the Republic of Lithuania No. 1-407 on the Credibility of the Litas", Vilnius.

Bank of Slovenia, "Monthly Bulletin", Ljubljana, various issues.

Barisone, G., R. Driver, and S. Wren-Lewis, 2004, "Are Our FEERs Justified?", Journal of International Money and Finance, forthcoming.

Bauer, C., and B. Herz, 2004, "How Credible are the Exchange Rate Regimes of the EU Accession Countries? Empirical Evidence from Market Sentiments", Bayreuth, mimeo.

Baxter, M., 1994, "Real Exchange Rates and Real Interest Rate Differentials: Have We Missed the Business Cycle Relationship?", Journal of Monetary Economics, Vol. 33, pp. 5-37.

Baxter, M., and R. G. King, 1999, "Measuring Business Cycles, Approximate Band-Pass Filters for Economic Time Series", Review of Economics and Statistics, Vol. 81, No. 4, pp. 575-593.

Bayoumi, T., P. Clark, S. Symansky, and M. Taylor, 1994, "The Robustness of Equilibrium Exchange Rate Calculations to Alternative Assumptions and Methodologies", in Williamson, J. (ed.), Estimating Equilibrium Exchange Rates, Institute of International Economics, Washington D.C., pp. 19-59.

Beblavý, M., 2002, "Exchange Rate and Exchange Rate Regime in Slovakia: Recent Developments", International Center for Economic Growth European Center Working Paper, No. 5.

Begg, D., L. Halpern, and Ch. Wyplosz, 1999, "Monetary and Exchange Rate Policies, EMU and Central and Eastern Europe", Forum Report on the Economic Policy Initiative, No. 5, CEPR, London.

Beguna, A., 2002, "Competitiveness and the Equilibrium Exchange Rate in Latvia", EuroFaculty Working Paper in Economics, No. 16, Riga.

Bénassy-Quéré, A., L. Fontagné, and A. Lahrèche-Révil, 2001, "Exchange-Rate Strategies in the Competition for Attracting Foreign Direct Investment", Journal of the Japanese and International Economies, Vol. 15, pp. 178-198.

Berensmann, K., 2002, "Currency Boards: A Monetary and Exchange Rate Policy Solution for Transition Countries: The Cases of Estonia and Lithuania", in Duwendag, D. (ed.), Schriften zur monetären Ökonomie, Bd. 45.

Berg, A., and C. Pattillo, 1999, "Are Currency Crises Predictable? A Test", IMF Staff Papers, Vol. 46, No. 2, International Monetary Fund, Washington D.C., pp. 107-138.

Bertsekas, D. P., 1976, "Dynamic Programming and Stochastic Control", Academic Press, New York.

Betton, S., M. D. Levi, and R. Uppal, 1995, "Index-Induced Errors and Purchasing Power Parity: Bounding the Possible Bias", Journal of International Financial Markets, Institutions and Money, Vol. 5, pp. 165-179.

Beveridge, S., and C. Nelson, 1981, "A New Approach to the Decomposition of Economic Time Series Into Permanent and Transitory Components", Journal of Monetary Economics, Vol. 33, No. 1, pp. 5-38.

Bitans, M., 2002. "Analysis of the Real Exchange Rate in Latvia: 1994–2001", Bank of Latvia Working Paper, Riga.

Blanchard, O. J., and D. Quah, 1989, "The Dynamic Effects of Aggregate Demand and Supply Disturbances", The American Economic Review, Vol. 79, No. 4, pp. 655-673.

Bofinger, P., 2004, "Exchange Rate Policies and Institutional Arrangements in the Transition Process to European Monetary Union", Paper prepared for the Workshop of the Pierre Werner Chair, EUI Florence, October.

Borensztein, E., and P. Masson, 1993, "Exchange Arrangements of Previously Centrally Planned Economies", in International Monetary Fund (ed.), Financial Sector Reforms and Exchange Arrangements in Europe, Occasional Paper, No. 102, Washington D.C., pp. 37-57.

Borowski, D., and C. Couharde, 2003, "The Exchange Rate Macroeconomic Balance Approach: New Methodology and Results for the Euro, the Dollar, the Yen and the Pound Sterling", Open economies review, Vol. 14, pp. 169–190.

Breuer, J. B., 1994, "An Assessment of the Evidence on Purchasing Power Parity", in Williamson, J. (ed.), Estimating Equilibrium Exchange Rates, Institute of International Economics, Washington D. C, pp. 245-277.

Brüggemann, A., and T. Linne, 2002, "Are the Central and Eastern European transition countries still vulnerable to a financial crisis? Results from the signals approach", Bank of Finland Discussion Paper, No. 5, Helsinki.

Bubula, A., and I. Ötker-Robe, 2002, "The Evolution of Exchange Rate Regimes Since 1990: Evidence from De Facto Policies", IMF Working Paper, No. 155, Washington D.C.

Budina, N., W. Maliszewski, G. de Menil, and G. Turlea, 2002, "Money, Inflation and Output in Romania, 1992-2000", Delta Working Paper, No. 15, Paris.

Bulgarian National Bank, "Monthly Bulletin", Sofia, various issues.

Burgess, R., S. Fabrizio, and Y. Xiao, "Competitiveness in the Baltics in the Run-Up to EU Accession", IMF Country Report, No. 114, Washington D.C.

Calvo, A. G., and C. Reinhart, 2002, "Fear of Floating", The Quarterly Journal of Economics, 2002, Vol. 117, Issue 2, pp. 379-408.

Canzoneri, M. R., R. Cumby, and B. Diba, 1999, "Relative Labor Productivity and the Real Exchange Rate in the Long Run: Evidence from a Panel of OECD Countries", Journal of International Economics, Vol. 47, Issue 2, pp. 245-266.

Cassel, G., 1922, "Money and Foreign Exchange After 1914", London.

Chen, B., S. McCoskey, and C. Kao, 1999, "Estimation and Inference of a Cointegrated Regression in Panel Data: A Monte Carlo Study", American Journal of Mathematical and Management Sciences, Vol. 19, pp. 75-114.

Chen C.-F., C.-H. Shen, and C. A. Wang, 2003, "Big Mac PPP and Consumer Price PPP", mimeo.

Cheung, Y. and K. Lai, 1993, "Finite-Sample Sizes of Johansen's Likelihood Ratio Tests for Cointegration", Oxford Bulletin of Economics and Statistics, Vol. 55, pp. 313-328.

Chinn, M. C., 2000, "Before the Fall: Were East Asian Currencies Overvalued?", Emerging Markets Review, Vol. 1, Issue 2, pp. 101-126.

Chobanov, D., and P. Sorsa, 2004, "Competitiveness in Bulgaria: An Assessment of the Real Effective Exchange Rate", IMF Working Paper, No. 37, Washington D.C.

Clarida, R., and J. Gali, 1994, "Sources of Real Exchange rate Fluctuations: How Important are Nominal Shocks?", Carnegie-Rochester Conference Series on Public Policy, No. 41, pp. 1-56.

Clark, P. B., and R. MacDonald, 1999, "Exchange Rates and Economic Fundamentals: A Methodological Comparison of BEERs and FEERs", in MacDonald, R., and J. L. Stein (eds.), Equilibrium exchange rates, Kluwer Academic Publisher, UK, pp. 285-322.

Clark, P. B., and R. MacDonald, 2000, "Filtering the BEER: A Permanent and Transitory Decomposition", IMF Working Paper, No. 144, Washington D.C.

Clements, K. W., and M. Semudram, 1983, "An International Comparison of the Price of Nontraded Goods", Weltwirtschaftliches Archiv, No. 119, pp. 356-363.

Clostermann, J., and W. Friedmann, 1998, "What Drives the Real Effective D-Mark Exchange Rate?", in Konjunkturpolitik, Applied Economics Quarterly, Vol. 44, No. 3, pp. 207-230.

Clostermann, J., and B. Schnatz, 2000, "The Determinants of the Euro-Dollar Exchange Rate Synthetic Fundamentals and a Non-existing Currency", Konjunkturpolitik, Applied Economics Quarterly, Vol. 46, No. 3, pp. 274-302.

Commission of the European Communities, 2004, "Strategy Paper of the European Commission on Progress in the Enlargement Process", Brussels.

Coudert, V., and C. Couharde, 2002, "Exchange Rate Regimes and Sustainable Parities for CEECs in the Run-up to EMU Membership", CEPII Working Paper, No. 15.

Crespo-Cuaresma, J., J. Fidrmuc, and R. MacDonald, 2003, "The Monetary Approach to the Exchange Rate in CEECs", Bank of Finland Discussion Paper, No. 14, Helsinki.

Cumby, R. E., 1997, "Forecasting Exchange Rates and Relative Prices With the Hamburger Standard: Is What You Want What You Get With McParity?", NBER Working Paper, No. 5675.

Cumby, R., and J. Huizinga, 1990, "The Predictability of Real Exchange Rate Changes in the Short Run and in the Long Run", NBER Working Paper, No. 3468.

Czech National Bank, "Annual Report", Prague, various issues.

Czech National Bank, 2003, "1993-2003", internet: http://www.cnb.cz/en/pdf/CNB_1993-2003_EN. pdf.

Daianu, D., and R. Vranceanu, 2001, "Subduing High Inflation in Romania. How to Better Monetary and Exchange Rate Mechanisms?", William Davidson Institute Working Paper, No. 402.

Darvas, Z., 2001, "Exchange Rate Pass-through and Real Exchange Rate in EU Candidate Countries", Economic Research Center of the Deutsche Bundesbank, Discussion Paper, No. 14, May, Frankfurt (Main).

De Broeck, M., and T. Sløk, 2001, "Interpreting Real Exchange Rate Movements in Transition Countries", IMF Working Paper, No. 56, Washington D.C.

De Gregorio, J., A. Giovannini, and H. Wolf, 1994, "International Evidence on Tradables and Nontradables Inflation", IMF Working Paper, No. 33, Washington D.C.

Desai, P., 2000, "Why Did the Ruble Collapse in August 1998?", American Economic Review: Papers and Proceedings, Vol. 90, No. 2, May, pp. 48-52.

Detken, C., A. Dieppe, J. Henry, C. Marin, and F. Smets, 2002, "Model Uncertainty and the Equilibrium Value of the Real Effective Euro Exchange Rate", ECB Working Paper No. 160.

Deutsche Bundesbank, 2002, "Fundamentale Bestimmungsfaktoren der realen Wechselkursentwicklung in den mittel- und osteuropäischen Beitrittsländern", Monatsbericht, October, Frankfurt (Main).

Dibooglu, S., 1996, "Real Disturbances, Relative Prices and Purchasing Power Parity", Journal of Macroeconomics, No. 18, pp. 69-87.

Dickey, D. A., and W. A. Fuller, 1979, "Distribution of the estimators for autoregressive time series with a unit root", Journal of the American Statistical Association, No. 74, pp. 427-431.

Doisy, M., and A. Hervé, 2003, "Les Déficits Courants des PECO: Quelles Implications pour leur Entrée dans l'Union Européenne et la Zone Euro?", Economie Internationale, No. 93, 1er trimester, pp. 59-88.

Driver, R., and P. F. Westaway, 2004, "Concepts of Equilibrium Exchange Rates", Bank of England Working Paper, forthcoming.

Drummond, P., S. Fabrizio, P. Madrid, and S. Mitra, 2004, "Hungary: Selected Issues", IMF Country Report, No. 146, Washington D.C.

Edison, H., 1987, "Purchasing Power Parity in the Long Run: A Test of the Dollar/Pound Exchange rate (1890-1978)", Journal of Money, Credit, and Banking, No. 19, pp. 376-387.

Edwards, S., 1994, "Real and Monetary Determinants of Real Exchange Rate Behavior: Theory and Evidence from Developing Countries", in Williamson, J. (ed.), Estimating Equilibrium Exchange Rates, Institute of International Economics, Washington D.C., pp. 61-91.

Égert, B., 2002a, "Estimating the Impact of the Balassa-Samuelson Effect on Inflation and the Real Exchange Rate During the Transition", Economic Systems, Vol. 1, No. 1, pp. 1–16.

Égert, B., 2002b, "Investigating the Balassa-Samuelson Hypothesis in the Transition: Do We Understand What We See? A Panel Study", Economics of Transition, Vol. 10, No. 2, pp. 273–309.

Égert, B., 2004, "Assessing Equilibrium Exchange Rates in CEE Acceding Countries: Can We Have DEER with BEER without FEER? A Critical Survey of the Literature", Bank of Finland Discussion Paper, No. 1, Helsinki.

Égert, B., and A. Lahrèche-Révil, 2003, "Estimating the Fundamental Equilibrium Exchange Rate of Central and Eastern European Countries: The Challenge of Euro Adoption", Review of World Economics, Weltwirtschaftliches Archiv, Vol. 139, pp. 683-708.

Égert, B., and K. Lommatzsch, 2004, "Equilibrium Exchange Rates in the Transition: The Tradable Price-Based Real Appreciation and Estimation Uncertainty", Bank of Finland Discussion Paper, No. 9, Helsinki.

Elbadawi, I. A., 1994, "Estimating Long-Run Equilibrium Real Exchange Rates", in Williamson, J. (ed.), Estimating Equilibrium Exchange Rates, Institute of International Economics, Washington D.C., pp. 93-131.

European Central Bank, 2004, "Convergence Report", Frankfurt (Main).

Faruqee, H., 1995, "Long-Run Determinants of the Real Exchange Rate: A Stock-Flow Perspective", IMF Staff Papers, Vol. 42, No. 1, Washington D.C., pp. 80-107.

Faruqee, H., P. Isard, and P. R. Masson, 1999, "A Macroeconomic Balance Framework for Estimating Equilibrium Exchange Rates", in MacDonald, R., and J. L. Stein (eds.), Equilibrium exchange rates, Kluwer Academic Publisher, UK, pp. 103-133.

Feyzioglu, T., 1997, "Estimating the Equilibrium Real Exchange Rate: An Application to Finland", IMF Working Paper, No. 109, Washington D.C.

Filipozzi, F., 2000, "Equilibrium Exchange Rate of the Estonian Kroon, Its Dynamics and Its Impacts of Deviations", Bank of Estonia Working Paper No. 2, Tallinn.

Fischer, S., 2001, "Exchange Rate Regimes: Is the Bipolar View Correct?", Journal of Economic Perspectives, Vol. 15, No. 2, pp. 3-24.

Fischer, C., 2002, "Real Currency Appreciation in Accession Countries: Balassa-Samuelson and Investment Demand", Deutsche Bundesbank Discussion Paper, No. 19, July, Frankfurt (Main).

Fischer, S., R. Sahay, and C. A. Végh, 1996, "Stabilization and Growth in Transition Economies: The Early Experience", Journal of Economic Perspectives, Vol. 10, No. 2, pp. 45-66.

Frait, J, and L. Komárek, 1999, "Long-run determinants of the real equilibrium koruna exchange rate", Czech National Bank Working Paper, No. 4 (in Czech).

Frankel, J. A., 1986, "International Capital Mobility and Crowding out in the U.S. Economy: Imperfect Integration of Financial Markets or Goods Markets?", in Hafer, R. (ed.), How open is the US Economy, Lexington Books, Lexington.

Frankel, J. A., and M. Mussa, 1988, "Exchange Rates and the Balance of Payments", in Jones, R., and P. Kenen (eds.), Handbook of International Economics, Vol. 2, Elsevier Science, pp. 687-693.

Frankel, J. A., and A. Rose, 1996, "A Panel Project on Purchasing Power Parity: Mean-Reversion Within and Between Countries", Journal of International Economics, Vol. 40, No. 1-2, pp. 209-224.

Fröhlich, H.-P., 1992, "Währungspolitische Reformen in Osteuropa", Beiträge zur Wirtschafts- und Sozialpolitik, No. 197, Köln.

Frömmel, M., and F. Schobert, 2004, "Exchange Rate Regimes in Central and Eastern European Countries – Deeds vs. Words", mimeo, Hanover.

Funke, M., and J. Rahn, 2004, "Just How Undervalued is the Chinese Renminbi?", The World Economy, forthcoming.

Gagnon, J. E., 1996, "Net Foreign Assets and Equilibrium Exchange Rates: Panel Evidence", International Finance Discussion Papers, No. 574, Board of Governors of the Federal Reserve System, Washington D.C.

Garry, J., and A. Vanags, 1995, "Inflation, Exchange Rate and Central-Bank Policy in a Transition Economy: An Analysis of the Latvian Experience, 1992-1994", Queen Mary University of London Working Paper Series, No. 333.

Gaspar, P., 1995, "Exchange-Rate Policies in Economies in Transition", Institute for World Economics, Hungarian Academic Sciences Working Papers, No. 56, Budapest.

Golinelli, R., and R. Orsi, 2002, "Modelling Inflation in EU Accession Countries: The Case of the Czech Republic, Hungary and Poland", in Charemza, W. W., and K. Strzala (eds.), East European Transition and EU Enlargement: A Quantitative Approach, Springer Verlag, Berlin, pp. 267–290.

Gonzalo, J., and C. W. Granger, 1995, "Estimation of Common Long-Memory Components in Cointegrated Systems," Journal of Business & Economic Statistics, Vol. 13, pp. 27-35.

Groen, J. J. J., and F. Kleibergen, 2003, "Likelihood-Based Cointegration Analysis in Panels of Vector Error-Correction Models", Journal of Business & Economic Statistics, Vol. 21, No. 2, pp. 295-318.

Gulde, A.-M., 1999, "The Role of the Currency Board in Bulgaria's Stabilization", Finance & Development, Vol. 36, No. 9, September, pp. 36-29.

Hadri, K., 2000, "Testing for Stationarity in Heterogeneous Panel Data", Econometrics Journal, Vol. 3, pp. 148-161.

Hakkio, C., 1984, "A Reexamination of Purchasing Power Parity", Journal of International Economics, Vol. 17, pp. 265–277.

Hall, S., S. Lazarova, and G. Urga, 1999, "A Principal Components Analysis of Common Stochastic Trends in Heterogeneous Panel Data: Some Monte Carlo Evidence", Oxford Bulletin of Economics and Statistics, Vol. 61, pp. 749-767.

Halpern, L., and C. Wyplosz, 2001, "Economic Transformation and Real Exchange Rates in the 2000s: The Balassa-Samuelson Connection", UN Economic Survey of Europe, pp. 227-239.

Hansen, B. E., 1992, "Tests for Parameter Instability in Regressions with I(1) Processes", Journal of Business & Economic Statistics, Vol. 10, No. 3, pp. 321-335.

Hansen, J., and W. Roeger, 2000, "Estimation of Real Equilibrium Exchange Rates", European Commission Economic Paper, No. 144.

Harris, R. D. F., and E. Tzavalis, 1999, "Inference for Unit Roots in Dynamic Panels Where the Time Dimension is Fixed", Journal of Econometrics, Vol. 91, pp. 201-226.

Harvey, A. C., and A. Jaeger, 1993, "Detrending, Stylized Facts and the Business Cycle", Journal of Applied Econometrics, Vol. 8, Issue 3, pp. 231-47.

Hausman, J. A., 1978, "Specification Tests in Econometrics", Econometrica, Vol. 46, No. 6, pp. 1251– 1271.

Hodrick, R. J., and E. C. Prescott, 1997, "Post-war U.S. Business Cycles: An Empirical Investigation", Journal of Money, Credit and Banking, Vol. 29, Issue 1, pp. 1-16.

Hristov, K., 2002, "Fundamental Equilibrium Exchange Rates and Currency Boards: Evidence from Argentina and Estonia in the 90's", Bulgarian National Bank Discussion Papers, No. 22, Sofia.

Hughes, G., 1991, "Foreign Exchange, Prices and Economic Activity in Bulgaria", Centre for Economic Policy Research, Discussion Paper Series, No. 549, London.

Huizinga, J., 1987, "An Empirical Investigation of the Long-Run Behavior of Real Exchange Rates", Carnegie-Rochester Conference Series on Public Policy, No. 27, pp. 149-214.

Im, K. S., M. H. Pesaran, and Y. Shin, 2003, "Testing for unit roots in heterogenous panels", Journal of Econometrics, Vol. 115, pp. 53-74.

Im, K. S., M. H. Pesaran, and R. P. Smith, 1996, "Dynamic Linear Models in Heterogeneous Panels", in Mátyás, L., and P. Sevestre (eds.), The Econometrics of Panel Data: A Handbook of Theory with Applications, 2nd Revised Edition, Kluwer Academic Publishers, Dordrecht.

International Monetary Fund, "Exchange Rate Arrangements and Exchange Restrictions: Annual Report", Washington D.C., various issues.

International Monetary Fund, 1994, "Lithuania, Economic Review", No. 6, International Monetary Fund, Washington D.C.

International Monetary Fund, 1998, "Republic of Slovakia: Recent Economic Developments", IMF Staff Country Report, No. 60, Washington D.C.

International Monetary Fund, 2002, "Exchange rate arrangements and exchange restrictions: annual report", Washington D.C.

Isard, P., and H. Faruqee, 1998, "Exchange Rate Assessment: Extensions of Macroeconomic Balance Approach", IMF Occasional Paper, No. 167, Washington D.C.

Isard, P., H. Faruqee, G. R. Kincaid, and M. Fetherston, 2001, "Methodology for Current Account and Exchange Rate Assessments", IMF Occasional Papers, No. 209, Washington D.C.

Johansen, S., 1995, "Likelihood-Based Inference in Cointegrated Vector Auto-Regressive Models", Oxford University Press, Oxford.

Johansen, S., and K. Juselius, 1990, "Maximum Likelihood Estimation and Inference on Cointegration with Applications to the Demand for Money", Oxford Bulletin of Economics and Statistics, No. 52, Issue 2, pp. 169-210.

Johansen, S., and K. Juselius, 1992, "Testing Structural Hypothesis in a Multivariate Cointegration Analysis of the PPP and the UIP for the UK", Journal of Econometrics, Vol. 53, No. 3, pp. 211-244.

Juselius, K., 1991, "Long-run Relations in a Well Defined Statistical Model for the Data Generating Process: Cointegration Analysis of the PPP and UIP Relations Between Denmark and Germany", in Gruber, J. (ed.), Econometric Decision Models: New Methods of Modelling and Applications, Springer Verlag, New York.

Kakkar, V., and M. Ogaki, 1999, "Real Exchange Rates and Nontradables: A Relative Price Approach", Journal of Empirical Finance, Vol. 6, Issue 3, pp. 193-215.

Kaminsky, G., and C. M. Reinhart, 1999, "The Twin Crisis: The Causes of Banking and Balance-of-Payments Crisis", The American Economic Review, Vol. 89, No. 3, pp. 473-500.

Kao, C., 1999, "Spurious Regression and Residual-Based Tests for Cointegration in Panel Data", Journal of Econometrics, No. 90, Issue 1, pp. 1-44.

Kao, C., and B. Chen, 1995, "On the Estimation and Inference of a Cointegrated Regression in Panel Data when the Cross-section and the Time-series Dimensions are Comparable in Magnitude", manuscript, Centre for Policy Research, Syracuse University.

Kao, C., and M. H. Chiang, 2000, "On the Estimation and Inference of a Cointegrated Regression in Panel Data", Advances in Econometrics, Vol. 15, pp. 179-222.

Kazaks, M., 2000, "Real Exchange Rate Appreciation and Loss of Competitiveness. The Case of Latvia", Presented at the Second Seminar of Managing Economic Transition in Eastern Europe, May 24, 2000, University College London, School of Slavonic and East European Studies.

Kemme, D. M., and W. Teng, 2000, "Determinants of the Real Exchange Rate, Misalignment and Implications for Growth in Poland", Economic Systems, Vol. 24, No. 2, pp. 171-205.

Kharas, H., B. Pinto, and S. Ulatov, 2001, "An Analysis of Russia's 1998 Meltdown: Fundamentals and Market Signals", Brookings Papers on Economic Activity, Vol. 1, pp. 1-67.

Kim, B. Y., and I. Korhonen, 2002, "Equilibrium Exchange Rates in Transition Countries: Evidence from Dynamic Heterogeneous Panel Models", Bank of Finland Discussion Paper, No. 15, Helsinki.

Knöbl, A., A. Sutt, and B. Zavoico, 1996, "The Estonian Currency Board: Its Introduction and Role in the Early Success of Estonia's Transition to a Market Economy", IMF Working Paper, No. 2, Washington D.C.

Krajnyák, K., and J. Zettelmeyer, 1998, "Competitiveness in Transition Economies: What Scope for Real Appreciation?", IMF Staff Papers, Vol. 45, No. 2, Washington D.C., pp. 309-362.

Kravis, I. B., Z. Kennessey, A. W. Heston, and R. Summers, 1975, "A System of International Comparisons of Gross Products and Purchasing Power", Johns Hopkins Press, Baltimore.

Lane, P. R., and G. M. Milesi-Ferretti, 2000, "The Transfer Problem Revisited: Net Foreign Assets and Liabilities for Industrial and Developing Countries", CEPR Discussion Paper, No. 2511, London.

Lane, P. R., and G. M. Milesi-Ferretti, 2001, "The External Wealth of Nations: Measures of Foreign Assets and Liabilities for Industrial and Developing Countries", Journal of International Economics, Vol. 55, No. 2, pp. 263-294.

Lane, P. R., and G. M. Milesi-Ferretti, 2002, "External Wealth, the Trade Balance, and the Real Exchange Rate", European Economic Review, No. 46, Issue 6, pp. 1049-1071.

Larsson, R., J. Lyhagen, and M. Löthgren, 1998, "Likelihood-Based Cointegration Tests in Heterogeneous Panels", Economics and Finance Working Paper, No. 250, Stockholm School of Economics, Sweden.

Lattemäe, R., 2003, "EMU Accession Issues in Baltic Countries", Ezoneplus Working Paper, No. 17A, May.

Levin, A., C.-F. Lin, and C-S. Chu, 2002, "Unit Root Tests in Panel Data: Asymptotic and Finite Sample Properties", Journal of Econometrics, Vol. 108, Issue 1, pp. 1–24.

Levy-Yeyati, E., and F. Sturzenegger, 2000, "Classifying Exchange Rate Regimes: Deeds vs. Words", mimeo, Universidad Torcuato Di Tella, November.

MacDonald, R., 1996, "Panel Unit Root Tests and Real Exchange Rates", Economic Letters, Vol. 50, pp. 7-11.

MacDonald, R., 2000, "Concepts to Calculate Equilibrium Exchange Rates: An Overview", Deutsche Bundesbank Discussion Paper, No 3, Frankfurt (Main).

MacDonald, R., and I. W. Marsh, 1997, "On Casselian PPP, Cointegration and Exchange Rate Forecasting", Review of Economics and Statistics, Vol. 79, pp. 655-664.

MacDonald R., and M. P. Taylor, 1994, "The Monetary Approach to the Exchange Rate: Rational Expectations, Long-Run Equilibrium and Forecasting", Journal of International Money and Finance, Vol. 13, Issue 3, pp. 267-276.

Maddala, G. S., and S. Wu, 1999, "A Comparative Study of Unit Root Tests With Panel Data and a New Simple Test", Oxford Bulletin of Economics and Statistics, Vol. 61, Issue 4, pp. 631-652.

Maeso-Fernandez, F., C. Osbat, and B. Schnatz, 2001, "Determinants of the Euro Real Effective Exchange Rate: A BEER/PEER Approach", ECB Working Paper, No. 85, November, Frankfurt.

Maeso-Fernandez, F., C. Osbat, and B. Schnatz, 2004, "Towards the Estimation of Equilibrium Exchange Rates for CEE Acceding Countries: Methodological Issues and a Panel Cointegration Perspective", ECB Working Paper, No. 353, April, Frankfurt.

Magyar Nemzeti Bank, "Annual Report", Budapest, various issues.

Maurin, L., 2001, "Fundamental Determinants of RER for Transition Countries", in Stierle, M. H., and T. Birringer (eds.), Economics of Transition: Theory, Experiences and EUEnlargement, Verlag für Wissenschaft und Forschung, Berlin, pp. 427-442.

McCoskey, S. K., and C. Kao, 1998, "A Residual-based Test for the Null of Cointegration in Panel Data", Econometric Reviews, Vol. 17, pp. 57-84.

Mundell, R. A., 1997, "The Great Contractions in Transition Economies", in Blejer, M. I., and M. Skreb (eds.), Macroeconomic Stabilization in Transition Economies, Cambridge University Press, pp. 73-99.

National Bank of Poland, "Annual Report", Warsaw, various issues.

National Bank of Romania, "Annual Report", Bucharest, various issues.

National Bank of Romania, 2003, "Annual Report", Bucharest.

National Bank of Slovakia, "Annual Report", Bratislava, various issues.

Nuti, D. M., 2000, "The Polish Zloty 1990-1999: Success and Under-Performance", American Economic Review, Vol. 90, No. 2, pp. 53-58.

Obstfeld, M., and K. Rogoff, 1995, "Exchange Rate Dynamics Redux", Journal of Political Economy, Vol. 103, No. 3, pp. 624–60.

O'Connell, P. G., 1998, "The Overvaluation of Purchasing Power Parity", Journal of International Economics, No. 44, pp. 1-19.

Oesterreichische Nationalbank, 1994, "Darstellung der Wechselkurspolitik in ausgewählten Reformländern", West-Ost Journal, No. 5-6, Wien, pp. 23-26.

Oh, K. Y., 1996, "Purchasing Power Parity and the Unit Root Tests Using Panel Data", Journal of International Money and Finance, Vol. 15, pp. 405-418.

Ong, L. L., 2003, "The Big Mac Index: Applications of Purchasing Power Parity", Palgrave MacMilan, New York.

Pakko, M. R., and P. S. Pollard, 1996, "For Here or To Go? Purchasing Power Parity and the Big Mac", Federal Reserve Bank of St. Louis Review, Vol. 78, No. 1, pp. 3-22.

Papell, D. H., 1997, "Searching for Stationarity: Purchasing Power Parity Under the Current Float", Journal of International Economics, Vol. 43, pp. 313-332.

Papell, D. H., 2002, "The Great Appreciation, the Great Depreciation, and the Purchasing Power Parity Hypothesis", Journal of International Economics, Vol. 57, pp. 51-82.

Parsley, D. C., and S.-J. Wei, 2004, "A Prism into the PPP Puzzles: The Microfoundations of the Big Mac Real Exchange Rates", mimeo.

Pavlov, K. N., 1999, "Currency Board Solution in Bulgaria", Paper for the NATO Research Fellowship Programme, internet: http://www.nato.int/acad.

Pedroni, P., 1999, "Critical Values for Cointegration Tests in Heterogeneous Panels with Multiple Regressors", Oxford Bulletin of Economics and Statistics, Vol. 61, No. 4, pp. 653-670.

Pedroni, P., 2000, "Fully-Modified OLS for Heterogeneous Cointegrated Panels", Advances in Econometrics, Vol. 15, pp. 93-130.

Pedroni, P., 2001, "Purchasing Power Parity Tests in Cointegrated Panels", The Review of Economics and Statistics, Vol. 83, No. 4, pp. 727-731.

Pedroni, P., 2004, "Panel Cointegration; Asymptotic and Finite Sample Properties of Pooled Time Series Tests with an Application to the Purchasing Power Parity Hypothesis," forthcoming in Econometric Theory.

Perron, P., 1989, "The Great Crash, the Oil Price Shock and the Unit Root Hypothesis", Econometrica, Vol. 57, Issue 6, pp. 1361-1401.

Perron, P., 1997, "Further Evidence from Breaking Trend Functions in Macroeconomic Variables", Journal of Econometrics, Vol. 80, Issue 2, pp. 355-385.

Pesaran, M. H., and P. R. Smith, 1995, "Estimating Long-run Relationships from Dynamic Heterogeneous Panels", Journal of Econometrics, Vol. 68, pp. 79-113.

Pesaran, M. H., Y. Shin, and P. R. Smith, 1999, "Pooled Mean Group Estimation of Dynamic Heterogeneous Panels", Journal of the American Statistical Association, Vol. 94, pp. 621-634.

Phillips, P. C. B., and B. E. Hansen, 1990, "Statistical Inference in Instrumental Variable Regression with I (1) Processes", Review of Economics Studies, Vol. 57, No. 1, pp. 99-125.

Quah, D., 1994, "Exploiting Cross-section Variations for Unit Root Inference in Dynamic Data", Economics Letters, Vol. 44, pp. 9-19.

Rahn, J., 2003, "Bilateral Equilibrium Exchange Rates of the EU Accession Countries Against the Euro", Bank of Finland Discussion Paper, No. 11, Helsinki.

Randveer, M., and M. Rell, 2002, "The Relationship Between Competitiveness and Real Exchange Rate in Estonia", Eesti Pank Research Paper, Tallinn.

Rawdanowicz, Ł. W., 2003, "Poland's Accession to EMU - Choosing the Exchange Rate Parity", Studies & Analyses, No. 247, Center for Social and Economic Research, Warsaw.

Reimers, H. E., 1992, "Comparisons of Tests of Multivariate Cointegration", Statistical Papers, Vol. 33, pp. 335-359.

Rogoff, K., 1996, "The Purchasing Power Parity Puzzle", Journal of Economic Literature, Vol. 34, pp. 647-668.

Rudgalvis, K., 1996, "Establishing a New Currency and Exchange Rate Determination: The Case of Lithuania", Centre of Economic Reform and Transformation Discussion Paper, No. 4, Edinburgh.

Saavalainen, T., 1995, "Stabilization in the Baltic Countries: A Comparative Analysis", IMF Working Paper, No. 44, Washington D.C.

Saikkonen, P., 1991, "Asymptotically Efficient Estimation of Cointegration Regressions", Econometric Theory, Vol. 7, Issue 1, pp. 1-21.

Samuelson, P., 1964, "Theoretical Notes on Trade Problems", Review of Economics and Statistics, Vol. 46, No. 2, pp. 145–154.

Sardà-Pons, J., and J. Pérez-Lacasta, 2003, "Exchange Rate and Long Run Equilibrium in Transition Economies", International Advances in Economic Research, Vol. 9, No. 1, pp. 35-50.

Schnabl, G., 2004, "De Jure Versus de Facto Exchange Rate Stabilization in Central and Eastern Europe", Aussenwirtschaft, Bd. 59, Heft 2, pp. 171-190.

Schuler, K., 2002, "Introduction to Currency Boards", internet: http://users.erols.com/kurrency/webdiss1.htm.

Scutaru, C., and A. Ghita, 1999, "Chaos and Order in Transition: Social Costs (Inflation, Unemployment) and Exchange Rate Policy; Case of Romania", Leicester University, Department of Economics, Faculty of Social Sciences.

Sepp, U., R. Lättemäe, and M. Randveer, 2002, "History and Sustainability of the CBA in Estonia", in Sepp, U., and M. Randveer (eds.), Alternative Monetary regimes in Entry to EMU, Bank of Estonia, Tallinn.

Sepp, U., and M. Randveer, 2002, "Aspects of the Sustainability of Estonian Currency Board Arrangement", Working Paper of Eesti Pank, No. 5, Tallinn.

Sinn, H. W., and M. Reutter, 2001, "The Minimum Inflation Rate for Euroland", NBER Working Paper, No. 8085.

Šmídková, K., R. Barrell, and D. Holland, 2002, "Estimates of Fundamental Real Exchange Rates for the Five EU Pre-Accession Countries", Czech National Bank Working Paper Series, No. 3, Prague.

Stein, J. L., 1994, "The Natural Real Exchange Rate of the US Dollar and Determinants of Capital Flows", in Williamson, J. (ed.), Estimating Equilibrium Exchange Rates, Institute of International Economics, Washington D.C., pp. 133-175.

Stein, J. L., 1999, "The Evolution of the Real Value of the US Dollar Relative to the G7 Currencies", in MacDonald, R., and J. L. Stein (eds.), Equilibrium exchange rates, Kluwer Academic Publisher, London, pp. 67-101.

Stein, J. L., 2002, "The Equilibrium Real Exchange Rate of the Euro: An Evaluation of Research", CESifo Economic Studies, Zeitschrift für empirische Wirtschaftsforschung, Vol. 43, No. 3, pp. 349–381.

Stock, J., and M. W. Watson, 1993, "A Simple Estimator of Cointegrating Vectors in Higher Order Integrated Systems", Econometrica , Vol. 61, No. 4, pp. 783-820.

Taylor, A. M., 2001, "Potential Pitfalls for the Purchasing-Power-Parity Puzzle? Sampling and Specification Biases in Mean-Reversion Tests of the Law of One Price", Econometrica, Vol. 69, pp. 473-498.

The Economist, various issues from 1990-2004.

Vasileva, E., 2002, "Currency Board and the Bulgarian Experience", Agency for Economic Analysis and Forecasting, mimeo, Sofia.

Vetlov, I., 2002, "Analysis of the Real Exchange Rate and Competitiveness in Lithuania", Eesti Pank Research Paper.

Von Hagen, J., and J. Zhou, 2002, "De Facto and Official Exchange Rate Regimes in Transition Economies", ZEI Working Paper, No. 13, Bonn.

Wadhwani, S. B., 1999, "Currency Puzzles", Speech delivered at the LSE, September 16.

Williamson, J., 1983, "The Exchange Rate System", Institute for International Economics, Washington D.C.

Williamson, J., 1991, "The Economic Opening of Eastern Europe", in Williamson, J. (ed.), Currency Convertibility in Eastern Europe, Washington D.C.

Williamson, J., 1994, "Estimates of FEERS", in Williamson, J. (ed.), Estimating Equilibrium Exchange Rates, Institute of International Economics, Washington D.C., pp. 177-244.

Williamson, J., 1995, "Currency Boards are not the Answer", News release at the institute for international economics, internet: http://www.iie.com/publications/newsreleases/cboard.htm.

Wren-Lewis, S., 1992, "On the Analytical Foundations of the Fundamental Equilibrium Exchange Rate", in Hargreaves, C. P. (ed.), Macroeconomic Modelling of the Long Run, E. Elgar Publishing, London.

Wu, J.-L., and S. Wu, 2001, "Is Purchasing Power Parity Overvalued?", Journal of Money, Credit and Banking, Vol. 33, pp. 804-812.

Peter Lang · Europäischer Verlag der Wissenschaften

Alexander Mende

Order Flow Analyses and Foreign Exchange Dealing

Frankfurt am Main, Berlin, Bern, Bruxelles, New York, Oxford, Wien, 2005.
139 pp., num. fig., tab. and graf.
Studien zu Internationalen Wirtschaftsbeziehungen.
Edited by Michael Frenkel. Vol. 4
ISBN 3-631-53571-6 / US-ISBN 0-8204-7689-7 · pb. € 27.50*

Traditional exchange rate modeling is in crisis. Fundamentals cannot explain exchange rates. Models using solely macro variables are bound to fail empirically, since they do not capture what is happening on foreign exchange markets. The question about the inner life of these markets arises. Since the middle of the 1990s, there is now an empirically motivated approach to exchange rates, based on the analysis of order flows. *Foreign exchange market microstructure* addresses the trading process and corresponding aspects of foreign exchange dealing. Analyses of order flows have become a promising field of research as cumulated flows are closely related to exchange rate movements. This investigation is made up of four related studies in the spirit of this new microstructure approach. It contributes to the existing literature by extending our knowledge of microstructure effects in the decision-making of foreign exchange dealers.

Contents: Order flow analysis and the microstructure approach to exchange rates · Asymmetric information and bid-ask spreads in foreign exchange dealing · Profit sources in foreign exchange trading · Tobin tax effects and foreign exchange market microstructure

FSC
www.fsc.org
MIX
Papier | Fördert
gute Waldnutzung
FSC® C083411

Zeitfracht Medien GmbH
Ferdinand-Jühlke-Straße 7
99095 Erfurt, Deutschland
produktsicherheit@kolibri360.de

Druck:
CPI Druckdienstleistungen GmbH
im Auftrag der
Zeitfracht Medien GmbH
Ein Unternehmen der Zeitfracht - Gruppe
Ferdinand-Jühlke-Str. 7
99095 Erfurt